GIANTKILLERS

GIANTKILLERS

THE TEAM AND THE LAW THAT HELP
WHISTLE-BLOWERS
RECOVER AMERICA'S STOLEN BILLIONS

HENRY
SCAMMELL

Atlantic Monthly Press
New York

Published simultaneously in Canada
Printed in the United States of America

FIRST EDITION

Library of Congress Cataloging-in-Publication Data
Scammell, Henry.
    Giantkillers : the team and the law that help whistle-blowers recover America's stolen billions / Henry Scammell.
        p. cm.
    ISBN 0-87113-909-X
    1. Popular actions—United States.   2. Citizen suits (Civil procedure)—United States.   3. Whistle blowing—Law and legislation—United States.   4. United States. False Claims Amendments Act of 1986   5. Corruption investigation—United States.   I. Title: Giantkillers.   II. Title.
KF8896.5.S28 2004
347.73'53—dc22 2003058311

Atlantic Monthly Press
841 Broadway
New York, NY 10003

04 05 06 07 08   10 9 8 7 6 5 4 3 2 1

SPECIAL THANKS TO:

Charles C. Thompson, whose careful, colorful, and richly detailed research into the history and early applications of the False Claims Act gave this book its start;

and Deborah Duffy, whose help at every step of this long project—with names, dates, numbers, connections, explanations, corrections, entire stories, unflagging cheerfulness, and endless patience—was indispensable in bringing it to a happy ending.

There is no kind of dishonesty into which otherwise good people more easily and frequently fall than that of defrauding the government.

—Benjamin Franklin

The men of Israel said, "Have you seen [Goliath]?
Surely he has defied Israel, and the man who kills him
the king will enrich with great riches."

David chose five smooth stones from the brook. His sling was in his hand. He drew near the Philistine.

—1 Samuel, 17

C O N T E N T S

A NEW AMERICAN HERO

In 1986, with government contractors stealing an estimated 10 percent of the total federal budget, Congress passed a newly strengthened anticorruption law. Ordinary citizens who knew of fraud could file lawsuits on behalf of the United States to recover money stolen from the public treasury, and they would share in the result. In the years since, despite massive institutional resistance, the False Claims Act has emerged as one of the nation's most potent weapons against corporate greed.

This is the story of that law: why it was needed, how it works, who brought it back to life, how it has survived the many attempts to kill it, and what it has accomplished.

Above all, it is the story of how a brave and endangered species, the corporate whistle-blower, at long last has earned recognition—and sometimes enormous rewards—as a new breed of American hero.

ONE

LAST MAN STANDING

I n the spring of 1969, some one hundred thousand American troops spread out on a long front west of Saigon and began walking inland toward a section of the Cambodian border between Angel's Wing and Parrot's Beak—two shapes suggested by turns in the boundary line on the campaign planners' maps. The goal was to push the Vietcong out of the country.

On April 12, about five miles from the border, an infantry company assigned to the advance of the operation wound its way in single-line formation along a jungle trail, through tall growths of thick bamboo that trembled with their passing. The usual point man for the hundred-man column was a slight, wiry twenty-one-year-old sergeant E-5, Emil Stache. But because Stache had just "gone short," entering the last thirty days before rotation home after eleven months of combat, he was assigned to carry the radio/telephone and moved back to number ten in the line.

Except for the backpack and a sweat-drenched towel to protect his neck, the former rubber worker from Akron, Ohio, was equipped pretty much like everyone before and behind him. He carried several twenty-round clips of ammunition taped bottom-to-bottom in pairs for quick reloading, and two canteens on each hip as defense against the dehydrating heat. He held his M-16 rifle in the classic hunter's cradle, resting the molded plastic fore end on his arm, his other hand gripping the neck of the stock, an index finger at the ready between the fire selector and the trigger guard.

Stache rounded a corner from behind a high, dense mound of fallen bamboo, following the column into a small, circular clearing of delicate, waist-high, green and yellow shoots. This whole front had been shelled repeatedly by American and Army of the Republic of Vietnam (ARVN) field artillery in the prior days and weeks, and the new growth covered recent scars. The troops ahead of him were walking through the open area in a gradual arc on a path that followed the curve of the surrounding trees, so that regardless of where they were in the line, each of them was nearly the same distance from the circle's center. The young sergeant had just emerged from the protection of the mound when someone in the lead, probably the point man who had replaced him, stepped into a wire that had been stretched at ankle height across the path, below the cover of new growth.

The wire led to a 155mm howitzer shell at the clearing's center. Like too much of the American ordnance in the Vietnam War, it was originally a dud. The enemy had rearmed it, bypassing the faulty impact fuse with an electric one. The normal kill radius for this type of ordnance is a hundred meters, about the length of a football field. The ten men in the van of the column, including Stache, were all within ten meters of the shell. The new switch clicked open. In an instant, a transcending whiteness consumed everything in the young sergeant's sight and a roar passed through his body. He was lifted into the air, then smashed to earth some thirty feet from the vanished trail, on top of the flattened undergrowth.

Deafened and dazed, he struggled to sit up, knowing from long experience that the blast was likely to be followed by the small arms fire of an enemy ambush. The rest of the company was still behind the large mound of dirt and decayed windfall, shielded from direct exposure to the explosion and shrapnel. Gaining his knees, Stache worked to free the radio pack from his back in order to call for security.

He could no longer feel his left arm. At first he was afraid it had been blown off, but he forced himself to look and saw it was still there. He then assumed it was just being held on by the shoulder harness of the radio pack, but when he moved the towel on his neck he could see a wide hole in his khaki T-shirt, and hamburger where the left side of his chest had been. The arm was still attached. With his right hand he freed the backpack and switched on the unit. When he spoke, his voice sounded like a distant echo in a tunnel, and the acknowledgment a barely audible whisper. He replaced the handset on the cradle, and it was smeared with blood; the blast had ruptured his eardrums.

In response to the call, members of the rifle company moved quickly forward from behind the protection of the mound to form a perimeter around the blast area, but as far as he could tell, the expected ambush wasn't happening. After another moment he rose tentatively to his feet, listening and watching, and when he sensed that it was at least momentarily safe, he returned to a quick inventory of his personal losses.

Except for the crater in his chest, the useless left arm, and his bleeding ears, he seemed to be in one piece.

Two of the other infantrymen in the clearing were also still alive, and perhaps there were more. Just a few yards beyond them, one of his oldest friends in the company was lying on the twisted underbrush, a piece of bright metal protruding from his pale temple, incongruously without blood. Stache had a field dressing in his pack, nothing more than cotton with gauze, but he felt certain it would make a difference if he could just get it open and apply it to his friend's injury. He was still struggling to remove the wrapping when the medics pushed past him to get to the fallen soldier. They turned him over, and Stache could see that the other side of the head was no longer there. The corpsmen turned their attention to Stache.

As they examined his wounds, a huge green twin-rotor medevac helicopter appeared over the edge of the surrounding trees, and with more of a purr than the roar his damaged ears expected, it settled into the area cleared by the blast. The medics strapped Stache onto a litter, carried it quickly under the whirling blades, and slid him inside as the Chinook rocked impatiently on its undercarriage like a nervous dragonfly. Others scrambled aboard, and he was pushed across the blood-slick deck to a position between two more litters, his life's liquids sloshing in his chest and then rising toward his throat. The machine lifted ponderously into the air.

Coolly, Stache decided he was going to live. He looked left and right at the two other survivors from the ten who had been in the line of the blast, and just as surely, he recognized that they would not.

Both were new kids in the platoon. One of them he knew only slightly, but the other, whose arms and legs had been blown off in the explosion, was already a friend. Stache turned to talk with him, offering some words of familiarity and comfort, but after only a few minutes the dying boy's sentences shortened and then slid into incoherence in the seductive, lazy wash of shock and morphine. Stache turned the other way. The second kid was assessing his losses just as Stache had done, but with a far different result: His hands groped across the empty space where his abdomen had been, and found instead the remnants of his spine. No matter how often Stache had seen that kind of thing—and in eleven months he had seen plenty—it still was hard to watch.

Less than fifteen minutes later, they arrived at the field hospital. The moment the Chinook came to earth, the doors slid open and a swarm of green-clad medical workers poured in, their swift, purposeful movements bringing sudden order to the scene of death and chaos. Triage workers searched for any with treatable injuries from among the dead and dying, and the litters were moved quickly onto rolling gurneys.

Things were changing fast. Stache asked two of the boys from the company to take a picture of him with his Kodak. They laughed at him and said he was crazy, but they all knew it was to record the passage, the end of his part in the war, on the doorsill of his exit from Vietnam. One of them reached into the bloodied pack that was still with him on the litter, and fished out the Instamatic. They waited until some of the others were moved, because they didn't want the photos to include any of the dead or their terrible wounds. Stache smoked a cigarette as the friend clicked off the shot, and reflected on the age that was ending. He wondered if he'd ever get to see the photo.

Before Stache finished the cigarette, two corpsmen arrived to move him to surgery, and at the same time someone gave an order for the rest of his company to move on. There were quick good-byes, and a moment later he was being lifted onto one of the operating tables inside the inflatable field hospital. The doctors turned him onto his right side, and at least two pairs of hands began to cut away his clothing with heavy shears. Now that he was facing the door, he could see the medical company's executive officer standing at the entrance, looking around the room.

Two teams were now working on the gaping wound, one in front and the other from behind, talking to each other through the hole that began in his chest and continued out his back. A doctor in front kept up a play-by-play for Stache on what they were seeing as they probed the injury. He told him the shrapnel had passed between the large vein that goes from the heart to the brain and the one that goes to the left arm. If the piece of metal had been just a few millimeters wider, or if it had a snag or burr big enough to cut either one of those veins, he would have bled out in two minutes. But it had come in flat, turned slightly when it hit the scapula, then taken most of the shoulder blade with it when it blew out his back.

The XO made one more survey of the room, then came over and looked down at Stache on the operating table. He had a few questions, he said, about the troops who had been in the clearing at the time of the explosion: how many, who they were, and what had happened. The doctors continued working front and back, cutting at the last of the clothing and washing the area around the wound with thick swabs of brownish-yellow disinfectant. When Stache finished with his answers, the officer shut the lid on his clipboard. "Where are your dog tags?"

He thought for a moment. "I guess I lost them."

"What's your blood type?"

"AB negative." It was relatively rare, and Stache had been told over a year earlier that if he wanted to get out of going to Vietnam, his blood type was an acceptable excuse because it couldn't be stockpiled in the field. But someone else would have had to go in his place, so he never asked for the exemption.

The XO shook his head and turned to one of the men in green scrubs. "Get on the horn and find AB negative." Looking back to Stache, he added, "We'll decide whether to ship you to the blood or the blood to you."

Just a few minutes later they located a source and made their decision to send him to another field hospital. By then the wound had been padded and wrapped, much of the crusted exterior blood had been washed from his body, and his torn and sodden combat clothing had been replaced by shapeless white hospital pajamas. The policy was to never close wounds in Vietnam because of the humidity and chance of infection; the hole in his chest would remain open until they airlifted him to Japan.

When the helicopter landed at another field hospital several miles nearer to Saigon, nobody was there to meet it. With some difficulty, Stache opened the door himself, climbed down, and walked alone to the aid station, the open part of the hospital where arriving patients register. There were several metal gurney tables with men lying on them. He approached a nurse at the desk, a major, who glanced up briefly and told him to wait on one of the folding chairs. He was cold; he knew it was from loss of blood and shock. He sat down, lit a cigarette, and drew the blanket about himself like a shroud.

Forty minutes after the blast, he still had received no sutures, his wounds remained open, and the blood—his rare, AB negative blood that should have kept him from ever going to Vietnam in the first place—was still streaming from both his chest and back. As the duty nurse passed by his chair on her way back to the desk, he said, "Ma'am? I'm feeling real light-headed and I'd like to lie down."

It didn't look like she was going to answer, but then she stopped and turned to look at him with open skepticism. "It wouldn't have anything to do with your smoking, would it?" she asked.

It took a moment to understand her meaning, but then he said, "Ma'am, it's not the cigarettes." He managed to lift himself unsteadily from the chair, and then he held open the wings of the blanket. "It's this."

The khaki front was still dry because with his right hand he had been holding it shut about the neck, his forearm shielding it from his leaking body. But opened it revealed his sodden pajamas, a crimson wick from shoulder to ankles. The pooled blood from where he had been sitting now spilled from the blanket, splashed onto his feet, and ran across the floor.

The major raised her clipboard like a shield and screamed. Perhaps she saw the boy before her as the bellyacher she had just sent back to battle, returned now in an instant dressed in slaughter. She threw the board aside, papers flying in all directions, and ran from the room.

Stache wasn't sure what to do. The major had turned down his request to put the chairs together and he knew better than to lie down anyway, but he could feel the darkness coming on and so he sat. Almost before he touched the seat, the nurse returned with two men in scrubs, all at a run. They hoisted him quickly onto a gurney, the orderlies full of chagrin for not having met the chopper, for not having known he had arrived, their apologies perhaps as much to soothe the distraught major as for him.

The gurney sped down the corridor to an operating room, and he was lifted swiftly onto the table. In almost that same moment the room was filled with people in green gowns and masks, and a brilliant light went on above his head. He turned his eyes. Plastic bags were hooked onto a metal stand beside the table, both his arms were being swabbed, and needles were being pushed into veins as conduits for the dark, frothed blood and crystal saline. A breathing cone was placed over the lower half of his face. Between the green bodies he caught the glint of drills and clamps and rows of shining knives. He drew three breaths, and for the second time that day was taken in completely by the whiteness.

T W O

QUALITY ASSURANCE

Before he was drafted, Emil Stache had worked for General Tire in Akron, Ohio. When he was discharged a year after his injuries, he returned to the comfort of the familiar. His job seniority had accumulated during his time in the army, and he moved up the ladder to a position in the company's physical testing laboratory. He married a girl he had met while he was in the army, and they had a son.

He liked the work, but in Akron, Ohio, practically the only thing anyone thought about was rubber. General Tire was the town's biggest employer, and there were dozens of other companies living off the same skilled labor pool. It was generally accepted that if you worked for a rubber company you stayed there until you retired. By 1978 he had gone from supervisor to head of the lab. But Emil was ready for a change. A year later, in 1979, he accepted a job with an independent testing lab and moved his family to California.

It was a whole new world. His work involved testing everything from space shuttle parts to airline toilets to nuclear warheads. In short order he got an even better offer, running the laboratory for a company that supplied hardware for the telephone industry. When the second company folded its California operations and moved back to Georgia, he called a friend named Al Muehlhausen who worked at Teledyne Relays in Hawthorne. Al had told him just a few days before that Teledyne Relays was looking for a supervisor in its Qualified Products List (QPL) laboratory. Emil got the job and reported to work on December 13, 1983.

An electronic relay is an automatic device that responds to a small change in current or voltage to activate a switch or other component in an electric circuit. They are used in everyday products, such as ignition systems for starting a car or living room thermostats for turning on a furnace. Because most of the relays manufactured by Teledyne were sold to the government, they were subject to far stricter manufacturing standards and more rigorous testing than relays used in household appliances. The government paid a premium for these high-reliability products to assure that they never failed.

To qualify as bidders on military projects, contractors had to build a testing and manufacturing facility that met the government's standards. They had to test their own products, giving the results of those tests periodically to the government to remain qualified. Once a company made it onto this "Qualified Products List," it could sell its military, or "MIL-Spec," components direct to one of the giant, systems-level government contractors like TRW or Hughes without going through any additional approvals, saving time and money.

Emil's new job was to test representative samples of Teledyne's relays for government projects and report the results on government forms to the Defense Electronics Supply Center in Dayton, Ohio. DESC periodically audited contractor facilities, usually once a year, to check out equipment and make sure testing procedures were up to standard.

Teledyne Relays was part of one of America's first large conglomerates. The parent company had been founded by two former Naval Academy roommates, and grew through a series of acquisitions based almost entirely on bottom-line performance. They bought up manufacturers of pool heaters, dental products, and television sets, fabricators of metal, and labs for measuring product fatigue. Most of the sixty-odd corporate parts were unrelated to each other or the whole in any way besides money, and the Relays unit was just one more such profit center. As long as the bottom line stayed positive, Teledyne's corporate relationship to divisional management was strictly hands-off.

The diversity of the corporate mix also meant that there was no centralized entity for the oversight of quality control. There was no reporting facility, no direction, and no meaningful standard for quality maintenance at the Teledyne corporate level.

When Emil started work, he discovered that the Relays Division had just been shaken from top to bottom by a drug scandal. Drugs in the workplace were a relatively new problem in the '70s, and in typical Teledyne style it was handled at the divisional level. Private detectives were hired to monitor employees. They accumulated evidence of widespread abuse, and known offenders were rounded up. Accused employees were presented with the evidence and given a chance to resign. In the massive wave of voluntary terminations that followed, one of the jobs that suddenly became open was supervisor of the Qualified Products List testing lab. Along with dozens of other recent hires, Emil owed his new position to that drug raid.

But if he was playing in a new arena, the rules of the game in quality assurance were basically the same as they had been in his prior jobs, all the way back to General Tire. He knew how to interpret specifications, and it didn't change things if they were now military specs; a specification was still just a set of instructions, and from the perspective of a laboratory director, the differences were a matter of semantics.

As soon as Emil started work with his new employer, it was immediately apparent to him that something was terribly wrong. His tests were revealing massive product failures—not just a fraction of a percentage point, but sometimes disqualifying the majority of products in the batch. When he spoke about it with his immediate boss and later with other division management, they all tried to explain it away. For the most part, they blamed the problem on antiquated testing equipment.

Despite their explanations, Emil formally noted the failures in his first report, in early 1984. He knew the company had an incentive to blame the problem on a cause that had nothing to do with the relays, and it was impossible, without another step, to know whether the failure rate was due to the testing equipment or to the devices themselves. If the company acknowledged it was producing defective products, the result could be financially disastrous. Most of the division's income was from relays sold for use in government systems ranging from the space shuttle to detonators for bombs. The government's most likely response would be to pull them off its Qualified Products List, halting the division's exsting government contracts and making it extremely difficult to get new ones.

Emil was relieved that management didn't seem to view his report as especially alarming, or to blame the failures on his inexperience in testing their product line, although the subject did come up. He just wanted to do his job and give honest reports and produce a good product.

Another part of the problem, Emil realized, was that he was new, and everyone was aware that he didn't really know that much about the product line or the equipment. He sure didn't want to start off like he was coming in there to cause trouble, that he was a wise guy with some kind of a spike out for the company.

Management told him that was all they wanted too. It took a lot of persuading and even more persistence, but eventually Emil got his bosses to agree to a change in the testing gear, and if necessary a second change, in order to eliminate the problem.

The first step was to replace all the relays in the testing circuits. That was done, but the product failure rate remained stratospheric. The second, far more costly step was to rebuild all the lab units with solid-state, nonmechanical components to improve the likelihood that any failures were in the products rather than in the testing systems.

After starting the changeover from mechanical to solid-state components, the company performed a series of electrical tests and recalibrations and more tests. Some glitches were expected, as normal. But the problem went further than that. At the end of these changes, either the testing system or the products themselves—or possibly both—still failed to meet the government's parameters.

Meanwhile, doubts began creeping in from another direction. Emil found himself wondering how the company had been able to keep shipping products prior to this without deliberately having rigged prior test results. Had they lied about the tests? Had they hidden their failures?

He had no direct proof, but he inferred that must have been the case. The only reports he had seen showed all good parts. He could find no laboratory documentation anywhere of earlier failures, but on investigating elsewhere in the company he found there was field evidence of failure everywhere its products were used.

He wondered how this failure rate was allowed to continue. Part of the answer was obvious: At that time the government ran the contracting process in a way that was strictly compartmentalized, with few channels for extending responsibility in either direction between one supplier and the next. Teledyne's responsibility began and ended at the component level. The component next went into a subassembly, then into an assembly, then into a system, with compartmentalized sign-offs at each plateau.

If the last contractor experienced a failure at the system level, for the government and everyone further down the feeding chain there was far greater incentive to sweep it under the rug than to deal with it directly. Nobody at Teledyne wanted to examine whether results of subsequent testing in assembly had been falsified as well. And there was no easy way for a contractor to see beyond his own partition clearly enough to challenge any supplier farther up the chain. Even if he could, it could mean going back and replacing and redoing everything. So instead, even as the failures mounted to the level of an epidemic, it was still more prudent to deal with each one as an aberration. If TRW, for example, sent back a Teledyne switch that failed in the field, the standard response was to dismiss it as just one more "isolated occurrence." It was an explanation that worked for everybody.

There was a similarly comfortable agreement within the division to explain away the failure rate in Emil's first report, when it had been unclear whether the parts themselves were at fault or if they'd been forced into an error mode by the test equipment. But six months later, the second batch of test results showed that the failure rate was even higher. Even though the company was about to replace the electromechanical parts of the testing equipment with solid-state components, the excuse was wearing thin. Moreover, this time Emil asked a question that he hadn't asked before: "Isn't this supposed to be reported to DESC?"

He already knew the answer, but sometimes the real information is in the tone of the reply. "Yeah," he was told, "we'll check into it." The question had drawn a line, and the impatient, distrustful response confirmed it. He was reminded that no one in the lab was allowed to communicate with DESC, and that meant when the government inspector came around even Emil could not talk to him directly unless someone else was present. That someone was always one of the experts, one of the design engineers who had developed the relay being tested, and it was obvious that the DESC inspectors held those experts in awe. Emil reported the failure rate to his superior, who in turn was the one telling him not to talk to anybody. There really wasn't anywhere else to go.

When samples continued to fail even after new testing equipment was in place, Emil was ordered to destroy the samples that had been tested and the documentation that went with them. When Emil got his orders to get rid of the samples and the paperwork, he went to the director of the lab, the friend who had brought him into the company. "You know, this isn't right."

His friend agreed. Like Emil, he had been in the service. But neither of them could figure out what to do about it.

"Well, I'm not going to scrap this stuff," Emil decided. "I'm going to take it home."

In the depths of this dilemma, the company suddenly came up with a solution. Emil was promoted out of the problem; his responsibilities no longer included the QPL testing area. Management's explanation was if they had to bring in a design engineer to complete the transition to solid-state equipment, it made sense for that same person to take over the testing once the new system was up and running. In Emil's new role he still had some initial involvement with the lab on paper, but soon those responsibilities were removed, and his connection with the testing process ended.

But that didn't end his interest. After the new solid-state testing facility was built, he was curious to know if the lab was still having failures. From time to time, he made a point of running into people he had brought into the company and who still worked in QPL. They verified his worst doubts: The changes in test equipment hadn't made any difference; the problem had been in the products all along, and they continued.

Emil knew he didn't have anything to worry about in asking questions of his former boss, Al Muehlhausen. They trusted each other, they both understood the inherently unpopular nature of their jobs, and they shared a common background in the military, although Al was older and had never served in Vietnam. Beyond the obvious ethical conflict between loyalty to the company and responsibility to the truth, each was aware of the high personal risk he faced in signing off on any product that he knew had failed in testing.

Emil was equally secure in his relationship with the lab staff. He had known most of them far longer than they had worked for Teledyne, and he was sure his friendships with them were stronger than any feelings they might have toward the company. But he was nowhere nearly as sanguine about how he was viewed from the other direction, by the people above him who had moved him up and out of the QPL laboratory.

He never deluded himself that in dealing with management he could indulge in the comfort of total openness. To the contrary, his survival owed to his early appreciation of how things worked, and he knew that in the unwritten culture of the division, rocking the boat was the same as jumping overboard. Company lore was filled with stories of engineers who had asked the wrong questions or pointed to obvious problems, only to be immediately removed to another job or terminated. He was smart enough to recognize his promotion for what it was: He had been dealt with, and he was lucky to have survived.

Some of the less fortunate were very close at hand. For example, all returns from the field came in to Production Control, and one day the manager of that area made the mistake of commenting on the high failure rate. He didn't make a big thing of it, and to those who claimed to have heard his remark, it seemed even casual, something like, "Hey, we sure are getting a lot of these back." But the next day he was gone, and everyone around him felt the company was making a forceful point: Doubting was disloyalty, and there was no room at Teledyne for troublemakers. Emil came to see these responses to returns or failure rates as the chorus of a tacit corporate mantra: "We developed this, DESC is our friend, we make the best product, nobody is going to do anything to us, we're untouchable."

By 1985, the Teledyne Relays operation employed some twelve hundred people, mostly in manufacturing and line assembly. Compared with the corporation as a whole—Teledyne had thirty-two thousand employees and annual sales of $6 billion—it was relatively small potatoes. But at the management level, the division was a dynamic, tightly knit organization. The group executive had developed close alliances with a select cadre of employees with whom he shared a boat and trailer and sometimes would go hunting. Emil realized there was no way he was ever going to penetrate that inner circle even if he'd wanted to, and he also knew that if he was viewed by any of its members as having broken its rules, his next move would not be up but out.

Neither the job change nor the implicit threat of termination, however, were enough incentive to keep him from attempting to bring up the failure rate with his new supervisor, the director of quality for the division. Not surprisingly, whenever he tried, he got nowhere.

"Don't tell me about that," his boss would interrupt, turning his head and waving the topic away. "I don't want to know."

It was the familiar don't-rock-the-boat mentality he had seen in the army: Teledyne was his boss's life, and he could see as clearly as Emil did that such questions put it all at risk. He was going to retire from there, and he didn't want those plans darkened by clouds of uncertainty or threatened by the suspicion of his peers.

He encouraged Emil to refocus on this same long view, but to Emil the connection between the problems in the QPL lab and the high rate of returns was inescapable, and his job was quality assurance and reliability, plain and simple. After a while the boss gave up trying to convert him, settling on another way of dealing with the problem. Whenever Emil raised an issue related to product quality—if he saw an attempt to sneak in a defective relay or to violate the strict military specs—the boss's answer became a quick, dismissive, "DESC says it's okay." That ended it. It was one thing to challenge the product. But for Emil to ask for proof, to suggest his boss was lying, would challenge the chain of command.

Emil knew that the booby-trapped howitzer shell in Vietnam, just like the failure rate at Teledyne, had been far from an isolated incident. He thought back to the time his company had gone through a thickly wooded area, and how after it stopped to rest he suddenly realized he was sitting on a 500-pound bomb that had been dropped from a B-52. The Vietcong didn't have anywhere near the amount of ordnance that the Americans did, and Emil estimated that as much as half of what the enemy used were American products that had failed in their original purpose. The Vietcong would move one, two, or three people at a time, each carrying nothing more than a bag of rice, a rifle with a bandolier of ammo, and often some marijuana. They applied classic guerrilla strategy to jungle warfare, deploying their battalions over a period of weeks and months and accruing more firepower simply by scavenging on America's carelessness. The Vietcong recycled American weapons and used them with catastrophic effect against the soldiers of the country that made them.

One day Emil sat down with his boss to talk about what he felt the failures really meant. "Why do bombs go off course? Why do planes fall out of the sky?" he asked. "Why did the *Challenger* explode?" The questions didn't produce any direct answers, but an expression of stony distrust descended on his boss's face like the visor of a helmet.

"Those things happened because something failed," Emil went on. "The parts we're building go into all these programs, and people get killed because of what we let slip through. I almost got killed and all my friends got killed because someone let this kind of stuff sneak by."

"I'm glad it wasn't me," his boss answered. And then, to make the point, he added, "But it wasn't."

He hadn't been in the military. He would never ride a rocket into space. And as long as all the consequences were for others, he didn't care.

Emil, by contrast, had vivid memories.

Whenever his wound was unpacked, doctors and nurses on other cases gathered by his bed, and all the patients on the ward who were able would raise themselves up on their elbows or crane for a look. Some called out with jokes or laughs and wry comments, but most just marveled. Here was this perfectly normal guy, wide awake, coherent, obviously in some degree of pain but tough about it, and when the bandages came off they could see in through one side of his body and straight out through the other. The daily ritual drew an audience like a bad wreck. They could see the tangled arteries still carrying blood, the gristle-clad bones, the muscles that were still connected, the tattered fabric of his skin, and the shrunken, disconnected tissue that was now ground-up meat going bad. It was like a big, expensive radio that had a hole smashed through it by a giant mallet but that miraculously still played.

Two months after the explosion, he was assigned to Forest Glen, an annex of Walter Reed Army Medical Center in Maryland, to complete his healing. Almost everyone around him was an amputee, and from his first look he knew it was going to be a very hard place. He was surrounded by young kids, double, triple, and quadruple amputees who couldn't even turn themselves over and whose lives had been blown to pieces. Some of them reacted to the terrible changes in their bodies by cutting off all associations with the past, refusing to see friends or even families. One of the boys in the ward had lost both legs and an arm, and when his girlfriend drove his car across the country for their first meeting since he had left for Vietnam, he wouldn't leave the ward to meet with her. Emil had seen this kind of thing before and he knew enough to stay out of it, but he hung around the ward. After a while, the kid asked to be rolled over to the window so he could look down into the parking lot to see his car. He looked down at the red 396 Chevelle with a stick shift that he would never drive again and silently grieved over his losses.

Emil was disgusted with his boss's attitude, but he had to be careful what he showed. Emil had been divorced in 1985, and he was now a single parent raising his teenaged son. Far from being some radical screaming from a soapbox, he saw himself as a team player who was simply trying to do the best he could in a bad situation. He was certain that the only way to correct the problem was from the inside.

Even if he'd been allowed to talk with the DESC agents, it seemed likely they'd have pretty much the same attitude as his bosses. The government was notorious for underpaying and overloading. In some cases the agents weren't even engineers, and they were expected to stay on top of twenty different sets of specifications at perhaps a hundred companies. Because they were so much less qualified than the experts whose work they monitored, they deferred to them on almost everything, taking care that even the most reasonable query was worded in a way that could never be mistaken for a challenge. When the company had meetings with DESC agents on interpretations of the rules, the sessions often involved open collaboration on how the company could get around the letter of the law. Besides, Teledyne invented the relays and wrote the specs for them, and under those circumstances when a young government inspector found something wrong, chances were good he was going to think the fault was his and not the product's.

In 1988, one of the leading quality control issues throughout the aerospace industry was the high failure rate associated with solder not making a good connection in electronic products. A frequent cause of the problem was inadequate metal plating on the surface to which the solder was intended to attach. The military expanded its specification in that area, especially for the High Reliability lines. It was a problem at Teledyne Relays as well, and Emil was chosen to become the resident expert on the subject. He was sent to China Lake, north of Los Angeles between the Mojave Desert and Death Valley, for a two-week course and certification. In 1989 he was recertified. But instead of building trust and strengthening his position within the company, his new expertise proved to be a further means of his undoing.

Because he understood the new standard better than anyone else and had been given responsibility for its application, it was no longer possible for management to blow off his objections with the usual claims of a specialized interpretation of the rules or a private understanding with DESC. That might still work with questions related to power surges or testing equipment, but when it came to solder, there were no deals, no looking the other way, no special cases. More and more frequently, as the problems increased, Emil's answer was a flat, unshakable refusal to sign off on the product. He found himself in a confrontation almost every week, with the vice president of engineering, with the production people, with the personnel in his own department. He realized he was developing a reputation within the company as the kind of person who had to be watched. It went beyond the nature of his job. More and more, he sensed the mistrust was personal, that it was about him.

In February 1990, one of his inspectors called Emil and said, "The QPL lots are failing solderability." Emil tested the failed lot and agreed with the inspector that they were bad. "Reject them," he told her. Then, almost as an afterthought, he added, "When you deliver them to the engineer for his evaluation, don't mention that these are QPL samples." Because the military line was so important, Emil knew that the engineer would never issue a rejection report.

The standard procedure is that the inspector writes up the rejection criteria, describing what's wrong, and the report is then delivered along with the defective part to the engineer in charge of that area. The engineer looks at it, makes his determination, sends it into the signatory cycle, and everyone agrees with whatever the engineer has decided.

When the inspector put the failed products on the engineer's desk, she simply said, "Rejected for solderability. Here's the rejection report." The engineer looked them over and agreed that the products should be rejected. Emil had figured he would incorrectly assume the products were not from the military line since those failuare rates usually weren't reported. A QPL failure was a potential threat to the certification of the whole product line and could mean the loss of millions of dollars. Once the engineer had confirmed the rejection, unknowingly triggering a requirement that Teledyne report the failure to the government, Emil stepped forward and dropped the bomb. "They're from the QPL," he said.

The explosion was instantaneous. "What are you trying to do?" the engineer yelled. "You're sandbagging me."

"If they're bad, they're bad," Emil answered. "Why does it make any difference where they came from?"

When Emil returned to his office a few minutes later, the phone on his desk was already ringing. The first call was from the vice president of engineering, and the question was repeated: "What are you trying to do?"

The next call, with the identical opening line, was from Emil's own vice president. The one after that, in which the incredulous query was repeated yet again, was from the director of the company.

Emil answered the question the same way each time. "It's a criterion," he said, "and we have to record it. It's not devastating—you have some bad plating. But you have to tell DESC."

As much as Emil resented the anger generated by his actions, he was just as aware as management that whatever happened next wasn't going to

be anywhere near as simple as his explanation made it sound. He had forced
the bosses into a dilemma. The right thing to do, as he enjoyed reminding
them, would be to report the failure to DESC. If DESC did the right thing
in return, Teledyne would be required to evaluate how much of the month's
production was affected, and there was no telling where it all might end.

A short time later, Emil was summoned to a meeting in the office
of the division's vice president of quality. Also present was the director
of quality, Emil's immediate superior in the chain of command. The confrontation started off civilly enough, but Emil sensed an air of deliberate tension.

They wasted little time getting to the bottom line. They were strip-
ping him of his responsibilities, essentially a demotion, but more important, a move that placed him in apparent limbo. Then the director asked
him, "What are you going to do?"

It was a small office. There were three chairs. The one assigned to
Emil was positioned with its back to the wall, and the other two were together facing it. Emil's answer was a weak "What do you mean?"

They each repeated the question. "What are you going to do?" the
vice president asked. The director echoed, "We want to know right now:
What are you going to do?"

Emil sensed that the tone in the room, along with his career, had taken
a sudden turn. They had just handed him a sword, and now they were
hoping he'd complete their job by falling on it. All he could think to do
was continue the chain of repetitions. "I don't understand. What do you
mean, 'What are you going to do?'" If they expected him to quit, which
was how it seemed, he wasn't going to make it easy for them.

The initial civility vanished in an instant. The director left his chair
and bent down in front of Emil, red-faced, his voiced filling the room. "We
want you to know that Teledyne will go toe-to-toe with you on any issue
you want to name." When Emil replied with nothing more than a bemused
stare, the director straightened up and looked back at his colleague for
affirmation. "Isn't that right?"

The vice president seemed to have a better sense that their strategy
of an assisted suicide wasn't working. But he was committed, and he played
it out. "Yes," he said, "that's correct."

Emil looked back and forth between his two antagonists. "Hey, guys,"
he said. But it was apparent that the time had long since passed for an appeal

to cordiality or even reason. "Fine," he said, holding his hands up in a small gesture of surrender. "Fine."

"Fine what?" the director asked.

"Fine," Emil repeated.

"We still want to know," the director said again. This time the tone was more subdued, like a late attempt to make it all sound reasonable.

No one had signaled that the meeting was over, but Emil stood up, then stopped at the door with his hand on the knob. "This has all just happened. I don't have any idea what I'm going to do."

And it was the truth. His son was nineteen and living with him, and he had house payments and other responsibilities. Most of all, he still thought of himself as a Teledyne employee, as someone who was loyal to the company and trying to do the job he was being paid for. Now he was being pushed to let it all go, to give it up in an instant, and he wasn't willing to do that.

Emil had been with Teledyne since he was thirty-five, and at the time of his demotion he was forty-two. He had risen up in management, and he knew that things essentially worked the same at the upper levels. To quit under these circumstances amounted to professional disaster. The company would be careful how it responded to reference checks, but there were ways to get the point across without leaving a record that could ever show up in court. At the very least, he was sure there wouldn't be any glowing recommendation.

When he left the office, he decided it was time to go down to Human Resources. One of the managers there was a fellow Vietnam veteran, and they'd always had a good relationship. As briefly as possible, Emil described the conversation of a few minutes earlier, and the events leading up to it. He finished the summary with an offer to meet privately with the president of the company. "I'll tell him everything that's going on. Other than that, I don't have any plans."

They discussed Emil's options, and agreed that his best choice until things settled down a bit would be to take a stress leave, which would keep the door open to his returning to the lower job.

The standard term for that kind of leave was ninety days. Once a week he met with a psychology student and collected disability. The therapist tried to get him to talk about his problem, but Emil knew there was no point—and possibly even some risk—in getting too specific.

During Emil's leave, the HR manager kept his promise to talk with to the president of the division. But the company president flatly rejected Emil's proposal to meet with him.

From then on, it was pretty much downhill. Two months into the leave, Emil learned that the director of quality had begun interviewing for his old job as manager of Quality Engineering and Reliability and was pressing the HR manager to hire someone before he came back. He succeeded, and the day before Emil had been scheduled to return, the new man started in his old job. But in the meantime, Emil's original schedule had changed. Teledyne had requested a second opinion on his fitness to return, and the second doctor extended his leave by another two weeks. When the director of quality learned of this, he went right back to the HR manager and asked him to hire someone for Emil's new, lower position as well. Again, a replacement reported to work on the day before Emil was scheduled back according to the revised schedule, effectively closing the door on any hope he might have had of returning to Teledyne.

Emil decided to move his case up a level, and he called the HR manager's boss, but by then it was evident that the tide was against him. The director of HR tried to talk him into resigning, and Emil turned him down.

"Well," the director said, "they've filled your old position and they filled your new position. If you're not willing to resign," he said shrugging, "then they're going to lay you off."

"Okay," Emil said. "Just send me the paperwork."

The HR director cocked his head for a moment, and then nodded and stood up. "Okay," he said. His tone suggested that the matter was at an end.

Emil stood up as well. He knew that it was not.

T H R E E

KILLING RANGE

T hroughout the stress leave, Emil had received a series of telephone calls at home from Al Muehlhausen, the former army man who had brought him into the company and who was his initial boss at Teledyne. Muehlhausen had majored in nuclear physics at Virginia Military Institute, served in active duty as a lieutenant, and had reached the rank of lieutenant colonel in the reserves by the time he went to work for Teledyne. The two men were still friends and had stayed in close touch even after Emil's promotion out of the testing lab to manager of Quality Engineering and Reliability. They were two of only three quality control managers in the division (the design engineer who replaced Emil in the QPL lab was the third), and they shared a common concern for the widening gap between the company's attitude toward quality control and the ethical and legal obligations of their jobs. With the start of Emil's stress leave, Muehlhausen began apprising him of developments that might have a bearing on when and whether he returned.

Muehlhausen had a second incentive for staying in touch with his colleague. After following the tortuous turns in Emil's career at Teledyne, he now sensed that at the age of fifty-six he was himself being maneuvered into the recently vacated hot seat, and that the division was intent on repeating its recent history.

Emil's leave lasted from the end of February through the middle of June. Near the end of May, Al called with a story that lent new substance to Emil's earlier suspicions. One of the technicians in the QPL laboratory had come into his office that day and told him that a lot of products were failing a part of the QPL testing regimen.

This placed Muehlhausen in a position that felt perilously close to where Emil had been only a few weeks before. Emil asked, "What do you want to do?"

"I'm going to take the Memorial Day weekend and think about it," Muehlhausen said. "But I want to know if you'll support me."

Emil hesitated. Support him how? They had talked this through a hundred times before. There was no one within the company who would listen, and they both knew reporting it to DESC would be worthless. "Al, I'm with you on this, but I don't know where to go."

"I don't either," Muehlhausen agreed. "But let's both give it some more thought, and we'll talk next week."

The following Tuesday, Muehlhausen called again. "I'm going to take it to the FBI."

"The FBI?" Emil repeated. "Why the FBI? Do they get involved in this kind of thing? It's not like it's a bank robbery."

They talked about it some more, but they kept returning to the familiar dead ends. The FBI seemed like a stretch, but at least someone there might be able to advise them on what to do next. "Okay," Emil agreed, knowing as he said it that they were about to cross a line.

When Muehlhausen phoned back, he told Emil he'd talked with the L.A. office and had made an appointment for both of them to meet with an agent two days later.

"That's the day after tomorrow," Emil answered, doing his best to sound matter-of-fact.

"The day after tomorrow," Al confirmed. "Noontime at Denny's."

Emil understood the reason for the hour. It had to be a time when Al could leave work without making explanations or excuses, and the Denny's in Hawthorne was about three miles from the plant—near enough to be convenient, far enough away that they wouldn't be likely to run into anyone they knew. Not that it would have made any difference even if they were seen; there was no reason two old friends couldn't get together for lunch, and it was unlikely anyone from Teledyne would recognize the third man at the table as an FBI agent.

They talked about what each of them would bring. Emil still had the samples from the failed lot from 1984, as well as the solder failures from 1989 and the rejection report that management had refused to sign. And Muehlhausen had the details on the latest hi-rel lot.

Two days later, a few minutes before noon, Emil spotted Al's car in the Denny's lot and pulled into an adjacent parking space. It was a hot day in early June, and after they greeted each other they looked around the lot and decided to wait inside. From the air-conditioned entrance area, they could survey each new arriving car.

"What's this guy's name?" Emil asked.

"McQuire," Al said. "I think he said Ken."

"Did he tell you what he looks like?"

Al shook his head. "Chances are, he looks like an FBI agent."

A car pulled into the entrance and drove slowly to the back of the lot. The single occupant was a male, probably in his middle thirties, and he was wearing a necktie and a white shirt. He pulled into a slot just a couple of spaces beyond their cars, and when he got out, despite the heat, he stopped long enough to put on a suit jacket. As he walked across the driveway, he pulled the jacket shut and buttoned it, but not before Emil and Al saw the handgun in a black holster on his belt.

"I'm just guessing, but . . ." Emil left the rest of it in the air.

After subdued introductions and brief handshakes, the three men ordered sandwiches and sat down in a booth. To Emil's and Al's surprise, Agent McQuire proved very knowledgeable about the electronics industry and military specifications. The situation they were describing was so widespread, he told them, that a special interagency task force had been created to investigate the sale of defective electronic equipment to the government. As a rule of thumb, the FBI wouldn't even bother to look into a case of this sort unless the amount the government had paid for the faulty products was over $100,000.

Emil glanced at Al. They hadn't discussed it beforehand, but both knew it was important that neither of them make any claims without the other's agreement. When Al nodded, Emil said, "This runs well over that."

"Far more," Al agreed. "Far, far more than a hundred thousand."

They took turns describing the situation at Teledyne, right up to the hi-rel lot that had failed just days before. They told McQuire they were both worried about their own liability because each of them had signed off, at the insistence of higher management, on products they all knew were defective. As manager of Quality Engineering, Emil had signed customer returns, and Al had signed for High Reliability lots as a lab manager.

"We want to see this stuff end," Emil said, "but we don't want Teledyne to turn it around and say, 'Yeah, this is a terrible surprise. And those are the guys who did it.'"

McQuire nodded to indicate he understood their problem. But he was carefully professional, and the gesture offered no assurances.

Emil told him about the parts he had brought with him in his car, but to his surprise the agent wasn't interested in even seeing them. "Tell me about this High Reliability lot from the other day."

Al described the tests, how they were supposed to be conducted and what they were designed to prove. He detailed the failures in the batch that had been sampled.

"Have they shipped yet?" When Al shook his head, McQuire asked, "Where are they going?"

"Sandia."

McQuire seemed satisfied with the answer. Sandia National Laboratory, in the barrens west of Albuquerque, was one the highest-security nuclear weapons research and development facilities in America. "Go ahead, then. Let them ship, and we'll intercept at the other end. Just tell us when."

And with that the meeting was over. The three walked together back into the heat of the parking lot and went their separate ways.

One week later, Al Muehlhausen closed the door of his office at Teledyne and dialed the FBI. After identifying himself to Agent McQuire, he said quietly, "I just wanted to let you know it's on the way."

Over the next few weeks, Al had several phone calls at work from McQuire or his colleagues. The calls were usually about technical issues related to basic design, how the products had been tested while they were still at Teledyne, or verifying the results as Al had reported them to his management. Al's side of these calls was low-key and matter-of-fact, and although he was careful to keep from being overheard, to any of his fellow employees the conversation no doubt would have sounded like business as usual.

Several weeks later, in mid-July, McQuire asked for a second meeting, again at Denny's. He wasn't the kind of person to give anything away, but at this meeting both Emil and Al were relieved to see that he seemed pleased. The shipment had indeed been intercepted at Sandia, and he told them that samples had been sent to an FBI contractor, where they were tested again. Five of the six switches, which had been intended for the trigger system in nuclear weapons, had failed to perform.

Teledyne was still unaware that the shipment had been intercepted, and the FBI had taken steps to ensure that this fact was kept secret. Sandia personnel had no particular ties to the company, and the very few who were involved in the interception were advised that disclosure would be a serious violation of the law. The new tests had been conducted on the other side of the country, at an equally secure facility in New Hampshire.

When Emil heard of the failures, he recalled again what the Vietcong had managed to do to their enemy with the Americans' own failed ordnance, and he was sickened at the thought of history repeating itself. Teledyne was still plodding along its old, familiar course of arrogance and deceit, as fat, dumb, and happy as ever. But Emil and Al derived some bitter satisfaction from the knowledge that now their huge, ugly cat was silently but ferociously clawing its way out of the bag.

When McQuire finished bringing them up to date, Emil asked, "What's next?"

"We want to pull a second sample."

For the next few minutes, the agent and Al discussed where the next batch of switches was headed and when it was likely to be shipped, McQuire methodically noting the plans for the interception on a pad of foolscap. When they finished, the FBI agent leaned back and looked at them thoughtfully, perhaps somewhat speculatively, across the table. And then he asked them, "Do you have a lawyer?"

Emil felt the hair rising on the back of his neck. If they were headed where the question seemed to be taking them, their worst misgivings were about to be proven true. His first thought was "I'm not a criminal—I've never been arrested in my life." But that isn't what came out. Instead, trying his best to remain cool, he said, "No, but we're going to get one."

If the question suggested that they had need for a criminal defense, McQuire didn't seem to be sending any such message in his tone or manner. He told them that they would need legal help to guide them through the process, and he even tried to explain a bit about how the system worked. Possibly he assumed they knew more about the law than they really did. In fact, they knew virtually nothing.

"Would you be able to give us some names?" Emil asked.

McQuire didn't appear to have expected the question. He thought for a moment. "I know a couple of former assistant U.S. attorneys who've gone into private practice," he said. "It wouldn't hurt to have someone who has dealt with this type of case before."

"Great," Emil said.

McQuire lifted his notes to a clean sheet on the pad. He wrote several lines, then tore out the page and passed it to Emil.

F O U R

T H E   R A I D

I n the latter part of August, Emil and Al met with a Los Angeles attorney named John Phillips. Trim, tanned, with light brown hair and quick, inquiring blue eyes, and appearing to be in his middle forties, Phillips greeted them with a firm handshake and an incongruously soft voice. After a series of false starts, they were suddenly hopeful of finding a good match.

The meeting with Phillips followed an attempt to contact Janet Goldstein, a former federal prosecutor on the FBI agent's list. Goldstein had left government service to join Phillips's public interest firm, but it turned out that she was on maternity leave. A colleague named Lauren Saunders told them Goldstein would be returning to work soon and suggested they come in. After Emil gave her a brief description of the fraud, Saunders told Al and Emil that Phillips had played a critical role in recent congressional amendments to the False Claims Act, the federal fraud law that might apply in a case against Teledyne. It was the first time either of them had heard of the act.

It was mildly disquieting to them that the specific rule that applied to stealing from the government might not be that old. But as they talked it over, Al and Emil found reassurance in the prospect of being represented by an expert. What better guide through their coming ordeal than the architect who had helped design the playing field?

It quickly became apparent that Phillips had already made himself familiar with the main facts in their case, as instead of having them repeat their well-rehearsed story yet another time, he asked if they had any questions about the law or about what was likely to lie ahead.

"Well, we're a bit concerned with why we need an attorney," Emil said. When he caught the brief expression of surprise on Phillips's face, he laughed nervously. "In fact, we're a *lot* concerned. We're the ones who

went to the FBI; they didn't come to us. We also know that one way for
Teledyne to defend itself in this situation is to blame the guys who reported them. Now we're beginning to wonder if the FBI is thinking the
same way."

Al added, "This whole thing is about quality control, and Emil and I
are two-thirds of the quality control managers for the whole division."

When Phillips held up his hand, Emil wasn't sure whether it was a
form of reassurance or a warning.

"We haven't spoken with the FBI about this case," Phillips said, "although of course, if we become your attorneys, we'll talk with them right
away. But just because they advised you to get counsel, you needn't worry
that you're the targets of an investigation." He laughed softly, and Emil
could see that the other attorneys at the table were amused as well. "If you
were targets, they wouldn't be giving you advice. They wouldn't be telling you anything."

For Emil, the statement lifted part of an enormous weight. Al appeared to be equally relieved, but they were both still uncertain about the
process they had set in motion and where it would take them.

"The reason you need a lawyer is to protect your interests," Phillips
said. He studied them for a moment, reading their reactions. "Has anyone
explained to you just what those interests are and how the law works?"

Emil thought about his lost job, his suddenly narrowed career hori-
zons, his uncertain future, and he shook his head. "Not really," he said,
meaning not at all.

The attorney leaned toward them with his forearms on the table, his
voice still low. "As Lauren has already told you, what Teledyne has done,
if it can be proven in court, appears to be a violation of the False Claims
Act." He paused, waiting for a response. When they remained silent, he
nodded. "I'd have been surprised if you knew anything about it, since most
lawyers still haven't heard of it either."

In the next several minutes, Phillips outlined the long history of the
act, from its origins in English common law to its recent modernization
and strengthening by Congress, based on amendments Phillips had suggested. "Under this law, anyone with knowledge that the government has
lost money through fraudulent schemes may sue for recovery of those funds
on behalf of the government. It's like being a private attorney general,

deputized to bring Teledyne to justice. You can jointly file a lawsuit on behalf of the government to make Teledyne repay the Treasury."

"You mean, *we're* the ones who go after Teledyne?" Emil asked, feeling suddenly as though what Phillips was telling them was pushing them both to the very end of the limb. "What about the FBI?"

"They did not send you to a lawyer because you're in trouble," Phillips explained, his tone still calm and reassuring. "It's because they knew about the law, just recently brought back to life, that allows people with knowledge of fraud to sue companies that are cheating the government. The law includes a reward, so the person receives a share of whatever the government collects as a result of their suit."

Phillips deliberately paused, watching them thoughtfully from the other side of the table as they took it in.

"Congress designed the law to encourage people like you to come forward with information about how the government has been defrauded," he said. "Having your own lawyer represent you as a party helps assure that the government acts on that information."

Emil slumped back in his chair. How many years, and what enormous pressures, had it taken before he and Al had even been willing to pick up the telephone and call in the law? Both of them had known when they went to the FBI that they were stepping past the point of no return, but they'd thought then that, at most, they were simply sharing knowledge, and were still protected by their anonymity, while others would be acting on what they told. What they were hearing now was altogether different.

Phillips told them that under the False Claims Act, a suit against Teledyne in their name and in the name of the government could be filed "under seal," assuring that it would not be made public, so that the government had time to investigate their allegations before alerting Teledyne to the charges. During that interim, the whistle-blowers and their attorney would work closely with government agents to pull together evidence and build a case. At the end of the investigation—which Phillips warned them could take months or even years—the government would decide whether or not to join the case. If the government chose to decline, the whistle-blowers—referred to in the law as "relators"—could continue the case on their own, essentially acting as the attorney general. Relators who pursue cases successfully on their own, he told them, might receive larger rewards.

"These cases can involve a lot of money," Phillips said, his tone still calm and reassuring. "A liable company could have to pay up to three times the government's losses plus five to ten thousand dollars for each false claim. Under the law, you as plaintiff would be entitled to at least fifteen percent, and as much as thirty percent, of whatever the government recovers."

Emil and Al looked at each other, both trying unsuccessfully to hide their astonishment.

"There's an old phrase that describes this type of suit," Phillips went on quietly, "so old, in fact, that it's Latin. It translates to 'Who brings an action for the king brings it for himself.' The first two words of that phrase are '*Qui tam.*' Your suit against Teledyne would be a *qui tam* case: *Emil Stache and Al Muehlhausen on behalf of the United States of America v. Teledyne.*"

Emil and Al were both silent. It was clear this was developing far, far differently from anything they had imagined; the attorney was about to raise the shade in a corner where neither of them had suspected, just a moment earlier, that there was even a window. Emil thought of saying something like, "We didn't get into this because we thought we were going to make any money," but he realized that was obvious to everyone in the room.

Phillips went on to explain the legal basis for a false claim. The certification that goes with every shipment is a representation that all the products in that order meet government specifications. Until just a few years earlier, before the law was rewritten to encourage individuals to pursue claims, it was unlikely that a large and powerful defense contractor like Teledyne would have a lot to worry about if that certification were untrue. There was little likelihood that the government would learn that the company was knowingly and systematically shipping defective products.

But with the rewritten law, all that had changed. Now, Phillips said, individuals like Emil and Al who knew about fraud could actually file suit in a federal court to remedy it.

Emil and Al knew what kind of paperwork went out with every batch of products. Even though most relays were shipped in large lots where the certificate of warranty covered a hundred switches at a time, Teledyne was producing and shipping hundreds of thousands of them every month. Uncertain he had grasped the concept correctly, Emil asked, "Am I hearing this right? We could be talking billions."

"If it comes to that," Phillips agreed. "But when a company gets caught submitting phony invoices—or certifying defective products—and they know the government can prove it, they're likely to try to settle the case rather than take it to trial. The government would probably settle based on its actual damages—with some multiplier—rather than rely on the penalties provision."

Emil fiddled with a pen for a moment, then laid it down again on the legal pad. He leaned back in his chair and looked at his folded hands. The concept of a settlement sounded too much like a way for Teledyne to get away with it, to slip out of the noose, at the best an anticlimax, at the worst a mere token. Regardless of whatever hopes Al Muehlhausen might still be nurturing for his future relationship with Teledyne, Emil knew with absolute certainty that once this case was out in the open, their careers were as good as dead. Nobody was going to cut any slack for either of them. With Teledyne's bottomless resources, a settlement meant the company could wriggle out of anything. But for himself and Al there would be no settling anything—no compromising, no negotiating, no token consequence: They were headed straight for a train wreck.

Phillips paused, and Emil looked up again. The lawyer seemed to be examining him tentatively from the other side of the table. "Let me explain again what's involved in settling," he said, and Emil wondered how many of his thoughts had been showing on his face.

"It doesn't mean striking a deal for five cents on the dollar. It doesn't mean getting off the hook. It means figuring out as closely as possible how much Teledyne was paid for the shipments that contained products that didn't work, then making them pay back those costs, plus an additional amount for the fraud."

A few days later Emil and Al had a second meeting with the law firm, this time to negotiate the terms of their relationship. By then Janet Goldstein was back from her maternity leave, and they both liked her immediately. She told them that they would not be meeting again with Ken McQuire. He had been transferred to another assignment, and the case was now being run by a multiagency task force.

Over the next two and a half months, Emil and Al spent countless hours with Janet Goldstein, an assistant United States attorney named Julie

Fox Blackshaw who was in charge of the criminal case that accompanied their civil suit, and agents assigned to the task force from the FBI, air force, NASA, the navy, and the army. The two men explained the quality control system at Teledyne in painstaking detail, helping the team assemble enough evidence to establish probable cause for a search warrant. They helped the government attorney and the agents decipher the military specifications governing relays, explained testing in detail, and described, a step at a time, how Teledyne routinely falsified test data. Based on the information they provided, the government was able to establish probable cause to get the search warrant.

In parallel with this effort, the two relators worked with Goldstein and her colleagues as they drafted a detailed legal complaint and "disclosure statement" which would become the government's primary source and road map in possible criminal and civil prosecution. They described how Teledyne products routinely failed tests, yet were sold to the government with the assurance they were failure-free. They chronicled the many failed relays and customer returns that had not been reported, as required, to the government. They helped the lawyers develop a theory of damages; based on the difference between the price of relays sold commercially and the amount Teledyne charged for relays that had been specially tested to ensure high reliability, it would be used by prosecutors to compute how much the fraud had cost the American taxpayer.

The civil false claims case was filed in mid-September, under seal, meaning that its contents were to be kept secret from everyone, including Teledyne. Emil had been terminated on July 3, and in the intervening weeks he spent his limited free time anxiously reading the employment ads and wondering if he would ever get another job. Despite the tremendous demands of the case, after ten weeks he found a position through the newspapers that was very similar to the one he had left, and he began working for his new employer the same week the case was filed. The pay was about the same, but the change meant he lost all his benefits, and in the smaller company he had a sense that his future was now limited. He was relieved that the stigma of his departure from Teledyne had not yet followed him into the street, but all that was subject to change on a moment's notice—possibly when the FBI made its move, and certainly when his new employer saw his name connected with the Teledyne case in the news.

It was equally obvious, at least to Emil, that things would change even more dramatically for Al. The FBI wanted him to stay on the job as long as possible because of the obvious advantage of having a man on the inside to guide them through the investigation. But the day would come when the case was unsealed, and Al gave no indication that he had made any plans for leaving once his role was revealed.

The demands of the case on Al's and Emil's time didn't end with the filing. To help the FBI in its coming search of Teledyne, the two relators provided agents with a detailed map of the facility, a list of witnesses to be interviewed during the raid, and guidance on the types of documents the government should seize, along with their locations. The government was afraid of leaks, but even if it succeeded in maintaining secrecy up to the moment of the raid, unless Emil and Al told agents exactly what they were looking for and where to find it, there was a risk that overlooked documents could be destroyed in the raid's aftermath.

A couple of weeks after the filing, on the night of October 1, 1990, Al Muehlhausen received a telephone call at home from the agent who had taken Agent Ken McQuire's place, advising him that the raid was scheduled for the following day.

He slept fitfully, got up somewhat earlier than usual, and drove to work with a growing sense of apprehension. He too knew that the story of his responsibility for the coming raid would eventually become public knowledge, but he was determined that nothing he said or did would provide the slightest hint of his role in what was about to happen.

The task force finally arrived, flashing badges and streaming down the halls with a fleet of rubber-wheeled dollies. The shock spread throughout the plant almost instantaneously, and the reaction was pandemonium. Employees ran back and forth between offices, making frantic phone calls to report on what was happening, seeking guidance from others in the company who were equally under siege, or offering empty assurances to panicked colleagues.

The agents, by contrast, were organized and calm, spreading through the plant, working their way systematically in teams of two through one office after another, interviewing employees, taking statements, collecting files. Dolly after dolly rolled by Al's office, stacked high with the records of thousands of tests falsely certifying the reliability of products that had been sold for tens of millions of dollars.

In order to deflect the suspicion of his colleagues, the government and Al had agreed in advance that when the raid occurred, he would be treated exactly the same way as everyone else in the company. That understanding had been confirmed on the telephone just the night before, so it was no surprise when the two agents assigned to his department sat down in his office and began the interview with the hard-nosed, no-nonsense tone of serious adversaries. If others in the department were paying attention, it would be clear to them that the agents weren't playing favorites, and Al was relieved. But when the door had been closed, and the three of them were separated from the scrutiny of his fellow workers, the tone of the inquiry didn't change. Suddenly uncomfortable, Al interrupted one of his interrogators to ask a question of his own.

"You both know who I am, right?"

The two agents examined him quizzically for a moment, then one of them consulted his clipboard. "You're Almon Muehlhausen." The tone suggested Al wasn't going to get very far if he was claiming to be someone else.

Al glanced around to be sure he hadn't missed something, that there was no one else in the room or within hearing. "I'm the one who brought this to the FBI."

Both of the agents looked considered Al for a moment, but neither replied.

"I'm the one who reported this case," Al repeated. "I'm the reason you're here."

Up to that moment, Al had assumed that all the agents involved in the raid would be fully informed. Each of them would know every detail of what he and Emil had shared with the FBI and later with the task force, and they'd certainly have been alerted to the identity of the man on the inside, their only ally within the company and the person who was taking all the chances. But all the agents did was look perplexed, and one of them said, "We don't have any information on that."

The other agent studied Al for a moment longer, perhaps with the slightest trace of sympathy. "There's no reason for anyone to tell us." Then, suddenly all business, he added, "Now that we're here, we have a job to do and we're looking for the same cooperation from everyone."

Al nodded; it made sense that not everyone in the task force would know, and the decision to not tell all of them might even have been made for his own protection. But the exchange—and the realization that the good guys didn't necessarily recognize him as one of their own—left him feeling more isolated than ever.

That feeling of separateness would grow as the day went on. From the moment the raid began, the assumption was nearly universal among employees that what was happening was the result of an informant. As Al's responsibilities took him elsewhere in the building, in response either to the demands of the government agents or to the normal obligations of his job, he never heard a single comment by a fellow employee suggesting the possibility that all of this was happening for a good reason, that the raid was taking place because something the company had done was seriously and fundamentally wrong. On the contrary, the only reason the federal agents were there was because of some individual's treachery, someone within the company whom all of them worked with every day. Someone they had trusted.

And whoever that person was, whoever had blown the whistle on his company and brought down this chaos on his colleagues and friends, Al heard more than once as the long day wore on, should be "taken outside, stood up against the wall, and fucking shot."

FIVE

SHODDY

More than a century before most Americans ever heard of Vietnam, the United States was facing a civil conflict of its own. And in that earlier war between the North and South, as in the latter one, corrupt profiteering was epidemic. Gunpowder was frequently adulterated with sawdust. Rifles didn't fire. At the start of the Civil War, Union uniforms exposed to rain would often dissolve and fall from the wearer in clots of sodden fiber.

The reason this happened to the uniforms was that often, instead of being woven, the cloth was held together with glue. The fabric was made from old materials that had been shredded, pounded to a pulp, mixed with a water-soluble sizing, and then rolled out like blotter paper. In the cotton-starved North, the resulting product, called "shoddy," was far cheaper to make than woven cloth. It could be cut and sewn and even ironed, and it gave a false appearance of reasonable quality. But under minimal stress or moisture, it lost all of its integrity and strength, and in a heavy rain it would quickly turn to oatmeal.

"Shoddy" was a word that soon came to be applied to almost anything that didn't hold together or do its intended job. It described soldiers' shoes so poorly made that they fell apart after the first week's wear, army blankets that lost their fibers after just a few nights in the field, and military overcoats that tattered in the first brisk wind.

In the American Civil War, the plague of shoddy craftsmanship went far beyond what soldiers wore or what kept them warm. In the early days of mobilization, heartless profiteering was viewed by many as almost a form of sport. The United States had existed for only eighty-seven years when the conflict began, the length of a long lifetime, and many citizens on either side of the Mason-Dixon line descended from parents or grandparents who had been born in a British colony and started life as subjects of a foreign power. In the old world, one class of society typically did the fighting, and another class would reap the profit.

The concept of a true, class-blind sharing in responsibility for the common good had been tested during the Revolution, but had lain relatively fallow in the years that followed independence. "We have changed our forms of government," Benjamin Rush, a signer of the Declaration of Independence, wrote in 1786, "but it remains yet to effect a revolution in our principles, opinions and manners so as to accommodate them to the forms of government we have adopted."

In the subsequent expansion of its frontiers, the new country seemed to place less value on public-spiritedness than on the adaptive skills of gifted loners. Title characters in the novels of James Fenimore Cooper, who died just a decade before the Civil War, included the solitary *Spy*, *Pathfinder*, and *Deerslayer*. On the darker side of human nature, another mid-century literary figure, first appearing as Melville's *Confidence Man* and evolving into the later river denizens of Mark Twain's Mississippi, paid wry, sardonic tribute to the sharp operator, the exploiter, the outsider who prospered by his wit and wile, usually at the expense of the law-abiding and righteous. By those lights, selling the same horse twice, or fleecing the gullible government with clothing that melted off its wearer's back, was almost a right of citizenship.

It was hardly practiced in secret. When the government bought carbines that didn't shoot, instead of forcing the makers to fix them, it sold them off in wholesale lots for $2 apiece just to get them out of inventory. The speculators who bought the defective weapons did nothing to repair them either, but instead turned around and sold them back to cooperative quartermasters at other locations—for eleven times the price they had paid for them as junk. Robber baron Jim Fisk, who made millions supplying worthless, moth-eaten blankets to the military, boasted, "You can sell anything to the government at almost any price you've got the guts to ask."

In the early days of the Civil War, the corruption extended all the way up to the secretary of war, a pinched, tweedy, white-thatched Pennsylvanian named Simon Cameron. Known behind his back as the "Winnebago Chief" for his alleged bilking of an Indian tribe before he came to Washington, Cameron enfranchised two cronies, New York governor Edwin Morgan and a former legislative aide named Alexander

Cummings, to disburse millions of dollars on military contracts. Both
Morgan and Cummings were involved in the carbine fraud, and the
latter's excesses included $140,000 in public funds for the rental of a yacht
and the squandering of another quarter million for such personal perks
as linen pantaloons, herring, pickles, ale, and porter. Other Cameron
cohorts were awarded contracts for a thousand cavalry horses at double
the going rate. When the animals were delivered to Louisville, Kentucky,
nearly half were found to be "blind, spavined [lame]... and with every
disease horseflesh is heir to."

Six months into the war, and in only the eighth month of his presidency, Abraham Lincoln criticized Cameron as "utterly ignorant and regardless of the course of things." That may have sounded harsh to some,
but to others who knew the secretary of war to be equally as generous with
himself as with his cronies, it seemed too kind. Cameron was hardly ignorant, for example, in repeatedly favoring two railroads in which he had
direct financial interests, the North Central and the Pennsylvania, for the
routing of Union war materials and troops. By January, Congress tired of
the blatant abuses and voted to censure the errant secretary. But Lincoln,
aware of Cameron's continuing political clout in strategically critical Pennsylvania, settled for kicking him out of the cabinet and into an ambassadorship. The disgraced Cameron left Washington in the middle of that
winter for far-off, frozen Russia.

Many of the congressmen who voted for Cameron's censure were
themselves guilty of the same type of offense. Several, for example, made
a regular practice of charging government suppliers a $50,000 "broker's
fee" on every million dollars in contracts let within their sphere of influence. Edwin Stanton replaced Cameron in the cabinet, but the corruption
and incompetence continued unabated. Gen. George McClellan, Union
commander of the Army of the Potomac, held shoddy goods and services
partly responsible for the failure of the campaign to capture Richmond in
the spring of 1862. For one example, defective artillery shells frequently
failed to detonate on impact or blew up prematurely in the cannons, kill-
ing Union troops. For another, the army's mobility was impaired by the
low quality of thousands of cavalry and draft horses used in that campaign.
"Worse than traitors in arms" was how a March 3, 1863 report from the
House Committee on Government Contracts described "men who pre-
tend loyalty to the flag, [but] feast and fatten on the misfortunes of the

nation, while patriot blood is crimsoning the plains ... and bodies of their countrymen are moldering in the dust."

There was no Justice Department in those days, and no effective national law enforcement agency. But not all the nation's leaders were crooks or plunderers, and as the predatory few continued to feast and fatten, the incensed majority searched for ways to purge this enemy from within their ranks. A Republican senator from Michigan, Jacob Howard, emerged as the leader of this effort. The ideal solution, Howard reasoned, would be legislation offering financial incentives to private citizens who took action against individuals and companies they knew were stealing from the government, a law that would make integrity almost as profitable as theft.

Howard was particularly indignant that the rifle recyclers and gunpowder adulterers had escaped punishment, and that Cameron had been rewarded with an ambassadorship rather than sent to prison. Defending his bill from the Senate floor, he railed against "frauds of a very gross character ... in the purchase and selling of small arms for the use of the Army." Lincoln, perhaps still smarting from criticisms of his leniency toward Cameron, embraced the new legislation with such enthusiasm that it quickly became known in the press as "Mr. Lincoln's Law."

Its official name was the False Claims Act, but the law was also frequently identified by the feature that allowed citizens to sue on the government's behalf, described in the Latin phrase "*Qui tam pro domino rege quam pro se ipso in hac parte sequitor*" ("Who brings an action for the king brings it for himself"). *Qui tam* laws had an ancient ancestry, tracing back to the thirteenth-century British courts of Henry III. It was a time when a large part of the civilized world was just emerging from the Dark Ages, there were virtually no police forces, and an otherwise obscure Yorkshire yeoman, taking the law into his own hands to right a financial wrong, gave rise to the legendary figure of Robin Hood. The main difference between *Robertus Hood, fugitivus,* listed on the Pipe Roll of 1230, and the first *qui tam* litigants of that same era was that the latter worked within the law and with the open encouragement of the king.

Statutes providing for *qui tam* suits stemming from old English law were imported to America and enacted by the first Congress. But once the new nation was up and running, these laws experienced a slow erosion and eventually were vitiated by the special interests they were intended to control. By fifty years before the Civil War, they had become so weak as to be useless. Jacob Howard hardly invented the concept, but he restored some of the weakened or deleted provisions to give *qui tam* law new teeth.

Actionable offenses under the law included the filing of a false invoice or voucher, conspiring to defraud, stealing, embezzling, concealing property, and delivering bogus receipts. Each individual act was punishable by a fine of $2,000—astronomical for its time—and in addition the offender had to repay two dollars for every dollar stolen, as well as all court costs incurred by the government or the private litigant acting on the government's behalf. Any such citizen who filed a successful false claims lawsuit was allowed to keep half of whatever was recovered, with the other half going to the federal treasury. The law also carried criminal penalties with a maximum fine of $5,000 and up to five years in prison. Not all such suits would be certain to prevail, of course, so a *qui tam* action was not without risk for the litigants on both sides.

By the time of the Spanish-American War, corruption in government contracting had once again become rampant. More United States soldiers in that conflict, quite literally, died in the mess hall than on the battlefield, the victims of poisoning by American beef that had been preserved in deadly formaldehyde by unscrupulous civilian contractors. Even Teddy Roosevelt, the "Hero of San Juan Hill," attested to the awful consequences of eating the tainted meat, and once again the result was an outpouring of public outrage. But this time, that was as far as it went. A military court of inquiry was convened, and after several days of often sickeningly graphic testimony the matter was dismissed without a single finding of culpability. Not one party to the conspiracy, either military or civilian, was ever held to account for a fraud that resulted in more deaths than from the entire Spanish arsenal.

Between 1863 and the start of World War II, the number of recorded *qui tam* cases stands at only ten, although it's possible, because of out-of-court settlements and a lack of publication, that the actual count is higher. By the time of the Japanese attack on Pearl Harbor, the feeding frenzy among unscrupulous contractors had resumed. The False Claims Act, designed to protect against such abuse, was unknown by the great majority of Americans, and viewed by most of the rest as irrelevant and arcane.

The firm of Curtiss-Wright, bearer of two of the proudest names in aviation, was caught selling the government defective engines for combat aircraft. The Glenn L. Martin Company, once builders of the giant flying boats that had flown some of the earliest commercial routes across both the Atlantic and Pacific, now knowingly built B-26 medium bombers with wings that were too short. In January 1943 the tanker *Schenectady,* built of substandard materials supplied by United States Steel and its subsidiary, Carnegie-Illinois Steel, broke in two shortly after launching. A special Senate investigative committee, chaired by Harry Truman of Missouri, was formed to look into these abuses, but its focus was more on maintaining the efficiency of the war machine than on the jailing of felons. Truman did manage to recover several billion dollars in a three-year period (the 1942 military procurement budget totaled $400 billion), but those responsible were routinely let off the hook.

In 1943, the federal government accused several defendants in the Pittsburgh shipyards of rigging bids. An enterprising attorney who had no prior knowledge of the conspiracy picked up a copy of the indictments at the courthouse and used them as the basis for filing a *qui tam* lawsuit on his own behalf. Certainly there was no intention in the law to offer a free ride to opportunists quick enough, and venal enough, to piggyback on government litigation—but neither was there anything in the law that said they couldn't. The Justice Department moved to dismiss the attorney's claim, and the battle went all the way to the Supreme Court. In one of those decisions where justice and strict adherence to the law go separate ways, both the government and the attorney won. Money was returned to the Treasury that would not otherwise have been recovered, and the court ruled that the relator was entitled to half of the recovered money, about $157,000, even though he knew nothing whatever about the fraud beyond the information contained in the government's indictments.

Predictably, lawyers all over the country began getting up earlier and reading the newspapers with new enthusiasm, looking for stories of federal indictments that might lead to similar opportunities. The Justice Department, never enthusiastic about *qui tam* law even before this latest assault, described the spate of suits that followed as "parasitic."

Almost as quickly, Congress set about to amend the False Claims Act, ostensibly as a response to this highly visible misuse of the *qui tam* provision, but also under far less visible pressure from industry. Most military contractors were anxious to remove this incentive to the reporting of corporate misfeasance and the launching of privately initiated lawsuits. The

Justice Department, never comfortable with civilian competition in the prosecution of government cases and jealous of the large rewards, was eager to cooperate, advocating that the *qui tam* provisions, which both empowered and rewarded the whistle-blower, simply be eliminated from what remained of the False Claims Act.

Congress was willing to go only partway. The relator's share was cut from half to no more than 10 percent in those cases where the government joined in the suit. In the unlikely circumstance that the government declined to participate and the litigation was successful anyway, the relator's share could go as high as 25 percent—still only half the amount provided for in the original law. And there was no minimum-share guarantee, so relators ran the risk of getting nothing for their efforts.

A key feature of the revisions eliminated exploitation of *qui tam* law by suits based on public information; a "government knowledge barrier" banned such litigation based on evidence already in the government's possession. Although aimed at the "parasitic" suits, it also had the effect, perhaps unintentionally, of precluding meritorious *qui tam* cases that were essentially unknown to anyone in the government responsible for fraud investigations. Some courts went so far as to conclude that if the information were anywhere in the government's possession—even if unread or buried somewhere in a dusty file and completely ignored—a *qui tam* lawsuit could not be brought.

As a result, although there were about a hundred *qui tam* cases between the date of those revisions in 1943 and the next substantial rewriting of the law in 1986, virtually all of them failed. When Wisconsin found that a nursing home was cheating both the state and federal governments, for example, the Seventh Circuit Court of Appeals threw out the state's *qui tam* suit because the federal government already knew about the theft. Wisconsin argued that the only reason that was true was because the Wisconsin investigators had told Washington about it.

The court's response suggested that the flaw was not in what the state had done, but in the law itself. The steady erosion had taken its toll. The False Claims Act had been worn back down to its gums.

By the start of the Reagan presidency, a new generation of predatory contractors had a virtual passkey to the government henhouse. The renewed emphasis on military spending saw hundreds of billions of dollars voted into the Pentagon sieve, with fraud and abuse attaining levels equal to the worst excesses of the Civil War. Fresh scandals aired almost nightly on the network news, most of them the result of tips to the press by disgusted insiders who had no other place to take their complaints than to the court of public opinion. Reports of venal horror stories, each more shameless than the one before it, became a form of popular entertainment.

On the B-52 bomber, a small plastic cap for the navigator's stool, worth approximately 17 cents, was sold to the government for $1,118.26, or 6,578 times as much as it actually cost.

The C5-A transport carried a ten-cup coffee maker, easily replaceable at Woolworth's, for which the American taxpayer was billed $7,622.

When the navy needed an ordinary claw hammer, instead of going to the hardware store and buying it off the shelf for $7.66 retail, it paid a defense contractor $435 for the exact same product.

The most famous such revelation, rising instantly to the level of a popular metaphor, was the flying toilet seat, a distinctly low-tech accessory for the P-3 subhunting aircraft that sold to the government for a high-flying $640. After that one made headlines, *Washington Post* editorial cartoonist Herblock regularly included a toilet seat in his caricatures of Caspar Weinberger, hanging it around the defense secretary's neck like a farcical albatross with the price tag flapping.

Not all of these stories were limited in their implications to comic-opera extravagance, waste, or simple stealing. In some of them, the bottom line was life or death.

For a year, the army systematically concealed deficits in the aiming mechanism for the Sergeant York, a mobile gun being developed for shooting down low-flying enemy aircraft. Named after the eagle-eyed Tennessee sharpshooter of World War I, the Sergeant York had a radar system that was so easily confused, the weapon might more accurately have honored the nearsighted Mr. Magoo. In one test of its effectiveness—a last one, as things turned out—when aimed at an incoming "enemy" helicopter, its radar and computers locked onto another target in the same general direction, which happened to be the whirring ceiling fan in a portable field toilet. This was too good a story to keep out of the papers, and in short order it was being told all over America. The Pentagon, already smarting from the exemplary potential in a simple toilet seat and anxious to avoid a similar association with an entire outhouse, quickly decided to cut its losses and scrap the project.

The misbegotten Bradley Fighting Vehicle had in common with the Sergeant York mobile field gun the fact that its name co-opted the reputation of an authentic American war hero, and that by the time the epic scope of the fiasco became public knowledge, the honoree was safely dead and therefore not likely to be represented by counsel. Designed for ambiguous and sometimes contradictory roles, the aluminum-armored hybrid was a mechanical crossbreed between an armadillo and a roadrunner. Its crew was sandwiched in above an arsenal of machine gun ammunition and antitank missiles and below huge plastic bladders containing the vehicle's fuel. A single hit by anything larger than a twenty-millimeter shell could produce instant and catastrophic results, potentially incinerating the crew or blowing them to pieces. True, the Bradley was equipped with a state-of-the-art halon fire suppression system, but that too was long on liabilities and short on assets; it couldn't put out the fire from burning ammunition, and the halon was so toxic that it either asphyxiated the occupants or forced them outside the vehicle to face enemy gunfire.

But unlike its strategic withdrawal from the Sergeant York, even after devastating footage on national television showed the Bradley burning like the Hindenburg in simulated combat trials and sinking like an anvil in the attempted amphibious crossing of a river, the Pentagon stood by its huge investment—by then in the billions—and paid little more than lip service to the vehicle's many defects. What was at stake was worth more than winning wars or saving lives; for the defense contractors who had produced it, the Bradley was one of the most productive cash cows in military history, at least in that one respect exceeding its designers' highest expectations.

If the Bradley was hard for taxpayers to swallow, the army's MRE (Meals Ready to Eat) program was literally nauseating. Intended to replace venerable C rations, by then in their forties, the space-age MREs came in convenient plastic packs that could be heated in boiling water or opened cold in combat conditions. There were two unexpected but frequent variations on the standard pouch, however, which were quickly dubbed "bloaters" and "leakers." Bloaters were MRE containers that blew up into putrid, gas-filled balloons as the result of microbial contaminants in the pouch. Some leakers may have experienced a brief midlife as bloaters, but the package had then ruptured, or had a hole to start with, and emitted foul fluids and noxious odors.

One shipment of MREs was returned to its plant of origin in Texas when the army discovered that the pouches were filled with maggots. The stench was so potent, even workers wearing masks became ill just disposing of them. But it was only after a story on the bloaters and leakers appeared on a national television newsmagazine that the army admitted, some eighty years after the formaldehyde-beef scandal of the Spanish-American War, that a number of soldiers had likewise been hospitalized with poisoning from the contaminated MRE rations. And only then were the first steps taken to remedy the problem at its cause.

A similar cover-up was orchestrated by the navy in defense of its enormously complex Aegis project. An amalgam of sophisticated seaborne radar, computers, and surface-to-air rockets ten years in development, Aegis was built to simultaneously track up to two hundred aerial targets and to control thirty killer missiles. But in sea tests against sixteen easy targets—easy because they were lobbed in one after another instead of all at the same time, as they would arrive in combat—the supershield missed all but five.

The navy was far more efficient than its dubious weapon, at least for a short time, in protecting itself against the cramping effect of congressional scrutiny or the potential embarrassment of publicity. The results of the sea trials were immediately classified, ostensibly for reasons of national security, and it was announced that the tests had been successful. When congressional overseers eventually learned they had been duped—again because not everyone involved in the fiasco interpreted "patriotic duty" as "staying silent"—the Aegis program was very nearly scuttled.

Back during the Vietnam years, when young Emil Stache was wounded and thousands of his countrymen and allies were routinely being maimed or killed by the enemy's recycling of defective American ordnance, the incentives and protection of Mr. Lincoln's Law were already almost obsolete. Some insiders, motivated by patriotism, an offended sense of right and wrong, or fear of being themselves blamed for the misdeeds they had witnessed, still occasionally revealed contractor abuses, but there were at least as many good reasons to remain silent. Their motives, and often their character, were routinely impugned by those they reported on; the whistle-blower seldom received a reward; and most paid a high personal price in lost trust, shattered reputations, and derailed careers. Compared with the number of offenses, reports of fraud were few and far between.

By the time Emil went to work for Teledyne fifteen years later, with the start of Reagan's buildup of the military, the pendulum had swung even further away from any form of legal protection, social support, or financial compensation for whistle-blowers; instead, swift, draconian reprisals were a virtual guarantee.

S I X

NO GOOD DEED
UNPUNISHED

O ne of the best-known examples of reprisal was the experience
of Robert Wityczak. His story, like Emil Stache's, begins in
Vietnam.

In June 1970, Wityczak was on a patrol with his marine unit thirty-
five miles southeast of Da Nang when he stepped on a land mine. He lost
his left leg at the hip, his right leg at the knee, and his left hand. Three
years later, with a hook in the place of his missing hand and a wheelchair
to get around in because there wasn't enough left of his leg for a prosthe-
sis, he went to work with the defense behemoth Rockwell International in
Downey, California, as a billing clerk. And he was glad to get the job.

At the outset, his work consisted of processing materials orders,
some bookkeeping, checking order changes, and follow-up on relationships with outside vendors. It gave him a window seat on an elaborate
scam through which Rockwell was systematically ripping off the government for millions.

The vista began to unfold when he discovered, in early 1974, that
Rockwell was illegally juggling charges between NASA's Apollo/Soyuz test
program and the B-1 bomber. The space shuttle contract had been awarded
to Rockwell at a fixed price, while the bomber was cost-plus. On a fixed price
job, the difference between the bid and the actual cost is the company's legitimate profit. But when billing at cost-plus, a contractor is reimbursed for
all reasonable costs it incurs, plus a stipulated profit. So every time Rockwell
shifted a bill from one project to the other, it was stealing twice—first by
increasing the profit margin on the fixed price project, and second by earn-
ing the markup as a fraudulent expense of the cost-plus contract.

Wityczak also found evidence of personal thefts. Rockwell engineers,
perhaps emboldened by the corporate example, were ordering items for

their own use and billing them to cost-plus government contracts. Wityczak told his group leader about orders for excessive quantities of twenty-four-karat gold polymide tape, exotic woods, and even wallpaper and carpeting. But he was never encouraged to put his reports in writing, and nothing ever happened as a consequence. When he came across some documents indicating illegal charge shifting and theft, he turned them over to a supervisor and another company official, who promised to pass them on to Rockwell security and the FBI. Wityczak waited, but nobody from either organization ever contacted him, and a year later he learned why: Instead of being passed along as promised, the evidence had been given back to the individuals responsible for the wrongdoing.

Three years into his employment, after consistently excellent performance reviews, Wityczak was promoted to a position in which he was ordered to participate in the false billing himself. Along with some thirty other employees, he was told to charge time to the space shuttle that had actually been spent on fixed-price projects elsewhere in the company. He went along at first, but the situation created in him unbearable tensions between loyalty to his employer and a strong sense of duty to his country, and by the end of 1977 he told his supervisors he couldn't keep it up. They were furious.

Their first reaction was to call him names—"anti-Rockwell," "anti-management," and, not infrequently, "pain in the ass." Often, they demanded that he sign blank time sheets that someone else would then fill in, inaccurately allocating his hours to those projects providing the highest return. His bosses were smarter than to fire him on the spot—but not much smarter. They stripped him of his confidential security clearance, limited his access to corporate billing documents, and excluded him from meetings. Eventually, Wityczak was transferred from his clerical job and, despite his obvious physical handicaps, assigned to straight manual labor.

For the next several months, he worked as a janitor, pushing a broom ahead of his wheelchair, keeping track of tools, sometimes even moving heavy objects. If the object of this reassignment was to persecute him into quitting, it didn't work. In 1981, he was moved again, this time to the machine shop.

The new job required him to unload and store parts on shelves that were between twelve and fourteen feet high. To reach the taller ones with the order picker, he had to stand on the wheelchair, balanced on the stump of his remaining leg. Frequently he fell, and sometimes those falls resulted in injury, but he'd get back in his wheelchair and keep on going. He loaded tools into boxes on wheels, then attached his hook to the carts, some weighing three hundred pounds, and used his right hand to steer the wheelchair as it dragged the heavy loads to various locations around the shop. The strain on his arm with the hook was sometimes excruciating, and more than once the burden on the wheelchair was enough to snap its axles. But even with his emotional and physical health deteriorating under the relentless persecution, he proved tougher than his bosses. Rockwell finally threw in the towel and fired him in May 1982.

Wityczak may not have believed he was able to do anything about the false billing, but this was a different matter. He responded with a suit for wrongful termination. Worst of all for Rockwell, he went public—not only with what the company had done to a wounded veteran, but with the far larger issue behind the harassment and firing: his unwillingness to go along with stealing from the taxpayer. "I gave a pretty good down payment for the privilege of living in this country," he told ABC's *20/20*, looking straight into the camera's eye, occasionally raising his hook for emphasis. A credible, immensely sympathetic witness, he had all the makings of a defense attorney's nightmare. Apparently that potential was not lost on his former employers.

A common condition in the settlement of cases before they come to trial is that the amount of damages be kept secret by both sides. Shortly after the *20/20* segment hit the air, Rockwell paid Robert Wityczak an undisclosed amount to get rid of his wrongful termination suit and to turn off the unwelcome spotlight.

The most famous modern-day whistle-blower was A. Ernest Fitzgerald. He first came into prominent public view during the war in Vietnam. As assistant secretary of the air force for financial management, in late 1968 and early 1969 he testified to Senator William Proxmire's Joint Economic Committee on previously unreported problems in the development of the C-5A. The giant cargo plane, he revealed, had already exceeded its budget by more than $2 billion, and major technical flaws remained unsolved. Congress reacted with predictable expressions of concern, but Fitzgerald's disclosures produced an even stronger response, if not as publicly, back at the Pentagon. The air force generals for whom the cabinet is charged with civilian oversight were outraged that Fitzgerald had actually performed his job as required by law, and they demanded his immediate removal for letting the cat out of the bag.

That vengeful scenario played better in the Pentagon than in the White House, which, though no less vindictive, was more finely attuned to the importance of appearances. For the next several months he was allowed to keep his title, but almost none of his former responsibilities. By the end of the year, when enough time had elapsed to provide what the presidential staff was fond of calling "deniability" for an act of political reprisal, he was fired. Although any connection between Fitzgerald's testimony and his later fate was decried as a slander on the integrity of the executive branch of government, the order was recorded for posterity by the hidden microphones in Nixon's Oval Office, in the president's own voice. "He's been doin' this two or three times," the leader of the free world can be heard telling his chief of staff. "Get rid of that son of a bitch."

But like Banquo's ghost, Fitzgerald wouldn't go away. He appealed his firing to the Civil Service Commission, took a part-time job with Senator Proxmire's committee, and set to work on a book about government misspending, *The High Priests of Waste,* which became a best-seller. After four years of costly litigation, he was reinstated by the air force, although not to a position connected to the cabinet or with any meaningful responsibility; his make-work assignment, studying the standardization of nuts and bolts, was a transparent extension of his initial punishment. He filed two lawsuits against nine high-ranking officials in the Department of Defense, and as a tenth defendant he later added the president. Although a divided Supreme Court dismissed his damage suit against Nixon, five to four, Fitzgerald won his case to be restored to his old job and responsibilities.

Ten years after the man who had ordered his termination was carried into exile on the purifying tide of Watergate, Fitzgerald was still living up to his pedigree as the Pentagon's most vigilant watchdog. He called public attention, for example, to the infamous "antenna hexagon wrench" sold to the air force by General Dynamics for $9,609, pointing out that it cost approximately one dollar to manufacture and was nothing more than a standard Allen wrench with a fancy handle. He also shed unwelcome light on the shortcomings of Hughes Aircraft Company's aptly named Maverick antitank missile, a heat-seeking weapon with a troublesome inability to distinguish between a legitimate target and a hot rock.

One night in early 1983, Fitzgerald got a telephone call from someone identifying himself as Chuck Grassley. "I'm a senator from Iowa," the man said. "Are you the Fitzgerald who wrote *The High Priests of Waste?*"

The question was almost as surprising as the identity of the caller. Why would Senator Grassley, a well-known Midwestern conservative, be telephoning him at home, at night, to ask about a book written eleven years earlier? With trepidation that may have shown in his voice, he acknowledged that he was the author.

"Is all the stuff you wrote in that book true?"

The second question was hardly what he expected, and Fitzgerald, though still puzzled, suddenly felt more confident. Every fact, every allegation, had been scrupulously checked by the publisher, and subsequently examined in microscopic detail by Congress and the press. "Absolutely," he said, knowing he was on rock-solid ground.

"Are the same kinds of things going on in the Pentagon now?"

Fitzgerald was still guarded, but he was beginning to feel the first slight tugging of exhilaration. "Yes," he answered. He told the senator that the problem was worse than ever, because now the Pentagon was getting more money from Congress than it knew what to do with.

"Well," Grassley said, "it's time I learned more about it."

SEVEN

IN THE PUBLIC INTEREST

I n June 1969, a few weeks after the vanguard of Emil Stache's infantry company was blown to bits in Vietnam, John Phillips, then age twenty-six, graduated from Boalt Hall, the University of California school of law, in Berkeley. It was just six months into the presidency of Richard Nixon, and the nation was in turmoil. Although Phillips wasn't sure what kind of practice he wanted to pursue, one reason for his choice of a career as an attorney was a sense that the law represented a chance to make a difference in the world.

The youngest of three sons of the local Ford dealer, Phillips had grown up in Leechburg, Pennsylvania, a coal-mining and steel-rolling community of less than five thousand about twenty-five miles downwind of Pittsburgh. For a good part of the year, football was the only thing that really seemed to matter. In fact, support for the local team was so spirited, the capacity of the high school stadium was greater than the entire population of the town.

The road to Boalt Hall, however, contained a couple of major detours. Because of business reversals, his father was unable to commit to paying for college. The Selective Service draft was still in operation when John completed high school in 1960. His older brother had opted to get his military obligation out of the way before college by spending six months on active duty, then serving in the Army Reserves. Reluctantly, John decided to follow his example. Prior to enrolling at Notre Dame, where he had been admitted, he joined the Army Reserves. He trained for six months as a communications specialist at Fort Knox, then was released from active duty to serve out the rest of his commitment by attending monthly drills and putting in two weeks at a nearby camp each summer. But just as he was settling in as a freshman at Notre Dame in the fall of 1961, the Berlin Wall was erected almost overnight. Two weeks into the first semester of his freshman year, he found a thick envelope in his student mailbox containing bus tickets and orders from the Army Reserve to return to active service. The combined tours of duty delayed his graduation from Notre Dame by two years.

During his last two summers as an undergraduate, he worked at construction jobs in California. His experience with the West Coast lifestyle, so much freer and more relaxed than the one on the orderly, cloistered campus in Indiana, was a powerful magnet in his choice of graduate school. It would have been hard to find two educational institutions with more opposite cultures than Notre Dame and Berkeley, especially in the late sixties, at the height of the nationwide schism over the Vietnam War. Notre Dame had given him a strong sense of duty, and public responsibility had permeated every aspect of campus life. It was a sheltered, politically conservative environment in which people forged close, lasting relationships. At Berkeley, students constantly challenged authority and noisily protested the war in Vietnam. Then-Governor Ronald Reagan ordered the National Guard into action, and its presence on campus became as much a part of school life as the lectures. In the aftermath of its frequent clashes with student protesters, the scent of tear gas clung to everything.

Despite these distractions, John Phillips did very well in law school. As a student he became an editor of the *California Law Review,* an honor reserved for only the top 10 percent of the class. Soft-spoken and relatively conservative in appearance, he combined eclectic interests and the ability to grasp a wide range of legal issues with a capacity for intense focus. Before graduation, after interviews with firms in San Francisco, New York, and Washington, he was recruited as an associate with the premier law firm on the West Coast, O'Melveny & Myers in Los Angeles. The firm's reputation for encouraging attorneys to do pro bono work appealed to him. Lawyers were in short supply in those days, and even the most prestigious firms competed fiercely for the best and brightest among the newest crop of graduates. Some of his classmates shunned the large, entrenched practices in favor of pursuing more idealistic, lower-paying goals such as providing legal aid to the poor. But "public interest" law practices, as they are now known, did not yet exist. Phillips wanted to become familiar with the workings of a big law firm and also have the opportunity to pursue pro bono work. He had a vague plan to use his law degree for public service, but wasn't sure how.

Even with a fairly clear idea of what was in store for him, the transition from Berkeley to L.A., from idealistic student to practicing attorney, proved to be at least as much of a culture shock as the change from college to law school. The ethos of a corporate law firm was a long way from the view he'd had of his future while still in law school. From the inside, the sense of divergence was even greater. It was a solid and prestigious firm. He liked the people he worked with, the money was good, and if he put his nose to the grindstone and got along with everyone, he was reasonably assured of becoming a partner after about eight years. But when he saw how the majority of the work at the firm involved defending large corporations and the status quo, he became more and more uncertain as to whether a partnership would be worth the wait.

There were other problems, not so much with the focus of the work but with the changing dynamic of the times. Up to the date he was recruited, when two young women also joined as junior associates, all of the firm's one hundred attorneys were white males; only a few were Jewish. An important part of the way the lawyers related to each other was in weekly lunches sponsored by the firm at the private California Club, which excluded women, Jews, blacks, and other minorities from membership. Women had to enter through the back service entrance and were permitted to eat only in a private dining room reserved by the firm. Despite recent articles in the *Los Angeles Times* about the club's discrimination, the firm continued to hold its weekly lunches there. Phillips, a white male, talked with the other new associates and they, too, were uncomfortable with going to the club.

One reason Phillips had been attracted to O'Melveny was the reputation of Warren Christopher, a senior partner who had just returned to the firm after serving as deputy attorney general under Ramsey Clark in the Johnson administration. A proven liberal who was universally respected, Christopher had assured the new associates that the firm supported pro bono work, despite its impressive roster of corporate clients. After working at the firm for a month, Phillips agreed to call Christopher on behalf of the associates to tell him they found it objectionable that the firm would regularly schedule business lunches at a club that was discriminatory. During the call, he added that he and some of the other new associates would not be attending those lunches in the future. It was a pleasant enough exchange, and Christopher seemed genuinely interested in Phillips's perspective on a tradition that apparently had never been challenged. Almost immediately, the luncheon was changed to another venue. Over the next several days, Phillips got calls from a few partners who said they had always been uncomfortable with the way things had been, and thanking him for raising the issue.

The response was decidedly less collegial a year later when the turbulence created by one of his pro bono cases threatened to affect the firm's income. Phillips was representing a consumer group in connection with a proposition on a statewide ballot that would allow gas tax revenues to be used for mass transit rather than being restricted to the building of highways. Opponents of the program, a front group called Californians Against Street and Road Tax Traps, had mounted an expensive attack campaign, with billboards all over the state reading "More Taxes? Vote No on Prop 9." Raising taxes was anathema in California, and the misleading billboards (the proposition didn't raise taxes) seemed likely to have an impact on the outcome at the polls.

But the state had a law requiring full disclosure of the sources of funding for political advertising. When Phillips learned that the necessary affidavits had never been filed by the sponsors of the ads, he initiated a lawsuit to force them to reveal their donors. A few days later, in large part because of the filing of the lawsuit, the newspapers told voters that a principal contributor to the ad campaign was Union Oil, along with other members of the "highway lobby"—other oil companies, road builders, and cement makers. It was a legal and public relations triumph for the group John Phillips represented. Since a recent massive oil spill from a drilling platform off Santa Barbara—ranked among the worst environmental disasters up to that time—Union Oil had been one of the least popular companies in California.

Union Oil was O'Melveny & Myer's biggest fee-generating client. While many of the firm's attorneys were laboring full-time to defend Union Oil and other oil companies on the Santa Barbara case, John Phillips had gone off on his own, without seeking the approval of the firm, as its rules required, and revealed to the world that the state's top polluter had also violated the law by concealing its financial support of political advertising. When the president of Union Oil, Fred Hartley, learned that an O'Melveny attorney had been responsible for this latest embarrassment, he protested to the firm's management committee. Phillips was ordered to terminate his representation of the consumer group. (The disclosure case didn't stop with the end of his involvement, however. It was continued by Edmund G. "Jerry" Brown, who was running for the office of California's secretary of state and who later became governor.)

After several meetings with partners about how he came to represent the consumer group, Phillips received an ominous-sounding phone call from Christopher, who told him that he and the partner who had first interviewed him for the firm, John Roney, would like to come to his office to talk with him. He found it hard to focus on his work while he waited nearly an hour for them to show up. When they finally arrived, Christopher and Roney subtly encouraged him to quit. They explained to the young associate that the partners' lives and fortunes were tied up with the firm and the firm's clients. Associates who work for the company, they said, face certain restrictions when the firm might otherwise be adversely affected. They asked if he thought he could accept those restrictions.

Phillips knew his job was on the line, and he was not yet ready to trade a steady paycheck for an uncertain future. Tersely, he answered, "Yes." But he then raised the question of whether the firm had told Hartley that the young associate had been trying only to seek compliance with California election laws. They had no response.

It was an awkward exchange. With his capitulation, the two senior attorneys attempted a balm of inconsequential chitchat, but it failed to ease the strain. A minute or two later they left.

Although his relationship with most of his colleagues remained cordial, Phillips soon realized that he would never be comfortable in O'Melveny's corporate setting. He found other ways to challenge the establishment outside of the office, such as working on the Senate primary campaign of U.S. Representative George Brown. A leading opponent of the war in Vietnam, Brown was one of very few congressmen to question the Gulf of Tonkin resolution which gave President Johnson authority to commit U.S. troops to the conflict. (The resolution was in response to an earlier attack by North Vietnamese torpedo boats on American destroyers. Johnson's portrayal of the incident was later revealed to be a lie.) Meanwhile, Phillips and three of his O'Melveny colleagues were working on the details of a plan for starting a new "public interest" law firm that would focus on the main regional problems of southern California: environment, transportation, and civil rights. As a nonprofit entity, it would be a different kind of law firm than any that then existed. Phillips and his friends—Carlyle W. Hall, Brent Rushforth, and Ric Sutherland—were convinced it was an idea whose time had come. When they received a $5,000 grant in 1971 and the offer of free office space, Phillips resigned from O'Melveny to go out alone in pursuit of funding for his new firm's first-year budget.

The Ford Foundation turned down the first application because there wasn't enough money left in the foundation's budget. But it was clear its administrators were impressed with the concept and with the four young attorneys who were willing to trade their careers at a top law firm for a risky opportunity to do good. The foundation indicated they could come back and ask again if they were able to raise more of the needed start-up money from other sources. Six months later they were back, having raised $85,000 elsewhere. This time Ford gave them $75,000 to complete the projected first year's budget.

The Center for Law in the Public Interest opened its doors beneath a Wells Fargo Bank branch, in a windowless basement office suffused with the odors of greasy hamburgers and french fries from a restaurant down the hall. Dominating the office was a heavily worn, bright orange carpet of desperately tasteless, nearly psychedelic cheeriness. Because they could not afford to replace it, the carpet quickly became a kind of campy, self-mocking emblem of the new firm's earnestness.

Within six months, the new firm had moved into donated upscale space in West Los Angeles and had become so successful that it was the subject of an admiring front-page story in the *Wall Street Journal*. Under the headline "Stepping on Toes: Public Interest Firm on a Winning Streak Shakes Up California," the article marveled that the Center had lost only five of the first sixty cases it had filed since inception, becoming "one of the most effective of the hundred or so public interest law firms around the country." Its success in suits related to the use of land, the story continued, had "transformed the whole pattern of development in California."

Predictably, his new career track would sometimes place Phillips on a collision course with his old law firm. One longtime client of O'Melveny & Myers was the Northrop Corporation, a California-based aerospace and defense contractor. One day, Phillips watched on TV as Nixon's personal attorney, Herbert W. Kalmbach, testified at the Senate Watergate hearings about where he got some of the hush money to pay the burglars who had broken into the Democratic national headquarters. Kalmbach said he got $50,000 in cash from a safe in the office of the chairman of Northrop, Tom Jones. The office was not more than two hundred yards down the street from the Center. Attorneys for the Center developed a novel legal theory under existing securities law and filed a suit on behalf of Northrop's shareholders, alleging that the gift to the comically eponymous CREEP (Committee to Re-elect the President) was actually Northrop's money that Jones had pretended was his own to circumvent the laws on corporate contributions to political causes. Jones was subsequently forced to admit that this was corporate money when he pleaded guilty to felony charges.

The Center continued its case. By luck of the draw, the judge to whom it was assigned turned out to be an admirer of the Center's work. Phillips's former employer, O'Melveny and Myers, led by Warren Christopher, represented Northrop. At a status conference with all the attorneys, representing the cream of the L.A. legal establishment, the judge asked Phillips if this was the first case the Center had filed that was aimed at corporate reform, and Phillips admitted that it was. "Well," he smiled, "congratulations on breaking new ground." Then, still beaming, the judge turned to Warren Christopher. "We're going to make some new law."

All Christopher could do in return was smile back and acknowledge the case was "very challenging your honor, very challenging." At the meeting, the judge ordered that Jones be deposed, over the objections of his attorneys.

The attorneys wanted the deposition done in the familiar elegance of their downtown offices but Phillips, sensitive to the importance of home-court advantage, insisted on his right to take it at the Center's offices instead. A couple of desks were pushed together end-to-end, and enough chairs were rounded up to seat all of the participants. Phillips surveyed the cramped scene in advance of the meeting. All their furniture had been donated by other firms, and he noted wryly that no two chairs in the room were from the same set.

The downtown attorneys arrived with their ashen-faced and obviously ailing client. Phillips expected Jones to tell the truth in his deposition; he was now a convicted felon as the result of his earlier plea, and faced a certain prison sentence if subsequently convicted of perjury. But Phillips was not prepared for how astonishing that truth would turn out to be. Jones took his seat, and once sworn he proceeded to reveal that the donation came from millions in corporate funds that had been laundered through one of the firm's subsidiaries in Luxembourg, brought back in a corporate jet, and smuggled through customs in suitcases. The revelations didn't stop there. One of the principal functions of that subsidiary, Jones also testified, was to maintain a slush fund for bribing foreign officials, including occasional heads of state.

Phillips and his upstart enterprise forced an unusual settlement. Northrop had to work jointly with the Center for Law in the Public Interest to interview and select a new, independent board of directors, establish an audit and nominating committee consisting of independent board members, and rewrite many of the company bylaws and articles of incorporation to avoid any future repetition of its illegal actions.

Next, lawyers at the Center for Law in the Public Interest brought a shareholder suit against Phillips Petroleum to end the payment of corporate funds in foreign bribes. The Center again achieved a precedent-setting result, adding six new independent directors to the eleven-member board and further revising the bylaws and articles of incorporation. The Securities and Exchange Commission, which initially had shown no interest in whether or not U.S. companies paid foreign bribes, used disclosures in the Northrop and Phillips Petroleum cases to force compliance by other American companies doing business overseas. After the SEC announced that it would go easy on companies that voluntarily reported paying such bribes, more than four hundred corporations acknowledged that they had engaged in the illegal practice.

Growing directly out of these scandals was a push for legislation to stop American companies from paying bribes in foreign countries. The most common argument against its passage was that if the United States were to become the only prude at the party, the world's business would still go to the highest bidder and American companies would lose their advantage in important emerging markets. Paying bribes in foreign countries was viewed by most multinational corporations as a necessary cost of doing business abroad, especially in third-world nations. For many years the practice was exempt from prosecution under American law. With the growing globalization of the economy, however, the extent of American corporate involvement in such corruption became more generally known, and the feeling arose that if a company's shareholders could force compliance with a higher ethical standard, as the Center's lawsuit and subsequent cases had demonstrated, then so could Congress. The Foreign Corrupt Practices Act was voted into law.

Other cases brought by the Center were similarly instrumental in facilitating major social changes. Separate lawsuits against the Los Angeles Fire Department and the Los Angeles Police Department helped end a long history of discrimination in the hiring of African-Americans and Hispanics in those organizations, and set a precedent for forcing other fire and police departments in southern California to conform to the same high standard. The Center followed those victories with a number of successful cases against other police and fire departments for discriminating in the hiring of women and minorities.

The Center's best-known case was the very first one it filed, which it began working on in 1971 and which lasted twenty-four years: to enforce environmental and housing laws that were being routinely disregarded by state agencies in the construction of the Century Freeway in Los Angeles. The massive project primarily affected the most powerless. For years, virtually without opposition, state and federal agencies had routinely violated federal laws intended to protect those communities. To build the seventeen-mile stretch from downtown L.A. to near the airport, builders bulldozed the poorest neighborhoods, including Watts, bifurcating communities and ripping out housing without providing for any safe and sanitary replacement shelter, as required by law, for the people being displaced. The only promised job opportunities to emerge from the massive project were for white males who lived outside the area; there were none for the people whose lives were being disrupted. No consideration was given to mass transit as an alternative to the superhighway, as required by law.

Following years of court battles, a landmark agreement was reached by the Center for Law in the Public Interest with the state and federal governments to minimize the highway's harmful effects. After bulldozing through the poorest section of the city, instead of pushing aside the undefended residents along with the debris of their former homes and businesses, the state had to rebuild six thousand units of low-income housing and provide job training and job opportunities for women and minorities affected by the construction in their neighborhoods. A mass transit system, the region's first, was to be built down the highway's median. The road's design was modified and its route redirected to minimize its impact on the environment.

When the real costs had all been factored in and the construction was finally allowed to proceed, the price of the project had risen nearly fivefold, from $630 million to $2.6 billion. The cost of the additional work required by the settlement, which included funds for the construction of mass transit and the six thousand units of housing plus job training for displaced residents, came to $1.2 billion, or more than twice as much as the original estimates for the entire project.

Although the housing program sounded good on paper, implementation proved elusive. After three years, the state had built only a small handful of the promised units, and those were of poor quality. Moreover, the application process was so complicated and arbitrary, many of the new houses stood empty for six months or longer and were vandalized while applicants' paperwork was stuck in the system. Initially delighted by his victory, Phillips was disillusioned by this unexpected outcome.

Fed up, lawyers for the Center went back to court and proposed a radically different approach under which a private-public partnership would build the housing and find qualified tenants. The plan was accepted, and it turned around the housing program. A nonprofit agency was formed to build the units, giving private developers the incentive of an ownership interest and certain subsidies in exchange for reduced rents.

In December 1981, after John Lennon was shot dead in New York, Phillips decided to cash out all of his retirement funds and take an unpaid leave from the Center. He devoted all of his time to the launching of a campaign against what he called "the most egregious of special interests," the National Rifle Association, widely recognized as the most powerful lobbying organization in America.

The focus of this new effort was a ballot initiative that would create a trade-in program to freeze the number of handguns in circulation by requiring buyers to turn in an old handgun before they could purchase a new one. It also required that all handguns be registered, and mandated a six-month sentence for anyone caught carrying a concealed handgun; this was primarily aimed at reducing gang violence. It began promisingly enough, with hundreds of antihandgun volunteer canvassers obtaining the million signatures required to get the initiative onto the November ballot as Proposition 15. By demonstrating that the NRA was not invincible, Phillips hoped

to embolden legislators across the nation and in Congress to pass legislation for gun control, modeled on his proposed California proposition.

Big-city police departments throughout the state were in favor of the
idea, and it received strong backing on the editorial pages of virtually all
the major dailies in the state, including the powerful *Los Angeles Times*. The
next step was to raise money for advertising. Phillips and his group raised
about $800,000 for a TV and radio campaign. But the NRA spent $7 million on a misleading ad program that frightened people about crime and
falsely told them that if the proposition passed, private citizens would never
be able to buy handguns.

By election eve, polls showed that Proposition 15 was doomed. At
eight o'clock that night, an apprehensive and disconsolate Phillips arrived
at the Biltmore Hotel in downtown Los Angeles where supporters of Tom
Bradley (for governor), Jerry Brown (for senator), and Proposition 15 had
election eve gatherings. L.A. mayor Tom Bradley was the first African-
American to run for governor, and although polls had him ahead by six to
eight percentage points on election eve, there was uncertainty about
whether race might be a submerged factor that would only surface inside
the voting booth. One of the first people Phillips ran into was a *Los Angeles
Times* reporter who told him the prognosis was nowhere nearly as gloomy
as Phillips feared, that the latest *Times* polls showed Bradley and Brown,
both Democrats, still looking strong. Phillips had barely allowed his spir-
its to be restored by this cheerful fantasy when he saw the actual returns.
Reality descended like a hammer. In the closest gubernatorial contest in
the history of the state, Bradley was headed for defeat, and Governor Brown
was losing his bid for the United States Senate.

The polls had just closed when reporters, pollsters, and commenta-
tors started speculating that the handgun issue was to blame for Bradley's
loss. The NRA campaign against Proposition 15 had energized rural white
voters, who normally don't turn out in great numbers, and while voting
on the handgun control issue they voted against the African-American man
running for governor.

John Phillips was devastated by the loss of the referendum. He
blamed himself for having taken on a cause he didn't win—and that indeed, many people had told him he *couldn't* win—and for having goaded
a ferocious adversary into a response that appeared to have been so disastrous to others.

It seemed like a good time for a trip abroad. By then Phillips was married to a CBS television reporter named Linda Douglass, who had covered the elections. The couple had recently learned that a child was on its way, and even before they foresaw the disastrous outcome of the election, they had been planning a vacation as a last chance for a while to be alone together. Three weeks in Italy would give them both some time to recover from the campaign and to reflect on a future that promised change on every horizon.

Like most vacations, it wasn't quite long enough. When they got back to Los Angeles, Phillips had little more idea about what to do with himself than when they had left. Still sensitive to the stigma of the recent disaster and tired of hearing how he had single-handedly cost Democrats the governorship, he turned down most social invitations, avoiding friends and spending the holidays with Linda in relative seclusion.

The one-year leave of absence was over at the start of 1983. He returned to the Center for Law in the Public Interest in early January, still feeling edgy and unfocused. He asked a staff attorney to put together a memo on present and potential areas for the application of public interest law, and on how the Center could fund those cases. Later, when Phillips read the attorney's response, he was struck by one of the last items on the list. It was a law called the False Claims Act, designed primarily to combat defense fraud.

The law attracted his interest for two reasons. First, it empowered the whistle-blower to function in the role of a private attorney general seeking repayment of funds to the U.S. Treasury, and to share in the recovery. Second, the high concentration of defense contractors in southern California meant that a lot of the potential business was right in the Center's backyard. When Phillips did some research of his own, he learned that the law had been little used in the past fifty years, was now essentially dormant, and had some major flaws. He was also convinced that if the False Claims Act were revised and strengthened, it could have a major impact on public interest law.

During a subsequent series of staff meetings devoted to the False Claims Act, Phillips never found his enthusiasm for revitalizing the law matched by the other lawyers at the Center. Nor did any of his colleagues feel that it was even remotely possible he would be able to convince Congress to make his proposed changes. "Let me get this straight," a lawyer

challenged him at one of those meetings. "You're going to draft amendments to the False Claims Act, take them to Congress, get the revised law
passed, then bring cases under this law, successfully returning millions to
the government while at the same time rewarding whistle-blowers and their
attorneys?"

Phillips's only response was a weary, patient nod.

The colleague laughed. "It's pie-in-the-sky," he said. "You have about
as much chance with this as you did with getting your handgun initiative
passed."

Phillips listened to the objections. In the light of his recent experience, he too was determined to be skeptical about anything new that promised to change the world. But despite a conscious decision to not allow
himself to become too quickly hopeful, he felt a growing sense of excitement. At a time when defense contractors could literally outspend and
outstaff the legal resources of the United States government, here was a
concept offering unprecedented power to the private litigator, which
seemed to him to be the very essence of the democratic process. If a private-
public partnership could break the impasse in low-income housing in the
wake of the Century Freeway, why wouldn't a variation on that theme work
in fighting fraud? He'd look into it further, but whatever was wrong with
the law in its present form, Phillips told the attorneys at the table, could
be corrected. A revitalized False Claims Act offered a real benefit to the
public and could be an exciting new area of legal practice.

On and off over the next two years, Phillips evaluated the act, studied
its history, gained insights as to why it had not been successfully applied
in the past, and determined what needed to be done to improve it. The
more he learned, the more he was convinced of its potential. Eventually
the project took on a sense of mission. He wanted to revitalize what had
once been known as "Mr. Lincoln's Law," making as few changes as possible, preserving its original intent while updating it to the legal requirements of the late twentieth century. He began drafting revisions that would
meet those goals.

The first major change was removing the problematic "government
knowledge bar," which had been used to block whistle-blower cases any-
time information about the fraud was known to the government, even if
the information was deeply buried in files that would never otherwise have
seen the light of day.

The second key change was to give whistle-blowers a greater voice in their lawsuits by making them formal parties to their cases, which meant they could participate fully in all phases of the litigation. Previously, even though they initiated the case, they were forced to the sidelines and had no say in the outcome.

Next, the proposed revisions guaranteed whistle-blowers a minimum share of any recovery. A reward would also encourage whistle-blowers to take the risk of coming forward, and would encourage private attorneys to put their own resources into good cases. This would benefit the government by increasing the chances of successful prosecution and would level the playing field in fraud cases against huge corporations with vast resources.

Another change would be to provide job protection, with reinstatement and a doubling of back pay for whistle-blowers when they were fired.

Last, to encourage lawyers to take on smaller cases where the contingency fee would not offer sufficient incentive, whistle-blowers' attorneys, in addition to their share in the reward, would be compensated for their work on a successful *qui tam* case. Wrongdoers found liable would have to pay the standard hourly rates and case-related expenses of the whistle-blowers' attorneys. This provision for attorneys' fees would also make it clear that if large cases with big expenses were brought to successful conclusions, the defendant would be liable not only for his own legal costs, but those attorneys' fees and expenses incurred by the relators—reversing the normal rule under which each side paid its own costs.

Despite Phillips's growing excitement about the law, the attitude of most of his colleagues remained basically unchanged. A couple of them, perhaps weighing the disaster of Proposition 15 against his earlier long-term winning streak, seemed close to being caught up in his enthusiasm. But the rest were divided among the quietly noncommittal, the eye-rollers, and the active naysayers.

The arguments only seemed to increase Phillips's conviction about the law's potential. "Come on, the Republicans would love it because it has marketplace incentives and privatizes some government work instead of adding to the bureaucracy," he pointed out. "And the Democrats would come aboard because it goes after big companies who are cheating the taxpayer. It's a natural."

*   *   *

At nearly the same time as the strategy meeting at the Center, three thousand miles away in the nation's capital, the staff of Senator Charles Grassley of Iowa was having an astonishingly similar conversation. What could be done, Grassley challenged his team, to help improve the Justice Department's success rate in the prosecution of defense contractor fraud?

Grassley knew that the Justice Department routinely took to court only less than 10 percent of such cases it investigated in a typical year. The tremendous disparity between losses due to fraud and recoveries obtained by the government had received scant coverage in the press; neither side was anxious to invite public attention to the fact that the government was regularly outspent and outmaneuvered in its defense of the public interest.

Part of the problem was manpower. In important cases, where the United States might be represented by three or four lawyers, attorneys for the defense sometimes had dozens. As a result, many of the largest cases never even came to court, and in an industry where the annual theft rate was thought by some to be in the tens of billions, fewer than two hundred corporations or individuals had been prosecuted, and the average recovery had been well under $100,000.

One of Grassley's aides, Lisa Hovelson, told the senator about a little-known statute, the False Claims Act, that had been on the books since 1863. It had never gotten much use except as a threat, and it had been eviscerated by a powerful defense lobby during World War II. In its present form it was nearly worthless. But rewritten, it just might prove to be a good idea whose time had come again.

John Phillips was aware that Grassley was an outspoken critic of defense contractor fraud and of the Justice Department's frequent failure to pursue offending companies for repayment. He believed that Grassley could be a powerful advocate for amending and reviving the False Claims Act, since the Republicans controlled the Senate. He called the senator's office from Los Angeles and was put through to Lisa Hovelson.

He was surprised to discover that she was already familiar with the False Claims Act.

E I G H T

C L I F F H A N G E R

For Chuck Grassley, there had to be something tremendously appealing in the idea of a law that allowed the average citizen direct access to the court system to fight corruption at the national level—not least because it also seemed to be so peculiarly American. Grassley had spent most of his life in public service, serving in the Iowa State House from 1958 to 1974, followed by six years as a United States congressman. Since taking his seat in the Senate in 1981, his attacks on military misspending had made him the most popular politician in his home state, where his sons still grew corn and soybeans on the family farm. Along the way, he had learned some important lessons about how fraud and waste had become so institutionalized that they were routinely tolerated, even protected, by the government's watchdogs, and allowed to prosper. In almost every case that had come before his subcommittee, federal departments or agencies were implicated in the misconduct, often even to the extent of automatically siding with the miscreants when the time came for decisions about investigating complaints, enforcing the rules, prosecuting the lawbreakers, or recovering misappropriated funds.

It wasn't just that the bureaucrats were afraid of exposing their own involvement; more than anything else, their reluctance to prosecute the law appeared to be a matter of mind-set. Federal inspectors were typically not as experienced and almost never as well paid as the corporate managers whose work they oversaw. They were always outnumbered by their charges, and they were perceived as low-status outsiders in almost every industry they monitored. Even before his conversations with Fitzgerald, Grassley had a pretty good idea how those bureaucrats would react to any effort to revitalize the False Claims Act.

Lisa Hovelson had started working for the senator as an intern in her senior year at Iowa State and had made such a good impression on the senator and his staff that she was invited to stay on after graduation. A night law student at George Washington University, she had been a full-timer for only two years but at twenty-four had already made a name for herself as a competent, trusted aide.

There was only one main difference, Phillips learned, between what the senator and his staff were considering and what he envisioned for the law. Up to then, Grassley's staff had been focused on ways in which the statute would give the government more power through the Department of Justice to move aggressively against companies that were cheating the taxpayer. Phillips, by contrast, was more interested in providing incentives for insiders and their lawyers to go after corporate wrongdoers. This struck a responsive chord with Hovelson, since Grassley was a staunch advocate of whistle-blowers. After a cordial, productive conversation, he agreed to send Hovelson his detailed, section-by-section analysis of the law and the proposed amendments. A short time later, Phillips flew to Washington and met with Hovelson.

To make sure that the House of Representatives would also start working on the False Claims Act amendments, they agreed that Phillips would raise the issue with Congressman Howard Berman of Los Angeles. Phillips had known him socially in Los Angeles during Berman's years in the State Assembly, and had worked with him on public interest legislation. A former labor lawyer, he had become majority leader of the State Assembly in his first term—an unheard-of accomplishment—and was one of California's most respected and effective legislators. He decided to run for Congress in 1982 and was now in Washington as the representative of the state's 26th District. Because he quickly demonstrated the skills and intelligence that had served him so well in California, he was given a seat on the House Judiciary Committee—which, among other things, was responsible for any amendments to the False Claims Act.

Berman quickly saw the potential of a modernized act, and he agreed to introduce the legislation and shepherd it through the House. The logical next step was to get Berman to meet with Grassley. The former L.A. labor lawyer and the still-active Iowa farmer couldn't have been more dissimilar in career background, experience, or political convictions. Walking to Grassley's office, Phillips told his old friend that the meeting would go well. "You don't have a prior history with him, and I know his politics are a lot different from yours and mine," he acknowledged. "But he's been at the forefront of what this law is all about. You'll like him."

It turned out Phillips was right. Warm, sincere, incisive but with a gentle, self-deprecating humor, the senator made his visitors feel instantly at home. He spoke of the law and of his long battle against government waste and corruption with such unapologetic conviction, there were times when the visitors had to consciously remind themselves that their host was not some liberal Democratic zealot but a well-known conservative Republican.

The meeting concluded on a note of high optimism. It was agreed that Hovelson would handle the progress of the legislation in the Senate and that Berman and his staff, with assistance from Phillips, would focus on the House. Hovelson and Phillips made plans to talk on a regular basis, and twice as often in a crisis. The alliance would continue for the next two years.

Grassley endorsed the proposed *qui tam* amendments and sent out a "Dear Colleague" letter with a detailed discussion of the changes. The letter was published in the *Congressional Record*.

In 1985, with nine of the top ten defense contractors under investigation for stealing from the government, and in the glare of unrelenting media scrutiny of the Pentagon's procurement system, the effort to revive the False Claims Act received an unlikely boost: The Department of Justice also proposed amendments to the law. None of the department's suggestions, however, involved the *qui tam* provisions. When Hovelson met with DOJ attorneys on the subject, she learned why and received an eye-opening preview of the problems ahead. The government lawyers wasted no time in telling her they hated the proposed *qui tam* amendments.

The only reason for the onetime popularity of *qui tam* law, they said, was the early scarcity of police forces, but today, with America's one and a half million law enforcement officers, the concept was an anachronism. By empowering malcontents, its revival would make a deputy of every cowboy with a work problem. Rewards could amount to far more than a conscientious government prosecutor, for example, might ever receive in salary over a lifetime, and might bear no realistic relationship to the value of the service rendered. For that matter, allowing the whistle-blower, known in the law as the relator, and his attorney to participate in any portion of the recovery, which was at the heart of the law, might give rise to a new breed of predatory lawyers. And finally, what was the point of having a Department of Justice if every American could, in effect, become his own attorney general?

Hovelson had no trouble recognizing the issues behind these objections. However vigorously they may claim otherwise, lawyers are ranked according to the power of their clients—and there was no bigger or mightier client in the world than the United States of America. The decision to enter government service often involves a trade-off between the higher financial compensation offered by the private sector and the right to wield that enormous power. Under *qui tam* law, however, outsiders can also represent the United States, placing new and unwelcome pressures on the Department of Justice's control of what gets done, and how and when.

Government attorneys had always depended on the testimony of inside informants, but those informants had never had parity with the prosecutors. Government attorneys always had full control over the informants' rewards, and often over their fate. The most common payment for a federal informant wasn't money, but some form of largesse from the government's bottomless purse of power—to protect, to forgive, to look the other way, and even in some notorious cases to give permission. To elevate the standing of inside informants, to give them direct access to the courts not just as witnesses but as litigants on their own and the government's behalf, and perhaps even more devastatingly to invest their attorneys with powers similar to those of lawyers from the Department of Justice, was perceived by many of the government attorneys as a change in the basic conditions of their employment almost equal to a breach of contract. Private attorneys were interlopers on their turf.

When Hovelson got back to the office, she reported to Grassley that the Justice Department lawyers were going to be a major problem. They could be expected to offer resistance to any restoration of the *qui tam* provisions of the law. If the time ever came that the suggested revisions were enacted, they would likely erect further hurdles in putting it to work.

The department's requested changes in the non–*qui tam* portions of the act, however, were generally positive, strengthening some parts related to the department's powers and easing the burden on the government to prove its case. DOJ lawyers wanted the authority to subpoena documents and witnesses before filing a lawsuit in order to determine whether a suit was actually warranted. They sought to change the standard from "clear and convincing evidence" (which is close to the standard used to decide guilt in a criminal trial) to the more relaxed "preponderance of evidence." This would make it easier to prove fraud, by simply showing that it was more likely than not. They also proposed to increase the penalties and fines. The current version of the law required a thief to return two dollars for every dollar stolen—Justice was asking for the penalty to be raised to triple the misappropriated amount. Individual fines for each false transaction, set years earlier at $2,000, would rise to between $5,000 and $10,000 per infraction. The statute of limitations, then at six years, would be extended to ten.

Another problem in the old law was proving that the accused had a specific intent to defraud, the most common responses to which were "Gosh, no one ever told me it was against the law," "I only did what I was told to do," or "We've been doing things this way for as long as I've been with the company." Justice wanted to replace "specific intent" with the more easily provable standard of "reckless disregard" or deliberate ignorance of the false claim being made, which didn't require proof that someone intentionally defrauded the government.

But the proposed Justice Department changes completely ignored the *qui tam* provisions of the law. It was clear the department viewed the concept as a relic of the Civil War, with no possible application to modern law enforcement.

Grassley and Berman felt differently. While they agreed that the department's proposals would strengthen the hand of the prosecutors, they also wanted to change the dynamics and heighten the pressure in government fraud cases, in part by lighting a fire under the enforcers. They wanted the law to do again what it was originally designed for. That meant providing incentives that would encourage witnesses of fraud to step forward. It also meant increasing the legal and investigative resources available to the government in proving its claims. Contrary to the public's perception, the government was usually vastly outgunned when it went after a large corporation. Providing the means for whistle-blowers to support their cases with adequate legal resources was at least a partial answer to the common defense industry strategy of outspending and overwhelming the government.

Grassley and Berman knew it was important to get the Justice Department to endorse the amendments, and that a major sticking point was the *qui tam* provisions of the law. No endorsement was forthcoming. Phillips met with Associate Attorney General Stephen Trott, the number three man in Justice and the person responsible for formulating the department's position on the amendments. Trott had been a top prosecutor in the Los Angeles District Attorney's Office and a United States attorney before moving to Washington to work for his colleague from California, Attorney General Ed Meese. Phillips had known Trott in L.A. and hoped he could convince him to support the amendments.

Trott told Phillips that the key problem was the risk of private lawyers' getting in the way of successful government prosecutions. The Justice Department gets information all the time about crimes, he said. They get search warrants, set up wiretaps, and use other investigative tools to build a case—all before the criminals ever learn they're a target. That way, the Justice Department retains the advantage of surprise. The problem with the amendments, he explained, was that Justice would lose that kind of control. Private attorneys would grandstand about their cases publicly, hurting the department's ability to investigate as well as prosecute.

After listening to Trott's objections, Phillips suggested that the Justice Department's fear that reckless lawyers and their clients would play havoc with sensitive government cases could be answered by a simple safeguard. He suggested a provision that would require all *qui tam* suits to be filed under seal. That would mean there would be no notification of the defendants or publicity of any kind for at least sixty days after filing, and the seal could be extended for as long as the department could prove was necessary simply by petitioning the court, giving the government time to investigate the case and to interview witnesses and issue subpoenas without generating publicity or alerting suspects. This period of enforced silence would also give the Justice Department enough time, free from the pressure of a public spotlight, to evaluate whether a case was strong enough that it should get on board. If DOJ decided that it was not, that decision would nearly eliminate the likelihood that there would be any parallel criminal prosecution to be placed at risk. It wasn't going to keep *qui tam* lawyers or their clients out of court, but at least it would allow *qui tam* cases to be handled like any other investigation by the FBI and the Department of Justice.

For *qui tam* proponents, the seal provided a subtle but important added benefit. In effect, it would ensure that the government gave prompt attention to fraud allegations rather than allowing them to languish indefinitely in a courthouse filing cabinet. Although the department could seek extensions to the sixty-day deadline, the government would be held accountable in court for investigating all *qui tam* cases.

After adding the seal provision, Grassley's staff worked with the Justice Department to affix its imprimatur to the amendments. Grassley made it clear that the *qui tam* amendments had to be part of any False Claims Act reform. What he got was an uneasy, nearly reluctant endorsement. The department remained convinced that the *qui tam* provisions would offer no benefit in antifraud enforcement and would instead amount to an inconsequential nuisance.

In September, 1985, the political campaign to generate support for the bill went into high gear in Congress. A new hearing before Senator Grassley's subcommittee spotlighted real-life stories about whistle-blowers who got chewed up and destroyed by their employers for trying to stop or change illegal practices, in order to show clearly why the law was needed to help whistle-blowers and to protect them. Phillips contacted Robert Wityczak and drafted testimony that the Vietnam veteran offered the subcommittee from his wheelchair. Wityczak vividly described the climate in which a giant defense contractor, Rockwell International, had responded to his complaints of false billing and other forms of theft with harassment that bordered on torture and eventually with an unjust termination. "There is absolutely no encouragement or incentive for someone working in the defense industry to report fraud and the submission of false claims to the government," the triple amputee told the senators. "In my case I could not consciously work for a company stealing from the government to which I gave half my body."

Ernest Fitzgerald testified about his experiences blowing the whistle on the defense industry. John Phillips was called to testify as well, as the public interest attorney working with Senator Grassley and Representative Berman on the design of the bill before the subcommittee. He offered a perspective on the hazards whistle-blowers would have to face in filing a *qui tam* lawsuit. "These risks include, first and foremost, being fired by an employer, being harassed or threatened by employers or coworkers, and if fired, being blackballed from within the industry in which they work.

"These fears have a basis in fact, for 'whistle-blowers' have historically not been treated well within our system. They have divulged their information and then lost their jobs. Even if they were able to bring suit against their employer for a retaliatory firing, the cases might take years to prosecute and are a big drain on personal resources, without any guarantee of success.

"The good thing about this bill," Phillips concluded in a direct pitch to apply Reagan's free-market philosophy, "is that it contains marketplace incentives. It encourages people because they want to do their patriotic duty first, but they also have a substantial stake in the recovery."

A Cincinnati attorney, James Helmer, and his client, Jack Gravitt, described what had happened when Gravitt filed a *qui tam* lawsuit under the existing act. A marine veteran of Vietnam with two Purple Hearts, Gravitt had repeatedly warned GE about time-card cheating on air force contracts, and was ignored or rebuffed. Despite strong evidence that the case was worth far more, the Justice Department wanted to settle with GE for $234,000. Judge Carl Rubin sided with the relator and against the government; eventually the company paid more than $3.5 million on suits filed by Gravitt and three other whistle-blowers. The relators' shares alone were more than three times higher than the amount the government had been willing to accept for the entire recovery. But the matter didn't end with the settlement. Gravitt was harassed by his employer and then fired. Even after he was gone from his job, GE continued to seek revenge, forcing him to defend himself in a series of costly legal actions transparently designed to make him an example to other potential whistle-blowers.

The hearings concluded a few weeks later with a favorable report from the subcommittee, which sent it to the full committee for consideration.

But that was the easy part. The strategy for the amended law's passage was to keep the process below the radar so as not to set off the big guns of the defense industry lobby. However, once it did discover what was going on, the opposition could still use all kinds of tactics to shoot down the legislation.

When the full Senate Judiciary Committee, under the chairmanship of Republican senator Strom Thurmond, met on the bill shortly before Christmas, defense contractor lobbyists filled the hearing room. Having only recently awakened to the implications of a strong False Claims Act, they had convinced a few senators to propose that the committee table the bill. Much to Phillips's relief, Thurmond shot them down. Senator

Grassley's bill had been fully reviewed and the hearings had been held, he said. The committee was ready to vote. The bill passed easily. Lisa Hovelson drafted the committee report on the bill. On behalf of Senator Grassley, she emphasized how the law would bring out information from insiders and use private legal resources to help right the imbalance that existed in government cases against corporate defendants. The law also would put pressure on the DOJ to vigorously pursue fraud cases and get the maximum recovery.

In the aftermath of the vote, the defense industry broke into a sudden scramble to anchor the rug they sensed was about to be pulled from under their feet. "They want to maintain the status quo and escape liability for false claims," Republican senator William Cohen of Maine, a key supporter of the bill, said of the "lobbying stampede" that was now being launched by industry contractors to kill it.

Although the real muscle behind a lobbying effort is flexed in private—and even there any threat of retaliation or promise of a quid pro quo is far more often tacit than spoken aloud—it was becoming apparent to the defense industry that its efforts behind closed doors would be far more likely to succeed if the industry could somehow improve the climate of public opinion. Industry spokesmen, far less bashful in forums of their own choosing, predicted that future *qui tam* relators would be nothing more than "disgruntled former employees" shamelessly using the law to seek retaliation after being fired for reasons having nothing to do with fraud.

At a time when the public had just learned that nearly half the military contractors in America were being investigated for stealing from the government and that as much as ten cents on every dollar was being systematically looted from the public treasury—and after the moving testimony of Wityczak and Fitzgerald, both of whom had endured far more loss than gain in their defense of the public trust—some viewed this industry campaign to portray potential whistle-blowers as dishonest malcontents as preemptive, self-serving, and perhaps even a bit cynical.

Some, but not all. Behind the publicity barrage, a tough cadre of Senate diehards emerged through the smoke after the committee vote to repel this attack on the high bastions of what President Eisenhower had described in his final day in office as the military-industrial complex. Hovelson called Phillips to tell him they had a big problem: Holds had been put on the bill by several senators, including Jesse Helms ("Senator No" to detractors, and even to some admirers), Paula Hawkins of Florida, and James A. McClure of Idaho.

"What's a 'hold'?" Phillips asked.

Hovelson explained that it was an old Senate custom, much abused, that allows any senator to stop the progress of a bill. Holds were placed in secret, although the senator placing one usually became known. Business on the Senate floor was typically conducted under "unanimous consent" agreements. These allowed the Senate to move in an orderly manner, protecting valuable floor time from being eaten up by legislative maneuvering to prevent debate or action on a particular bill. A hold on a bill was a flag that told other senators they wouldn't be able to get unanimous consent. Rather than tying up the Senate, leaders scheduled floor time for bills on which action could be taken. Holds were often used to force changes in a bill or, in the case of the amendments to the False Claims Act, to block further action. The strategy was not to make a direct frontal attack on a bill that seemed so likely to capture the public imagination, but to keep it out of play and let it die by running out the clock.

Grassley was not about to let his bill die. He went from office to office, meeting with each senator who had placed a hold. It was apparent from the first such meeting that none of the dissenting senators had been armed in advance with powerful ammunition from any of the defense contractors they represented. It was one thing for politicians to put a hold on a bill because an important constituent says it's bad legislation and asks that it be stopped, but another to defend that act with coherent, credible reasons of their own. Grassley began by asking each of them, "Do you have specific criticisms? What changes do you want to make?" He also made it clear how strongly he felt about the bill. After a few predictable generalities and a lot of time spent smiling, each of the meetings came to a quiet, affable end as the opposing senators agreed to lift their hold. With his strong credentials as a conservative Republican, Grassley had gotten them to back down.

Led by Howard Berman, the House easily passed its version of the False Claims Act in June 1986. The Senate version came up for a vote the following month. The session was nearing its end and floor time was extremely scarce, so opponents could easily have blocked the bill again by scheduling inadequate time for debate and a vote, or no time at all. Fortunately, Senate majority leader Robert Dole was eyeing a run for the Republican presidential nomination. The first caucus in that race was in Grassley's state of Iowa. Dole made sure the bill got the necessary floor time, and it passed in the Senate as well.

The next step was reconciliation of the House and Senate versions of the law, which varied somewhat due to changes made along the legislative process. When the differences in a piece of legislation are substantial, standard practice is for participants from both chambers to meet in conference and reach a compromise. In this case, as in most legislation, the two approved forms were already enough alike that the adjustments could be made less formally. But though the differences were few, their potential consequences were substantial. In one version, for example, the relator's share of the recovery—set at half in the original law 122 years earlier—could vary according to the court's discretion at between 10 and 15 percent; in the other version the spread was from 15 to 25 percent. After consulting with Berman and Grassley, Phillips and Lisa Hovelson drew up a list of the differences and suggested how to reconcile them, basically fashioning a compromise bill from the strongest provisions of each version, and brought their proposals to separate meetings in the House and Senate.

The final bill reversed court-ordered limitations that had stymied *qui tam* law since the end of World War II. Relators were given a louder voice in the lawsuits; they now would be formal parties to it, giving them more rights. They would be able to object in open court if a Justice Department settlement was inadequate, but they couldn't veto it. The relator's share in successful cases was set at 15 to 25 percent if the government had entered the suit, and up to 30 percent if it hadn't. Losing defendants would have to pay the fees of winning *qui tam* lawyers, at regular hourly rates. Relators who were fired for blowing the whistle would be reinstated if they wanted to return to work, and paid two times the salaries they had lost.

Hovelson had worked out similar terms with the Senate, allowing both sides to feel they had achieved their objectives. Congress passed the final version of the revised False Claims Act in early October. All that remained was for President Reagan to sign it into law.

That last step would prove to be one of the most challenging hurdles in the race.

The first hint of a problem in the homestretch arose with the discovery of some typographical errors that required the White House to send the document back to Congress for correction. The turnaround ate up two critical weeks and set the table for the possibility of a pocket veto. If Congress is in session and the president doesn't sign a bill that has already been passed by Congress within ten days, it becomes law automatically. He also has the option of vetoing the bill and providing a message giving his reasons. However, if Congress has adjourned, as it now had, the bill automatically dies if the president doesn't sign it within ten days of adjournment. Unlike a formal veto, this "pocket veto" usually requires no explanation and often happens without public awareness. More problems arose over the next several days, none of them significant in itself but collectively increasing the possibility that the process was being deliberately managed in a way that would allow the bill to quietly expire.

As the delays accumulated and the silence stretched more ominously toward the deadline, speculation became more specific—that Reagan was being pressured to let the bill slip off the table. Although there was no tangible evidence, the suspicions began to focus on Defense Secretary Caspar Weinberger. The administration was worried about the passage of its defense budget, which was attracting unwelcome controversy and closer, even unfriendly, new scrutiny by Congress. It was also worried about any new development, such as an increase in *qui tam* lawsuits, likely to turn up new stories about $600 toilet seats and other government waste. The last thing the Defense Department wanted was new *qui tam* lawsuits that would expose more fraud, making it difficult to get a bigger defense budget passed through Congress.

Because 1986 was a congressional election year, that fall President Reagan was out campaigning across the country in support of Republican candidates. On October 27, the day the bill was scheduled to die, he was in Georgia, and the White House still had not given the slightest hint of the president's intentions concerning the law. Phillips was in regular contact with Lisa Hovelson, who had no information about Reagan's plans.

The previous day, John Phillips had decided he'd waited long enough. He had picked up the telephone and begun calling a short list of people with whom he had prior contact in the national media.

"There's a story here," he told each of them. "We understand that the defense industry is putting on the heat and Reagan isn't going to sign the bill. You should look into it."

A short time later, the White House Press Office received its first press query on the subject, from ABC Television News. Was it true the president was being pressured by the Pentagon and its contractors? Did he intend to sign the False Claims Act into law? The press officer didn't know the answer, but promised to find out and get back to the caller.

If, as Phillips hoped, that first query carried with it a faint scent of smoke, the next one, from the *New York Times* an hour later, should have suggested a serious fire. The tone of the query was equally businesslike, and it was nearly identical to the first, but this time the answer was far more decisive. The Press Office was well aware that Reagan would come off in the media, a week before elections, as a captive of the defense industry if he allowed the False Claims Act amendments to die, especially when one of the law's strongest supporters was a conservative Republican.

By the time NBC called early that afternoon, there wasn't any need for the reporter to finish the question. "There's no story here," he was told. "The president will be signing the bill today."

John Phillips was never able to find out whether the president had taken the bill with him on the campaign trip or if a copy had to be flown down by special courier from Washington that afternoon. Either way, at just a few minutes before five o'clock, Ronald Reagan sat down at his desk on Air Force One in Georgia and signed the document that Charles Grassley, Howard Berman, John Phillips, and Lisa Hovelson had labored on for the previous two years. The False Claims Act, its teeth restored and stronger than ever before, was once again the law of the land.

N I N E

FIRST LIGHT

"**T**here is so much potential for good," a prominent plaintiffs' lawyer said of the new law, "that I think the contractors will kill it. They will just wait until the heat dies down."

Even in the euphoria of the legislative victory, Phillips was aware of the many risks to the revised act. Reagan had sent Grassley a cordial letter of congratulations for his role in creating "a more effective tool for the prosecution and recovery of losses suffered through fraud against the United States government." But unless they were reading over the senator's shoulder, most Americans—including those with the greatest need to know—had still never heard of the False Claims Act. Phillips knew that the law had to be publicized, so that potential whistle-blowers would become aware of this important potential weapon. And it would be easier to get publicity for the law once there were some successful cases to point to.

To educate the public about the new law, Phillips contacted a number of reporters to see if they would be interested in doing a story about it. One of the first big news articles about the revised law appeared on the front page of the *Los Angeles Times*. It described how readers with private knowledge of theft from the government could do their patriotic duty so that instead of losing their jobs and even their careers as usually happened in the past, they could be rewarded for their service, and even get rich. The article was followed by a brief spate of similar pieces on television. Gradually the story of the law was heard by employees of government contractors throughout southern California.

Calls poured in, but Phillips knew he had to be selective about the cases he took. In addition to the traditional limitations of manpower and money, a practice concentrating on False Claims Act cases faced considerations peculiar to the law itself. As with other civil lawsuits, each one would be a gamble, because it would be taken on the contingency of success. But with a *qui tam* case, which might very well involve enormous front-end expenses, the bet would be placed on a horse that had never run a race. Even if such a case were to be initiated by the federal government and not merely a private citizen, it could take years to complete. Corporations would be expected to respond to the new law with vigorous opposition. In the deep-pockets world of government contracting, outspending often translated to outlasting. A strategy based on staying power was all the more likely when the opposition was a private citizen.

There were a lot of other unknowns. Since no one had ever brought a *qui tam* suit under the revised law, it was impossible to accurately guess the likely size of relators' rewards. There was also no history of how to proceed with a case. No one could predict the outcome of future constitutional challenges, which were sure to be made. And lurking at the outskirts of these unknowns was the question of how deep and how enduring the Justice Department's hostility was toward the whistle-blower law.

Sorting facts and testing evidence represented a potentially large preliminary investment by a *qui tam* attorney. In a start-up environment it could be disastrous to spend a lot of time and money on false leads or on cases that turned out to be based less on an employer's wrongdoing than on the plaintiff's desire for personal revenge.

But motivation and character were important to most people, and public opinion, either positive or negative, could have potential political consequences regarding the law's future. The way in which the press reported on the first relators and on the merits of their cases would be critical in shaping that opinion. As they had in the past, lawyers whose clients were accused of stealing from the government could be counted on to paint the accusers in the darkest possible colors, hoping to paint the law itself with that same brush.

Phillips expected that future *qui tam* litigants would be driven, like those in the past, by integrity and patriotic duty, and that they would have calculated the new equation between the risk to their careers and personal lives and the financial protection the law gave them for standing up for the truth. He hoped that some people who had tried to stop fraud by their employers in the past and gotten nowhere might be encouraged by the new law to try again, and that others with knowledge of wrongdoing who were previously unwilling to step forward might now be more likely to take such risks.

Phillips was sure the False Claims Act would find far wider application, over time, than just within the defense industry. But since there were so many defense contractors in southern California, and because that is where he lived, he assumed that at the start most of his cases would come from that sector of the economy. When the telephone finally rang—a delayed consequence of the piece in the *Los Angeles Times*—it turned out the caller had no connection with the defense industry. Far from it: He identified himself as Dr. Paul Michelson, from La Jolla, an upscale university town just north of San Diego, and he was an ophthalmologist. "The story says the law is about stealing from the government," he said to Phillips half apologetically. "So I thought, why not Medicare?"

"That's right, why not?" Phillips replied, although on the face of it the call was a nearly comical anticlimax. He recognized the potential for fraud in any part of the economy that did business with the government, including physicians and hospitals contracting with Medicare. But there was the presumption of a higher ethical standard in a profession dedicated to saving lives than in a sector like defense where the focus was often in the opposite direction. Besides that, it had not occurred to him that the size of individual cases in the medical field could ever approach the level of abuse that had been associated with big-ticket items like bombers and battleships. He didn't want to say anything that would give his caller the feeling of being turned away, but neither did he want to offer a false hope. It was hard to imagine a less likely relator than an eye doctor.

Michelson thought he detected a hint of uncertainty in Phillips's response, and in turn he became even more tentative about the appropriateness of his call, asking for a copy of the law so he could decide for himself whether it was relevant to his particular situation. Phillips had to tell him that the revised False Claims Act was still so new, it was not yet available in print. The best thing, they both decided, was for the doctor to come on up to Los Angeles for a preliminary meeting with Phillips and his colleagues.

Michelson turned out to be a pleasant, low-key man of forty-four, with a slightly diffident demeanor and a precise, analytical mind. His wife, he said with a hint of self-deprecation, described him as "obsessed" with the events that had changed his life. He had turned to the False Claims Act as a last resort.

The story began nine years earlier. A graduate of Johns Hopkins School of Medicine, Michelson was teaching at Harvard when the prestigious Scripps Clinic and Research Foundation recruited him in 1977 to come to California and put together a new division of ophthalmology. He began hiring top-ranked doctors, and two years into the assignment he recruited his younger brother, Dr. Joseph Michelson. Three years after that, in 1981, Paul brought in another key player in the story, a bright, young doctor named Raymond Chan.

In 1983, when Paul came out on the losing end of a policy difference with Scripps management, he was demoted and replaced as division head by his younger brother. The strained relationship between the two siblings was part of the problem even before the change, and it didn't improve now that Joseph had Paul's old job. On the positive side, Paul was somewhat relieved to be free of the administrative stresses, and he made every effort to put the rivalry behind him and get on with the practice of medicine. One day, as he was making a routine notation in the department's laser log, he discovered a series of earlier entries that set off an immediate alarm. According to the record, Dr. Chan was routinely performing a very complex operation, called a resection, and reporting it as an outpatient procedure.

Paul Michelson had seen only two resections in his entire career—a burn case in Africa, and a child who had been attacked by a wild boar in Iran. The procedure involves the surgical removal, reconstruction, and reattachment of the eyelid, which is sewn closed after reattachment and then remains shut for three months. It requires an operating room and a full staff. There was no way it could have been performed by a single doctor with a laser, nor could it have been done as frequently as Chan claimed. It was unthinkable that the patient could have gone home on the same day as the surgery.

When Michelson checked Chan's office records, it was apparent that he had actually been performing blepharoplasties, minor cosmetic eyelid skin tucks, and misreporting them to collect a much higher fee from Medicare. As Michelson probed further, he found that Chan was frequently billing other laser procedures as scalpel surgery, for the same reason.

Michelson was offended by his colleague's greed, but he was far more concerned with the potential consequences of his actions to Chan's patients. In several cases involving glaucoma, he felt Chan was too quick to use argon laser therapy, often, he told the lawyers, before trying "the accepted, appropriate, safer, and far less expensive medication therapy" recommended by the American Association of Ophthalmology, and in some instances even before making a clear diagnosis.

One of Michelson's own patients, a pretty young girl whose only problem was that her eyes weren't producing enough tears, was automatically passed on to Chan one day when Michelson wasn't at the hospital. Although Michelson had advised her to use artificial tears and to cut down on the length of time she wore her contact lenses, Chan convinced her that he could cure her condition with a laser. When she returned the following day—to Michelson, not Chan—she was suffering from blistered burns on both corneas, was unable to open either eye, and was in great pain.

When he first became aware of the red flags raised by the entries in the laser log, Paul was no longer head of the department. But even after the change, his relationship with Chan was still cordial enough that he felt he could approach him as a concerned colleague in order to bring the situation out into the open. He started off casually, saying he noted Chan was getting a lot of glaucoma patients, and he wondered where they were all coming from. Chan responded with a guarded smile. When Paul pressed him, his noncommittal, indifferent response seemed deliberately designed to discourage further discussion. "In effect, he was telling me to go away, that it wasn't my business," Michelson said to the lawyers at that first meeting. "He was letting me know that he planned to continue doing things his way, and if I chose to do things differently, that was all right too."

Realizing he was getting nowhere by dealing directly with Chan, Michelson decided to follow accepted ethical protocol for such matters and take the problem to the head of the division. He told his brother there were too many things on the monthly report that didn't make sense and that could lead to serious trouble. He urged him to look into it. His brother said he'd do just that. When Paul walked back to his office, he decided he had done everything the situation required, and that it was time to let the matter drop.

The weeks passed, with no clues that anything had changed. It was always possible that his brother had settled the issue privately, that he had spoken with Chan in his capacity as division head and had simply laid down the law. But whatever steps Joseph had taken, or not taken, as a result of what he had been told, there was no question that Paul was now out of the loop. That was all right too. He had never enjoyed the interpersonal responsibilities that went along with running the division, and was glad the burden was on someone else's shoulders. But one day it came back to him with its full weight, and Paul realized that nothing had changed at all.

The occasion was the billing and coding of a minor laser procedure that Paul had performed on a patient's eyelid. His own secretary was out, so Paul had taken the file to the woman who handled such matters for Dr. Chan. When he picked it up a short time later, he gave it the usual quick review. "Wait a minute," he told her, "you've done this the wrong way. This isn't the procedure I performed."

The secretary looked at him defensively. "That's how Dr. Chan does it."

"But you're not billing this for the right thing," Michelson repeated. He pointed to the line on the paper describing the service that had been provided. "That's not what we did."

The secretary nodded in agreement, but with a coaxing smile. "You make a lot more money billing it this way."

Michelson felt a sinking in his stomach, but tried not to give away what was going through his mind, keeping up his end of the conversation as though he were really interested in learning how to improve his billings. Eventually, the secretary told him that Dr. Chan did all of his own coding, the clerical task of selecting standardized descriptions of what work has been done. Each code was reimbursed by the government at a fixed rate for Medicare patients, who accounted for about 80 percent of the foundation's business. Dr. Chan's choice of codes, she said, was usually based on which procedure paid the highest rate, rather than on what he had actually done.

Not only had Paul Michelson's complaints failed to put a stop to these practices, vice was now being advertised as virtue, with Chan's secretary serving as evangelist. Trying hard to contain his rage, Michelson went back to relate the conversation to his brother. This time Joseph seemed less concerned with placating Paul than before. Over the next several months Paul approached his brother again and again on the issue. Each time the only result was a sense of being stonewalled.

The problem persisted. Chan kept billing for procedures he hadn't performed. Patients were still being treated with expensive, risky, and inappropriate therapies for the sake of profit. Chan was being paid money he hadn't earned, and so was Scripps. In early 1985, Paul decided to take his complaint outside the division to Melvin A. Block, the chairman of the surgical department and a member of the foundation's clinical board of governors.

Although it appeared at first that his complaints at this higher level would be equally without result, it became apparent over the following months that this time Paul Michelson's crusade was about to produce a tangible consequence. Without explaining the context, his superiors began describing his attitude toward his coworkers as "incompatible." For the first time he heard the suggestion that Scripps might not renew his contract. Although he recognized clearly enough that this was a threat, he didn't take it as seriously as it was meant, and his complaints continued. In January 1986, Block called him into his office. He would be let go when his present contract expired on the last day of July.

Paul Michelson frequently found himself close to choking on the inequity of being punished for the transgressions of one errant colleague and the self-serving indifference of others. But he kept telling himself that the change was all for the best. He managed to do all the self-preserving things required for a seamless segue to the opening of a new practice on August 1—he would not miss a day of work—just a few blocks away from the scene of his painful exile.

But his nights were a different matter. From the time he was told he was no longer wanted, his sleep was visited by wrenching, painful dreams. They continued even after he had left it all behind and was well established in his new practice. On one particular night toward the end of summer, he awoke from a long chase, in which he had been pursuing his three tormentors through a field, to discover that he had just smashed a fist into his pillow only inches from the head of his sleeping wife. He lay for a long time staring into the dark, thinking about what was going on and trying to come up with a solution for dealing with it. His initial incredulity at the situation had graduated into a barely repressed anger that was eating him alive. He realized that even now it wouldn't go away unless he took some further positive action.

At this point, any hope for a resolution obviously no longer lay with Scripps. He didn't know of anyone with direct experience in dealing with such matters through the American Medical Association or the American Academy of Ophthalmology. But he had often heard both these organizations referred to as toothless tigers, traditionally aligned with power and in defense of the status quo. The Medical Board of California, which had authority over the licensing of physicians, didn't look much better, with a reputation for being underfunded, understaffed, ineffective, and notoriously slow. His only other apparent recourse was the United States Department of Health and Human Services, which maintained a widely publicized fraud hot line. Unfortunately, most of that publicity was negative, with several recent articles in professional publications criticizing the department's haphazard handling of Medicare fraud cases. Up to now, his ordeal had been relatively private. The wrong next move could turn him into a professional pariah, or even a national joke. He knew he had to do something, but he had no idea what that something might be.

Later that fall, his wife handed him the *Los Angeles Times* and pointed to the front-page story about the False Claims Act. Although Paul had misgivings about the law's focus on the defense industry, his wife reasoned that the principle was just as logically applicable to any other sector of the economy that did business with the government. Paul mulled it over for a few weeks before he made his call.

After they heard his story, Phillips and his two colleagues, attorneys Joel Reynolds and Lisa Foster, were convinced that Michelson had the makings of a strong legal case under the False Claims Act. They were equally impressed by the man himself. He told them he assumed he would be professionally and socially ostracized if he filed the suit. However, he felt so strongly about the moral rightness of his cause that he was willing to accept that consequence. His commitment to principle went further than that. The article in the *L.A. Times* had spelled out how the *qui tam* provision of the law allowed the whistle-blower to share in the recovery of stolen funds. Michelson told the attorneys that he wanted to assure that his motivation in this case escaped any possible taint of self-interest. He intended to donate all of his own profits from the litigation to charity.

Compared with the lawyers' expectations for cases involving the military, Michelson's estimate of the amount of Dr. Chan's false billings was almost minuscule. Based on his random checking of the files of thirty-seven Medicare patients treated by Chan between 1984 and the time of

Michelson's departure in mid-1986, Michelson had identified fraudulent charges of only $47,000. The sampling represented only about a seventh of the patients for whom Chan claimed to have prescribed laser therapy during his time at Scripps, suggesting a potential recovery somewhere in the area of a third of a million dollars. If the outcome included triple damages, as the False Claims Act allowed, the recovery could be worth as much as a million, which would yield at least $110,000 as the reward to Michelson.

Phillips told Michelson that he was inclined to take the case, but before they made a final decision, he wanted him to meet with Howard Daniels, an assistant United States attorney in Los Angeles. Daniels had earned a reputation as a tough, relentless prosecutor of individuals and companies who stole from the government, and Phillips wanted his evaluation of the doctor as a potential relator.

In the meantime, Phillips considered some of the other ramifications of this case as the first *qui tam* lawsuit under the amended act. Health services were the fastest-growing sector of the economy. The more he thought about it, the more he realized that the potential for abuse in Medicare billing was perhaps even larger than in defense. However, it was also likely to be a lot more diffuse, since health care providers comprised a network of mostly small contractors. The amount of money in the case against Chan and Scripps was tiny in comparison to that potential, but that wasn't all bad either. It would be easier for the public to stay focused on the issues, and harder for the law's detractors to claim that it was the whistle-blower, rather than the defendant, who was motivated by greed. Both Phillips and the Justice Department felt that Michelson's case represented a good precedent: a doctor doing the right thing, showing good character, offering solid evidence in a lawsuit they were sure they could win.

The impression Michelson brought home with him from the meeting with Phillips, Foster, and Reynolds was equally as positive as theirs had been of him. "These are the first lawyers I've ever met that didn't have any agenda besides doing the right thing," he told his wife, surprised to find himself sounding enthusiastic about a meeting he had approached so cautiously. "I knew Phillips would be smart, but the people who work with him are extremely bright as well." He thought for a moment. "I don't know exactly what I expected, but the one thing I *didn't* expect was that it would actually be fun."

A few days later, government attorney Daniels called John Phillips about his meeting with Michelson. "He's totally solid," he told Phillips. "He explains the case well, he's as sensitive to the legal issues as to the medical ones, and he has all the right motives. I'm impressed."

Phillips discussed the report with his colleagues, and the response was unanimous: The eye doctor would make an ideal relator. The first *qui tam* lawsuit under the revised False Claims Act was filed against Scripps and Chan in Los Angeles on April 29, 1987, six months after Reagan had signed it into law.

Early on, while the case was still under seal, Phillips and Michelson met with investigators from the Department of Health and Human Services, the government agency responsible for monitoring Medicare claims, to review Michelson's allegations. The problem, the HHS sleuths admitted, was that they didn't see anything in what either Chan or Scripps had done that was really wrong. Michelson wasn't surprised by their reaction, They weren't doctors, and even though they were nominally the agency's enforcers, they understood very little of the language of medicine, and almost nothing of the issues and alternatives related to the procedures for which Chan had filed his false claims. HHS had limited resources, so agency investigators often lacked the experience and background to understand medical procedures. "There are more red flags on these files than in Red Square on May Day," he told them. Then, patiently, translating as he went, he led them through the discrepancies a step at a time. By the time he finished, the investigators saw the flags just as clearly as he did.

At Michelson's insistence, his brother was not named in the action, even though he had been in charge of the division of ophthalmology at the time of the events in question. That generous decision had little impact on their relationship; by September, when the case became public, Paul and Joseph were no longer speaking to each other.

Up to then, that was the only serious consequence. But nobody yet knew about the lawsuit. Because there were so few models, especially in medicine, for what he had done, Paul Michelson and his wife had no idea what the reaction of his other colleagues or of neighbors and friends might be once the story became known. A lot of his professional associates already knew why he had left Scripps. Although there were the usual social realignments, those early consequences were predictable and relatively benign. With the unsealing of the case, and the revelation that he was no longer just a victim but had struck back, the Michelsons prepared for the worst. Separately and as a couple, both of them could lose many valued friends.

As it turned out, almost all of the agony was in the waiting. The result was far different from their expectations. When the story became public, many of the colleagues Michelson ran into during the course of his work made a special effort to let him know they understood what he had done and why, and that they approved. Others went out of their way to contact him with encouragement and support. The Michelsons received phone calls and letters from doctors, patients, neighbors, casual acquaintances they hardly remembered, and even people they had never met. To the Michelsons' amazement, despite their worst foreboding, the initial avalanche of affirmation was untainted by a single negative response from friends or colleagues.

In April of the following year, Scripps wound up settling its part of the case with an agreement to pay $335,000 in Medicare indemnity and $100,000 of its adversary's legal fees. Although the amounts were small—even trifling—the precedent was stunning. The False Claims Act worked, the *qui tam* provisions were enforceable, and the application of the law was no longer limited to the defense industry.

Negotiations with Chan dragged on for another couple of years. As the time approached for that settlement, Phillips began looking for opportunities to get the False Claims Act some more national publicity. Several media outlets expressed interest, including *60 Minutes*. The producer for the project, Sandy Socolow, told Phillips a big reason for his interest in the story was because of its unusual tensions, of doctor against doctor and (although Joseph was conspicuously absent from the suit) brother against brother.

Two camera crews were assigned to the segment, and network anchor Harry Reasoner was flown in from New York to report it. Paul Michelson did well in his interview, the background material fell nicely into place, and Reasoner had done the obligatory shot in front of the Scripps building to explain that the medical center's officials had refused to be interviewed. All that remained was for *60 Minutes* to get some footage of Dr. Chan. When Chan declined Reasoner's request for a sit-down interview, Phillips and his colleagues told *60 Minutes* where Chan was working and what kind of car he drove. The lawyers couldn't be there for the shoot, but there was no reason to think they'd be needed; a camera crew was assigned to ambush the doctor when he arrived for work. If, as they expected, they couldn't get Chan to face his interrogator, the next best thing would be some footage of him running away from the cameras.

On the chosen day, the team was waiting outside Chan's office building when one of the crew called out that their target was in view. A Mercedes had just turned onto the street and they all waited expectantly, ready to leap, as it pulled into the parking lot and the driver stepped out. But when he realized he was being approached by men with microphones and cameras, he suddenly jumped back into his car and sped away, apparently in a state of panic. The crew was satisfied they had gotten what they came for, and headed for the airport.

After the story had been put together in New York, Phillips asked the producers to send him the footage to make sure the crew had shot the right person. Four frames from the final scene were shot off a video monitor and sent back to his office in Los Angeles. Phillips looked at the face of the frightened driver. It was possible he was somewhere around Chan's age, but that was as far as it went. He wasn't even Asian; his complexion and features suggested Middle Eastern, Hispanic, or Mediterranean lineage. Phillips called Socolow with the bad news. A few hours later, the producer called back to say the story had been spiked by the show's executive producer, Don Hewitt, because it no longer had "enough tension."

Positive publicity can be life's blood to developing a new field of practice, and the decision came as a terrible disappointment. But by the time *60 Minutes* called it off, numerous other media outlets had picked up the story and Paul Michelson was well into his fifteen minutes of fame.

Michelson didn't seek that fame, and he didn't want it. And he didn't want the money that came with it. The final settlement with Chan called for repayment of only $250,000 to the government and the reimbursement of legal fees of $75,000. Chan was also required to perform four hundred hours of community service. Shortly after the Chan settlement, as he had privately promised at the outset of the case, Michelson gave away every last dollar. One of the principal beneficiaries was his alma mater, Johns Hopkins, where he helped establish a chair in medical ethics.

As it turned out, the money really wasn't all that important to the government, either, compared with the other benefits produced by the case.

Even though the financial recovery in the two settlements was lower than expected, a far more substantial benefit could be found in the model it provided for those who might follow in either Chan's or Michelson's footsteps. The case was widely reported in the medical trade press for ophthalmologists, sending a message to others who may have been tempted toward the same type of upcoding in order to increase revenues. The biggest promise of the False Claims Act was in the deterrence that comes from successful prosecutions. Health care fraud was suddenly far riskier, and honest initiatives safer, than either of them had been before.

Phillips had predicted another result of the Michelson case that was far easier to measure. Following news of the two settlements, his telephone began ringing off the hook with inquiries about the False Claims Act.

T E N

G R E A S Y   S P O O N

The final installment of Michelson's story, the government's settlement with Chan, appeared in the *San Diego Union* on July 31, 1990. That morning, a forty-two-year-old salesman named Jack Dowden read the article twice, first with the casual interest of a browser, and then with the muted excitement that sometimes comes with an unexpected discovery. He folded the paper and laid it on the breakfast table, weighing the relevance of what he had read. Then he reached for the telephone.

The following day he was in Los Angeles, telling his story to attorney Lauren Saunders in the offices of John Phillips, in a new firm recently established to focus on *qui tam* cases. Dowden knew enough about selling to recognize that this was a screening interview, and he provided the degree of detail necessary to establish his credibility. Until just two weeks earlier, he had been the regional sales manager for MetWest, a large medical laboratory chain, where he had supervised a force of twenty-five reps in a territory that included most of southern California. At the time, the market for clinical laboratory tests was about $20 billion annually, and MetWest's parent, MetPath, was one of the six leading independent companies in the field. Dowden had left his $70,000 job during the culmination of a longrunning dispute over billing practices. He said the company—indeed, the majority of the medical laboratory industry—was using an elaborate system of false claims to steal tens of millions of dollars from Medicare and Medicaid.

Saunders was interested enough to ask him some questions about how, but her tone and expression remained professionally neutral throughout the interview. When it was apparent that she thought she had heard enough, she excused herself, and a short time later she returned with two other attorneys. Dowden recognized John Phillips from the story in the newspaper. His colleague, a slight, quiet young woman named Mary Louise

Cohen, shook his hand as firmly as Phillips, with the same friendly smile and a look that was at once direct and subtly appraising. Cohen, a Harvard Law School classmate of Janet Goldstein's, had met Phillips when she was general counsel for Handgun Control, a nonprofit lobbying group in Washington, D.C. When they were all reseated and after a brief exchange of pleasantries, Phillips asked Dowden to describe the way in which he felt that money was being stolen from the government.

Dowden started off by warning them that it wasn't a simple story. He explained that the lab business worked on one fee schedule for doctors and another for patients; the doctors' fees were always discounted, and the patients' were as high as the market could bear. The lab had four possible payers: the patient, the doctor, an insurance company, or the government. Every year, the government complained about lab costs because it knew it was paying a higher reimbursement for the tests than doctors were. But the government never did anything about it, and the difference between what the government paid and what the doctors paid just got bigger every year. "It grew like stories about fishing," Dowden said, "where the first liar didn't have a prayer. One reason the government has never done anything about it is because they helped create the problem. Unlike the reimbursement system for other medical services, patients covered by Medicare and other government health insurance programs aren't required to co-pay on the cost of their lab tests, so they don't have the same opportunity to check on what those tests are and how much they cost."

A common practice among medical labs was to bundle nineteen or more blood chemistry tests that could be performed on a single machine using the same blood sample. The series of tests, called "Serial Multi-Channel Automated Chemistry," or "SMAC," included testing for frequently ordered items such as glucose, cholesterol, calcium, and sodium. Because the reimbursement for a SMAC was relatively low, Medicare would reimburse for the panel of tests even if the doctor needed only as few as two of the individual results. At that time, Medicaid paid around $19 for a SMAC panel, while doctors paid as little as $5.50 and no more than $7.

In 1987, one of the giants of the laboratory testing industry, National Health Laboratories, Inc. (NHL), began using the SMAC concept of bundled tests to trick doctors into ordering tests that were medically unnecessary. NHL added the HDL test, which looks for a lipoprotein that appears to decrease the risk of atherosclerosis, or hardened arteries. While the HDL test provides useful information when a patient's total cholesterol is high, there is no medical justification for including it as part of a routine blood screening. Medicare and Medicaid only reimburse for medical tests that are requested by a doctor and are necessary to prevent, diagnose, or treat an illness or injury.

When the lab added HDL to the SMAC panel, it initially increased the charge to doctors by a dollar or two, then later discounted the doctor's price so that it was actually cheaper than the original SMAC without the test. But this discount was never applied to the government, and the doctors were never told that when this newly expanded panel was billed to Medicare, the unwanted HDL test was charged as a separate item at an additional cost of $12.

At the time, Dowden was regional sales manager with a smaller testing company named Central Diagnostic Laboratories, and CDL did not go along with the practice even though NHL was its main competition in southern California. One day he was visiting an account in the South Bay, below Los Angeles. The doctor told him, "I'm getting the same thing from National Health Labs that you're giving me, but they're adding HDL at the same price."

"That's right," Jack acknowledged. "But the reason they're doing it is because they're billing Medicare separately."

The doctor looked shocked. "They couldn't possibly be doing that," he said. "It would be fraud."

"If I can show you proof that's what it's about, will you come back to my company?"

The doctor looked skeptical but said he would.

So Jack went to another doctor, rolled up a sleeve, and asked him to draw a blood specimen. It was sent off to NHL, and when the report returned it showed that the cholesterol test had been billed separately. Armed with the proof, he returned to the office in the South Bay. This time the doctor was too busy to see him. He dodged him for the next three visits until Dowden decided it wasn't worth the effort and gave up.

The HDL addition was so profitable that by 1989 NHL decided to do the same thing again with yet another unnecessary test. It began measuring ferritin on its SMAC panel and charged Medicare an additional $25. The ferritin test is a sophisticated method of detecting unusual iron disorders. As with the HDL, there is no medical justification for including it in routine blood screenings, especially when the SMAC panel already tested for iron. By adding the unwanted and unnecessary ferritin and HDL tests routinely to every order, NHL was able to bill Medicare $56 for each SMAC instead of the $19 the government had established for the basic panel. The actual cost to NHL was only a few cents per sample, so the enormous difference was almost all profit.

The problem got even closer to home in early 1989, when Jack's company, CDL, was taken over by MetPath. Jack was flown to the flagship MetPath facility in Teterboro, New Jersey, to meet the sales manager with whom he would be working and to tour the company's laboratories. His new colleague showed how they would take a tray of a hundred specimens and put it on a SMAC tester. A few minutes later, he picked up the same tray, walked another twenty feet, and placed it on another testing system for the HDL. Even doing it in two steps, it was cheaper and easier to run the whole tray—about a half hour for the hundred samples—and withhold the results from nonrequesting doctors than it would have been to break up the batch on the basis of who ordered it and who didn't. As a result of this demonstration, Jack realized his new employer would soon add HDL to every chemistry panel.

He was convinced this was wrong. He knew the practice would trick doctors into ordering tests they didn't need, which was against the law. A short time after the tour, when he met the future president of the company's California subsidiary, MetWest, Dowden told him what he had learned, and that he was opposed to it. The only immediate response was a quizzical look, followed by a slight shrug and what might have been a shaking of the head, suggesting disagreement.

Two days later, Dowden's boss, Jim Pitton, was far less ambiguous about the company's stand on his objection. Jack had been training salesmen up in Orange County, and Pitton said he wanted to get together with him that noontime. They agreed to meet at a restaurant in Westminster called the Greasy Spoon. Dowden liked Pitton and they had always gotten along well, but his boss wasted no time in coming right to the point of the meeting. "You talk too much," he said, in an obvious reference to his conversation with the president-designate of MetWest two days before. He then told Dowden to keep his mouth shut or he'd find himself out of a job. Pitton didn't sound angry and his tone was conversational; it wasn't so much a threat as just a friend explaining the facts of life.

Even though his new company was about to follow its competition in a practice that Dowden saw as unethical and illegal, it wasn't a change that would place him at any personal risk. What he would be asked to do was no different from what five hundred other salesmen in his industry were doing already, and in fact it could mean $600 or $700 extra in monthly commissions from Medicare payments alone. Dowden assumed that Pitton had done some of the same math, and he left the restaurant feeling angry and marooned. He tried to think of where else he might try to make his case before the company got caught up in the web.

Sometime earlier, he had heard a rumor in the industry that there was a small task force of federal investigators in San Diego assigned to watch National Health Laboratories for billing irregularities. It had occurred to him that if he could find out where they were, he could tell them what he knew and all hell would break loose. Initially, he had considered such a move strictly as a competitive stratagem against a company that he felt was eating his lunch. Now the idea offered the additional appeal of providing a cautionary model that might save his own company from taking the same crooked path. The day after his meeting at the Greasy Spoon, Dowden made a few calls and learned that the investigators were with the Office of Inspector General, assigned to the Department of Health and Human Services. That afternoon, he walked into the HHS offices in downtown San Diego and asked for an IG agent in charge of the investigation of National Health Laboratories.

The meeting was a long way from what he had expected. At first he was encouraged by the fact that his visit was taken seriously enough that two investigators participated in the interview. He told them he thought NHL was committing fraud, and he was worried that his own company was about to do the same thing. But very early on, he sensed that neither one of them was all that interested in what he had to say. They seemed distracted, and Dowden wondered if what he was telling them was over their heads.

"Do you know what a chemistry panel is?" he asked. If they knew anything at all about the field in which they were conducting their investigation, the question was so basic it risked being seen as insulting, so he tried to make it sound casual, with no hint that he might be testing their competence. To his astonishment, they both said no, as if they had never heard of it.

"Well, what about HDL cholesterol?" He was still trying to be offhand, but when they answered no to that as well, he realized his mission was in serious trouble. "How about ferritin?" Again, they shook their heads. Considering the business they were in, Dowden couldn't have been more discouraged if they'd said they didn't know how to read or tell time. It was going to be a hard sell, and he hesitated, pondering where to go next. The pause, apparently, was the break the investigators had been waiting for.

"What we're interested in is kickbacks," one of them said.

"Kickbacks or volume discounts," the other added, suddenly animated now that they were switching over to their own agenda. Dowden sat back in his chair and tried not to show the letdown.

Volume discounts were a form of incentive, like the frequent flier miles offered by airlines, by which some laboratories rewarded their most productive physician clients. There was nothing wrong with offering price breaks per se, and wholesale schedules are a normal part of almost every kind of business. But when the government is paying the bill and the entire credit for the discount goes instead to the physician placing the order, then the practice becomes a bribe and the discount is a form of stealing.

Years earlier, long before he ever got into the testing business, Jack Dowden had seen a segment on *60 Minutes* in which a lab salesman was taped talking to a physician, offering to rent closet space in the doctor's office for the storage of test tubes. The offer was morally equivalent to giving the doctor a television set in exchange for his business—another incentive, along with hams, turkeys, liquor, theater tickets, and even expensive vacation trips, that was standard bait in the early competition for lab business. When the government finally woke up to the fact that these bribes were being paid with public money, the labs responded by switching to a different kind of lure, hiding the bribe as a fake rental contract or in some similar disguise.

"That's all you're interested in?" he asked the two agents. "Kickbacks and volume discounts?"

They looked at him guardedly, and the one Jack had figured was the senior of the two said, "That's where we're focusing."

The other added, "It's where the abuses are."

In shifting the conversation's center of gravity from Dowden's subject to their own, the two investigators were striving for familiar ground on which they would be able to take control of the interview. Dowden didn't want that to happen. He sat up in his chair and leaned toward them. "Well, guys," he said, "that isn't where it's at. What you're looking at is only a pimple. I'm here to show you the whole elephant's ass."

In San Diego alone, he told them, National Health Laboratories was making $20 apiece on a thousand HDL tests every day. There were no kickbacks involved, and no volume discounts. The reason most doctors went along with it was because they didn't understand how NHL was billing the parts of the tests they didn't need.

The two agents listened patiently, but through the whole explanation Dowden felt that he never had their full attention. It was obvious they hadn't bothered to learn much about the field they were investigating, and maybe they had decided his story was too complex for them. Afraid that he was going to lose the sale and anxious for some kind of response that would reengage them, he asked what they thought would be a reasonable next step. The senior investigator said they wanted to talk it over with their boss.

It could have been a brush-off, but it wasn't. The following day, they invited him back to meet with Arthur Roy, who was in charge of the NHL investigation.

Dowden went through the whole story again. This time he didn't assume that Roy knew any more than the two agents from the day before, so he took the time to describe what the add-on tests were intended to measure, and how the government was being billed at an inflated rate for results the doctors didn't order. Ferritin, for example, was an indicator of how the body stored iron, and although it was relevant to patients with anemia, another test, the complete blood count or CBC, determined the same thing and a lot more besides. When Dowden finished his explanation, Roy nodded politely, and then asked him what he knew about volume discounts and kickbacks.

If Dowden had been in some profession other than sales, he might simply have given up. Instead, he repeated his response of the day before about the pimple and the elephant, and passed the ball right back to Roy. "Look," Dowden went on, "I've been in the testing business for nine years, and in all the thousands of times I've interviewed doctors about what tests they want included in their chemistry panel, not a single one ever asked for ferritin. It's the kind of test they order one at a time, as needed, and not in a panel where it gets measured every time someone draws blood. Yet somehow this inconsequential test got added to the chemistry panels of National Health Laboratories in 1989, and every time they run the panel, a separate bill goes out to the government as though the ferritin were being tested all by itself. Check it out," he said. "It won't take much to find out if what I've told you is true."

Two weeks later, near the end of February, Dowden got a telephone call at home. It was Arthur Roy from the inspector general's office. He said he was looking into the ferritin testing at National Health Laboratories, and he needed some competitive figures for comparison. He asked Dowden how much of that same kind of testing MetWest billed in a given period. Encouraged by the question, Dowden went straight to the company's files as soon as he got to the office. In those days, MetWest's total laboratory billings were about $80 million a year, and of that amount, the portion related to tests for ferritin was a minuscule $27,000.

"That ought to prove ferritin isn't a very important test," he told Roy. "How does MetWest stack up against NHL?"

The only numbers Roy had from National Health Laboratories were for the current month, and just for the San Diego office. But in that one location, which had an annual business volume of only $5 million, NHL's Medicare billings for ferritin testing in the month of February alone were $78,000, or triple the MetWest companywide total for both Medicare and non-Medicare for the entire year. NHL hadn't added ferritin to the SMAC panels until just the year before, in 1989. In short order, this inconsequential test that hardly any doctor ever ordered and that cost NHL almost nothing would account for billings by that one testing company alone of $20 million a year.

Dowden wasn't the kind of person who needed to share his anxieties with his friends or coworkers, and he never told anybody, either at work or elsewhere, that he was talking with the government about his company's competition. At one point his wife, who wasn't working at the time, happened to be at home while he was on the telephone with Roy, and when he hung up she told him she didn't want to see him doing anything that would get them into trouble. He explained only enough to try to put her at ease, and even though he could tell he hadn't been entirely successful in that effort, she was willing to let the matter drop.

Within a month after their luncheon at the Greasy Spoon, Dowden had two more warnings from his friend and boss, Jim Pitton, about the dangers of opposing their newly merged company's plans for including HDL testing in the SMAC panels. The first of the two was at a hotel in Los Angeles where Dowden was training salespeople, not the best venue for a give-and-take discussion about company ethics. But the second time he met with Pitton in a large corporate office in Orange County just after the merger with MetPath, and this time Dowden was ready for him. He told him in detail why he thought adding HDL to the SMAC panels was wrong, and why the company could get into trouble if it went ahead with its plan.

Perhaps the argument really changed Pitton's mind, or maybe he just decided to let Dowden think so. But by the end of the detailed recital, he agreed that the practice would amount to fraud, and he even agreed that if MetPath went ahead as planned, which was all but certain, neither of them should have anything to do with putting the plan into action.

"Jim," Dowden asked, "where do you suppose this is all going?"

The question may have sounded somewhat rhetorical, like, "Whatever will become of us?" or "Woe is me," or maybe Pitton was stumped for an answer, but when he didn't reply, Dowden outlined what was going to happen next. "The company is going to send out a letter to two thousand doctors saying we're about to up the price of a SMAC panel by a buck. For that small increase, we're going to include an HDL, which is a real bargain. But if any doctors think that even a dollar is too much, then they should just call their rep."

Pitton nodded. He knew that such a letter would be sent out, and he looked uncertain as to where Dowden was headed.

"Jim, someone is going to sign that letter."

"Yes," Pitton said, suddenly understanding.

Dowden nodded. "If you tell me right now that you intend to be the person who signs that letter, you are a fool."

His boss was still nodding as he took it in. Whoever sent out that letter would be seen as the company's prime mover in the promotion of a scam. If Pitton signed it, he agreed, he would be a fool.

A few weeks later, as Dowden had prophesied, the notice that HDL was being added to the SMAC panels went out to all the doctors in their market area. The name at the bottom was "Jim Pitton." Now it was Dowden's turn to shake his head. Apparently his boss had been convinced that the new organization prized team spirit over personal integrity, and that the only way to get along was to go along. He wondered if the cost of maintaining his lifestyle and an expensive mortgage had featured in Pitton's change of heart as well.

The day after the notice went into the mail, Dowden met with the two investigators who had first interviewed him in San Diego and gave them a copy of the letter. MetWest, at MetPath's direction, would bill Medicare $27 for the new combination of HDL with the SMAC panel—an increase of $8 over the price of the previous panel, Dowden told them. Like NHL, MetPath and MetWest designed their order forms so that there was no option for a physician to order a panel of tests without the test for HDL. "I've been thinking . . . ," he said. "How about if I quit my job and go to work for the inspector general?"

Whatever else the agents may have felt about the proposal, they must have immediately realized how much more valuable Dowden would be to their developing case as a witness than as an investigator. While he was still an employee of MetWest, he offered an insider's access to information and a veteran's perspective on its significance, both of which were in short supply within their own office. When they realized he was serious about a job, one of them said they couldn't consider him for employment because of his age. Dowden protested that he was only forty-three. Yes, but that meant he wouldn't be able to put in twenty years and still retire at fifty-five, which was the agency's policy. As Dowden left the office he thought that here he had brought them the biggest case either one of them was ever likely to see in his lifetime, and they were telling him he was too old to go to work for the government.

He also realized the time was fast approaching when he would have to make a move, and if it wasn't to the IG's office, then it would have to be somewhere else, perhaps even to unemployment. He just couldn't see himself continuing in a job where what he did every day went against his conscience—and, although he apparently was still the only one who saw it that way, against the law.

The added strain, of course, was that he was juggling the requirements of his regular job with the challenges of assimilating the merger, all at the same time he was meeting with investigators who had targeted his entire industry. He had taken Pitton's warnings seriously about keeping his mouth shut, but sometimes the pressure was so great that he doubted he was doing a very good job of toeing the company line.

A case in point arose when MetPath invited all its managers to a national meeting in Philadelphia. At a hotel cocktail party one evening, he found himself in a conversation with a colleague and one of the MetPath corporate attorneys. The sales manager was explaining to Dowden how he had approached an account in San Francisco and offered him a 90 percent discount off physician's costs just to get his business, and even then he couldn't make the sale.

At first Dowden didn't respond, assuming the company lawyer would drop on him like a ton of bricks. But to his amazement, the attorney said nothing, reacting instead with the kind of polite, slightly abstracted interest one might take in a war story from an arena in which the listener had never seen combat, along with a look intended to suggest empathy for the salesman's hard lot in life. Dowden knew one reason for the gathering was to help build relationships and trust within the merging workforce, but this was something altogether different. He asked the salesman, "What the hell are you doing offering a ninety percent discount?"

In California, a discount was legal as long as the doctor passed the savings along to the patient. But unless the doctor was particularly attentive to his patient's financial interests—and to the law—it was far more likely the physician would interpret the offer as a bribe, the very thing the IG investigators were looking for at NHL. Dowden never made a doctor that kind of offer, and he didn't want to do business with someone who did. But he was nowhere nearly as angry with the sales manager as with the attorney, who acted as though what he was hearing were regular business. Dowden wanted to reach over and grab him by the throat. Instead, he held up his hand, both as a sign of peace and to head off an answer to his question, and excused himself from the table.

Even though Dowden put on the brakes and steered away from a noisy wreck, when two companies are working hard to integrate a merger and the corporate thrust is toward unity, this kind of exchange is not likely to pass without notice. Differences between individuals are often seen as contests between the merging cultures, and quickly magnified by any suggestion of friction or defiance.

On June 1, 1990, at a sales conference in Los Angeles, Dowden was told that his field force and his territory were both being cut in half. He was assured it had nothing to do with his performance.

The main subject at the sales meeting was equally hard to swallow. MetWest was planning to add two more unnecessary tests to the chemistry panels in the coming year. In addition to the superfluous HDL test, it was going to measure protein-bound glucose and iron-binding capacity, and eventually these too would be billed out to the patient and to Medicare as separate tests. The sales force had to go around to all the doctors in the customer base and collect signatures to show that they wanted the tests included on the panel. There was almost no incentive for the doctor, so the sales pitch was based on the promise that the tests were free. There was no mention of the plans for direct billing to the patients and to Medicare.

Dowden was angry all the way home. That night he called Jim Pitton and told him he was going to quit. The following morning he drove to work and submitted his resignation.

Dowden also had a financial interest in a drawing station, a facility in San Diego where local doctors sent patients to have their blood taken. He'd put up some of his own money to get the venture started at a time when the assets of his original company were frozen during negotiations over the merger with MetPath. Although he estimated the appreciated value of his investment in the business to be over $300,000 on the open market, he was unable to find another buyer on short notice and settled with MetPath for $180,000, still several times his actual cost. The agreement, signed on June 12, also stipulated that he would stay out of the lab business for two years.

At about that same time, he heard again from Arthur Roy, who drove him downtown for an interview in the IG team's offices at Health and Human Services. Roy led him to a small meeting room, and when they were seated Dowden turned around and saw that another investigator, someone he had not met and who was not now identified, was stationed right outside the door, apparently as Roy's legal witness to their conversation. It seemed odd, but he thought that must be the way these things worked.

It wasn't until the first question that he began to suspect otherwise. Roy wasn't at all interested in hearing about needless add-ons to SMAC panels, or that the elephant Dowden had pointed to five months earlier now filled the room. All he wanted to talk about was the original pimple. "Come on," he said, his tone halfway between coaxing and impatient, "give me something on volume discounts and kickbacks."

"My God," Dowden answered. He couldn't believe it.

What he didn't know—and what his lawyers learned only years later—was that the government's investigators had gone to Carol Lam, the assistant United States attorney in charge of the grand jury, and she had rebuffed them. She said she wasn't interested in Jack Dowden's allegations.

Dowden had a salesman's skill for explaining things, and although his presentation to John Phillips, Mary Louise Cohen, and Lauren Saunders was laid out methodically and without any trace of polemics, there were moments when his quiet assurance seemed to be struggling, just below the surface, with something like frustration. Perhaps he was distracted by the lawyers' unrevealing demeanor—friendly and receptive but carefully professional, resistant to a salesman's natural need for affirmation.

Or perhaps it was a growing awareness, as he attempted to reduce his story to the simplest of terms, that he was attempting to unravel a yarn so badly knotted as to be inaccessible to anyone except the thieves themselves.

E L E V E N

ROUGH ROAD TO FAT CITY

The problem wasn't whether or not they understood him, Phillips assured Dowden at the end of their meeting. The problem was their limited knowledge of the regulations on health care reimbursement. "At this point, we don't even know if what these labs are doing violates the False Claims Act. It sounds like it does, and it's an absolutely outrageous practice. But we have to be realistic about the hurdles we'll face at the Justice Department. They'll say, 'Where's the fraud? The doctors did order the tests as indicated by the boxes checked off on the forms, and the tests were done.'"

It wasn't the answer Dowden was hoping for; he had a hard time accepting the possibility that anything based on so much secrecy and deceit could somehow still be legal. On the other hand, he knew how it looked. Here's this one, solitary salesman with a complaint against an entire industry, and there doesn't appear to be anyone else on earth—including the government's own enforcers—who thinks his story is anything more than sour grapes. But if the lawyer's answer meant they were willing to look into it, then there was still hope.

Phillips also warned him that the government could be unwilling to join the *qui tam* case. If that happened, he said, there were a couple of alternatives by which they might still be able to stop the fraudulent billing practice. One would be to talk with Representative Henry Waxman, who chaired a health care oversight committee in Congress and who might be willing to hold hearings on the abuse. The other would be to pursue a *qui tam* case on their own, although he warned that such a lawsuit was less likely to succeed without government participation.

Dowden weighed that possible outcome. While it would satisfy the biggest part of his motivation in approaching the government investigators a few months before, it was a distinct anticlimax to the slam dunk he had been hoping for. His original goal was to get National Health Laboratories into enough trouble that he wouldn't be forced by his own company to do the same thing. But now, even though he was no longer in the business, he was offended by the prospect that a company might be allowed to keep everything it had stolen right up until it was caught with its hand in the cookie jar and the government made it stop. Phillips appeared to be reading his thoughts.

"This isn't just about the False Claims Act. It's also about the rules that govern Medicare. Until we're sure that those rules aren't flawed in a way that allows contractors to get away with this kind of thing, we don't want to mislead you about your chances of prevailing in court. If you decide you want to go ahead with this, the best we can promise at this point is that we'll take it to that next step."

Dowden stood up. "Sounds good," he said, and they shook hands all around. He left the office wondering if the trip to Los Angeles would turn out to have been a waste of time. The idea of a personal reward was appealing, but he had only learned of such a possibility the day before, from the story in the newspaper, and it wasn't all that hard to let go of the idea that he might gain financially from doing something that he had started for altogether different reasons several months before. In the interim, even though his goal was still pretty much the same, his motivation had shifted. Since this all had started, he had given up his job over the issue and had been shut out of the industry in which he had made his living. If all that came of this was that the government eventually got around to telling the testing industry to quit stealing—or worse, if nothing happened at all—then giving everything up would have been for naught. He would be remembered only as a troublemaker, and no one would ever see that he had been right. By the time he got home, he had resolved to do everything possible to make sure that didn't happen.

The following day, he sat down at the desk in his study and began to write out everything he had explained to the three lawyers. A few days after Phillips received this treatise, Dowden called him on the telephone and asked if it had convinced him that what he was reporting amounted to fraud. Phillips said it was helpful, but the answer still would depend on what he learned about the rules for billing Medicare.

Dowden started looking for a job. Even though his termination agreement with MetWest kept him out of the lab business for the next two years, he had been a salesman for most of his working life, so he figured he should be able to sell anything. He went to work in a Chevrolet dealership in San Diego, where despite his selling background, the first few weeks were a disaster. Fortunately, MetPath was buying out his interest in the drawing station in installments, and the first $40,000 check arrived that August.

On the seventeenth of that month, Lauren Saunders mailed off a long letter to Dr. Peter Budetti, a specialist in health care law at George Washington University in the District of Columbia. A follow-up to a telephone conversation between Budetti and John Phillips, the letter outlined what the attorneys had learned from Dowden, describing the added tests as "an outrageous fraud against the government" potentially involving millions of dollars. If anyone could tell them whether the testing labs were breaking the law, Budetti was the man.

Dowden received his copy of the letter within a few days of the check from MetWest, and it encouraged a tentative, slowly forming hope the pending litigation might hold a key to his long-term future. Maybe he was going to find vindication after all, and at the end there might even be some kind of reward. The payments on the lab might provide the means for surviving long enough for that to happen.

Meanwhile, if his prior experience as a salesman had any relevance at all to his new calling, in which the only real requirement for employment was the absence of a criminal record, it was in the degree to which it had honed his tenacity. He settled into his position with the dealership, passing long stretches of time alone in his cubicle with an eye on the front door, doggedly absorbing the indignities and disappointments and boredom of his new work, until finally he began to make some money. Eventually he became so good that there were times when he outsold every other salesman in the store. But even then the most he ever made in a single month was only $3,000, or half his salary as a sales manager in the industry from which he was now barred, and there were lots of weeks in between when he sold nothing at all. When there are no commissions, dealers have to pay their nonproducing salesmen the minimum wage. They don't like doing it.

Based in part on Budetti's affirmative response, the lawsuit against National Health Laboratories, MetPath, and MetWest was filed in April 1991. The plaintiffs in the suit were the United States of America, the State of California, and Jack Dowden.

The filing was a milestone, but there was no reliable way to estimate how long the three defendants could drag out the process, and still no solid assurances of the result. There was nothing more for Dowden to do once the legal mechanism was set in motion. Because it was under seal nobody had any idea of his role in the case and he couldn't discuss it. He plodded along with the Chevy dealer until he finally got fired for failing to sell enough cars to earn the equivalent of the minimum wage. He sold for the next few months at another couple of dealerships, without substantially changing his luck, then circled back to his old job and was once again selling Chevrolets.

Meanwhile, at the Department of Justice, the senior trial attorney assigned to the case seemed to be having trouble understanding how the False Claims Act applied to Dowden's allegations. Luckily for Dowden, a new government attorney joined the Justice team. A graduate of Yale Law School and not yet thirty, Larry Freedman quickly grasped the key concepts and seemed eager to get on with the investigation.

Lauren Saunders made an appointment with Freedman at the department's Civil Division in Washington on August 8. She was surprised, she told him, that four months after filing their case and over a year and a half after Dowden had first gone to the inspector general, the government's agents still appeared to know little about the practices described in the complaint, or about why she and her colleagues felt those practices would be found illegal.

Saunders was encouraged when Freedman asked her to prepare a memorandum on theories of liability. A magna cum laude Harvard Law School graduate who had recently left a prestigious clerkship on the District of Columbia Court of Appeals, she was well suited for the task. Saunders worked on the arguments over the next ninety days, and on November 25, 1991, she sent Freedman a tightly detailed road map for the government's potential prosecution of criminal and civil cases against the laboratories. "The case is even stronger than I thought," she told him. She came back from a subsequent meeting with Freedman confident that the Justice Department would now investigate the allegations and take the case seriously.

Back in San Diego, the criminal investigators finally appeared to understand what Dowden had been trying for so long to tell them. And Assistant United States Attorney Carol Lam, who had been working on possible criminal prosecution related to the volume discount side of the investigation, now began working closely with Freedman on NHL's addition of ferritin and HDL tests to the SMAC panels. Under the pressure of a possible grand jury indictment, NHL began to show a new interest in resolving Dowden's false claims lawsuit.

Meanwhile, Jack Dowden's pay once more dropped to the minimum wage and he was fired by the Chevy dealer for a second time. At that point, he decided a year and a half was long enough in the car business. Thinking he ought to do better with a product he could care about, he got a job selling used boats. He did all right for a little while, but then things slowed down there as well. In November 1992, after just eight months, he was on the beach again.

By then, however, the ship that had been wavering on his horizon like a distant mirage for the prior two and a half years had gathered substance and appeared at last to be heading into port. Although the Justice Department had still not joined the case, Freedman told Phillips that he was demanding a settlement in the tens of millions of dollars. When Dowden heard this news, the necessity of looking for another job no longer seemed anywhere nearly as urgent. Savoring the irony of his dazzling prospects in the aftermath of being fired from a job that paid the minimum wage, he decided to sit back and wait to see how it all played out.

The settlement demand shocked NHL's attorney. Frank Rothman was the former head of a Hollywood movie studio and the husband of a federal judge. He later complained to Phillips, a longtime acquaintance, that Freedman had been a hard negotiator. "The kid was very, very tough to deal with."

On December 18, 1992, at 5 P.M. Pacific time, after the closing of the stock markets, the Department of Justice announced that it had settled its case against National Health Laboratories. Rather than face trial, the company had agreed to pay the United States government $100 million in restitution, plus $10 million to the states whose health care systems it had swindled, and an additional $1 million criminal fine. The Justice Department had demanded more. But in light of the company's precarious financial condition, that was determined to be the most NHL could pay and survive. The announcement came just a little more than two years after

Jack Dowden walked into John Phillips's office and twenty months after the filing of his case.

As in all *qui tam* cases, especially the early ones, what was at issue was far more than money. The settlement was the first of its kind in the laboratory industry, and it sent a powerful message. NHL was required to publicly acknowledge wrongdoing, although the confession was carefully worded to limit the monetary consequences. The company admitted only to having submitted false claims for unnecessary blood tests to a Department of Defense program that administers health care services for the families of military personnel. If NHL had been forced to acknowledge stealing the much larger amounts it had received from similar false billings to Medicare or Medicaid, the result would have been mandatory prohibition against future participation in either of those programs, and the company would have very likely gone out of business. But even the limited admission was enough to end the practice.

Although the announcement rocked the testing industry and was viewed by most observers as a huge victory for the False Claims Act, to those on the inside of the case the government's press release about the settlement was equally notable for what it left out.

It ignored the treble damages provision of the False Claims Act, which would have yielded an amount six times higher than the settlement, instead of letting the company keep half of what it stole.

Nothing was said about the provision in the False Claims Act for fines of up to $10,000 per offense if the case actually went to court—potentially, a financially crushing lever that might move a defendant to accept responsibility in a full and timely manner.

The chief executive officer of NHL, Robert Draper, would later receive a six-month sentence, serving half of it in jail and half at home with an electronic ankle bracelet, and a fine of $500,000. But even while he was in jail, the company kept right on doing business with the very government programs it had swindled.

The company's onetime controlling stockholder, financier Ronald Perelman, made out better than anyone, including the federal government. A suit by some of his fellow shareholders claimed that the company had inflated its growth and revenues by systematically submitting false medical claims to the government, and that NHL hadn't disclosed to the public that it was under investigation by the government. Perelman had sold

55 million of those inflated shares in 1991–1992 for a yield of over a billion dollars. When the value of NHL's stock nosedived on the first day of trading after the settlement of the false claims case, those 55 million shares were owned by others; Perelman had taken his money and moved on. NHL's insurance settled the shareholders' suit for $64 million. Perelman paid nothing.

The biggest omissions of the press release were any mention of Jack Dowden, whose relentless pursuit of justice had given the case its focus and led to the huge government recovery, and of his attorneys, without whose counsel and tenacity the case could not have had its successful outcome. Instead, virtually all the accolades were directed to Carol Lam, the assistant U.S. attorney whose initial disdain for the lawsuit had nearly persuaded the government to disown it.

Despite the False Claims Act's guarantee of at least a 15 percent share to a successful relator, four months after the settlement with NHL the government was still refusing to pay Jack Dowden a cent. He flew to Washington to have his deposition taken at the Justice Department by Larry Freedman. One of the questions was whether the company's illegal activities "didn't appear to be common knowledge" to the federal investigators Dowden had first met in San Diego in 1990. No, he replied, the agents had no knowledge of these practices until he told them, and even then they didn't understand why they were illegal.

On May 5, knowing that Freedman's recommendation for Dowden's share had been forwarded to the new attorney general, Dowden's lawyers wrote to Janet Reno, once more outlining the facts of the case, and asking her help in bringing it to an equitable solution. Three weeks later, Jack Dowden was awarded a relator's fee of $15 million, the minimum amount allowable under the False Claims Act, which was all he or his attorney had asked for. He collected the first payment, nearly $5 million, in July.

The following month, Larry Freedman invited him back to Washington, this time as an ally, to enlist his perspective on the still-pending case against MetPath. Unlike NHL, the company had gone to the trouble of getting written releases from doctors saying they approved the extra tests being added to the panels. Freedman had reviewed the physicians' signature forms, and found several on which either the doctor or the salesman had written in the word "free." Dowden looked at the cards and shook his head. "There's your point," he told Freedman. "They wrote that in because they wanted to be sure they weren't going to get a bill for something that was worthless to them. And 'free' means nobody has to pay—not the doctor, not the patient, not Medicaid. It proves a salesman told them it was being offered for nothing. And that was a lie."

In mid-September, while Dowden and his wife were on a cruise to Alaska, he got a telephone call from his attorneys. MetPath was in settlement negotiations with the government. Both Dowden and his lawyers knew MetPath had been more careful than NHL in the information it provided to doctors about the addition of tests to the SMAC panels. And unlike NHL, MetPath had never added the ferritin tests. Even so, the settlement offer of $23 million seemed too low, and Dowden and the lawyers agreed that the Justice Department should be urged to counter with a higher number.

The next day, he got a second phone call, saying the negotiated figure was nearly $40 million. This time his attorneys recommended acceptance of the offer. This was still less than Dowden figured MetPath had managed to steal, but he understood that it would be difficult to persuade the court to reject such a large settlement. Under the False Claims Act, relators can object in court to settlements, but they don't have veto power. So Dowden agreed to the deal. Again, despite his central role in the prosecution and recovery, Dowden requested only the minimum of 15 percent as his relator's share. This time, the government was quick to agree.

In October, Dowden moved into a million-dollar home, surrounded by similar dwellings of the rich and powerful, in the elegant, storybook village of Point Loma. From his living room, he could look down across a terraced slope of pristine, tiled rooftops, perfect lawns, and manicured grounds to the sparkling blue waters of San Diego Harbor and the beckoning sea beyond. The former Chevrolet salesman bought himself a Lexus, and a Jaguar for his wife. But he knew the battle wasn't over.

The crime he'd reported was not the kind of thing normally associated with violence, but what he did had changed a lot of lives. Even after they moved into their million-dollar home, his wife's best friend was afraid to get into the same car with her. When Jack applied to the local country club, he felt obligated to tell them he was responsible for sending one of its members to jail. It let him in anyway. Because membership rosters are alphabetical, his name and address were listed directly opposite those of Robert Draper, the man he helped send to prison.

Justice had a different spin. Assistant United States Attorney Carol Lam told reporters she had never met with either Dowden or Phillips in the course of the investigation, and that the outcome owed nothing to either of them.

On January 16, 1994, *60 Minutes* aired a segment on the False Claims Act, and it included a look at the role of the relator in the case against NHL. Reporter Lesley Stahl asked Lam if the $100 million settlement was a direct result of Dowden's lawsuit.

"That is absolutely not true," Lam said, looking offended by the suggestion that the government needed any help from the people it represents. "We would have gotten exactly the same result even if his lawsuit had never been filed."

"Then why did Dowden get fifteen million dollars out of it?"

"Because, I assume, that's what the law says he's entitled to get. Basically, he got fifteen million dollars for giving the government a tip."

Again, the real story was in what was left out. Lam did not tell the reporters she had received summaries of every interview between Dowden and the agents who worked for her from the time he first walked into their offices in 1990. She said nothing of the fact that the initial investigation of NHL had been directed elsewhere, or that she had turned her back on Dowden's information and later disparaged the facts reported by government investigators that were the basis for his suit, apparently because she didn't understand how those practices were against the law. She left out the fact that she had received a copy of the memorandum on theories of liability that Saunders had written for the government's lead attorney on the civil case.

The former U.S. attorney general William Barr was even less subtle in his choice between defending turf or the law. He referred to *qui tam* attorneys as "bounty hunters," and while acknowledging that they pursued the public's interest, he decried their motives as mercenary. "They get a piece of the action," he said, as though the practice were unique to the False Claims Act and contingency fees had been invented by Satan.

"Just think, Lesley: When the government sues, we go through great pains to ensure that the agents and the lawyers have no financial interest. In fact, it's a crime for a government lawyer to have a financial interest in any matter they're looking at. But what this does, it lets any Tom, Dick, or

Harry get some financial interest in the matter and then bring the suit in the name of the government. And that's wrong."

Throughout the entire three years since he'd first told his story to the indifferent government agents in San Diego, and continuing beyond the time of the settlement, Jack Dowden's fortunes had seemed to vary less with the merits of his case than with the whims and follies of an enormous, recalcitrant bureaucracy. Even after his receipt of the first payment, while the Justice Department was using his complaints against NHL and MetPath as a template for follow-up cases against other companies engaged in the same practices, it still failed to fully acknowledge his contribution.

At the end of the segment on *60 Minutes,* the camera came back to Jack Dowden. Despite Lesley Stahl's attempts to coax him into a somewhat more ennobling posture, he appeared to revel in his fortune, insisting that he now spent all his time at nothing more useful than golf, boating, and the enjoyment of his wealth. Some viewers may have been put off by the apparent callousness of this claim on the good life, although probably the majority interpreted his admission, and the insistent, slightly defiant smile that went with it, as nothing more than hard-earned satisfaction. But Dowden may not have been all that concerned with how he appeared to the world at large.

More likely, he was performing for viewers much nearer at hand— at his old company, at NHL, in the Inspector General's Office and the Justice Department, the friends he had left behind and the new neighbors right next door. For them, his look was less a gloating smile than a calculated, laid-back, in-your-face, kiss-my-ass expression of triumph. Against all odds, Jack Dowden had finally and decisively made his point. And he had decided that living well was indeed the best revenge.

TWELVE

MAN IN THE MIDDLE

J ack Dowden wasn't the only whistle-blower to run into opposition from government lawyers who had been eager partners in prosecution only to become strangers in the sharing of credit and adversaries in the allocation of rewards. Another dramatic case in point was one of the two other clients of John Phillips and Mary Louise Cohen whose stories were told in the *60 Minutes* piece featuring Dowden. This second relator was a mild-mannered, middle-aged man with prematurely white hair and gold-rimmed glasses. He was the whistle-blower in a landmark case against the world's largest company, which was also America's third-biggest defense contractor.

When he first contacted John Phillips by telephone in the summer of 1987, he gave his name as John Wallace. He said he was an American working in another country and that he wanted to talk with an attorney about a potential *qui tam* lawsuit the next time he was back in the States. He was audibly nervous and unwilling to supply any real information on his case, suspecting that the international phone call might be monitored. Phillips was used to potential clients being guarded and apprehensive when they first spoke with him, and he agreed to the requested meeting.

Wearing a gray suit, white shirt, and light-colored tie, the visitor looked just like what he said he was, a mid-level manager for a defense contractor. He said his company's products were widely used in military jets in America and abroad, as well as in commercial airliners around the world. He gave up the information cautiously, still as circumspect and apparently nervous as when he had called for the appointment. He had proof, he went on, that his employer was colluding with the air force of a foreign country to defraud the U.S. government of millions. But if word got back that he had even participated in, let alone called, this meeting, he was certain the foreign general at the center of the fraud would have him killed rather than risk exposure. Phillips responded with an overview of how the False Claims Act worked, but he knew better than to push for more information than was being offered.

They met twice again over the next two years, and in those subsequent meetings the man in gray filled in more and more of the missing details. He revealed that his employer was General Electric and that he worked for the Aircraft Engines Division, headquartered in Evendale, Ohio. The foreign client was the Israeli Air Force.

In the early 1980s, he said, GE was awarded a major contract for F16 engines on Israeli Air Force jets. In beating out longtime rival Pratt & Whitney in a hard-fought competition, the company owed much of its victory to the long-standing relationships between its International Programs Division manager, Herb Steindler, and high-ranking military and government officials in Israel. In particular, Steindler was a close personal friend of Rami Dotan, the fierce-looking, saturnine air force lieutenant colonel in charge of engine procurement who soon became a general on the strength of his leadership with the F16 program.

In 1984, Wallace said, he established an office in Tel Aviv, and for the next four years he acted as GE's liaison with the government of Israel and with the country's air force. Although he was nominally manager of GE's aircraft engine business there, his primary role was not as a decision maker but as a facilitator of the information flow in both directions between the clients in Israel and the real managers in the United States. This meant he had to be present at discussions between GE personnel and representatives of the Israeli Air Force or government, and relayed messages back and forth between the two sides.

For GE, the contract had implications that went far beyond the initial sale. Because of Israel's military reputation in the Middle East, the country's every move was watched closely by neighboring nations, which frequently emulated its decisions on equipment. Shortly after the announcement that Israel was replacing its Pratt & Whitney engines on the F16, GE received similar orders from the air forces of Turkey and Greece, and then from Egypt, for a total of over a billion dollars in new business. With so much resting on this highly visible relationship, the company had an enormous incentive to make sure Israel remained a happy customer.

GE's contract with the Israeli Air Force was worth $415 million. A support contract for tools, equipment, training, and upgraded facilities added $40 million more. In 1988, another order was received for sixty-six more engines and nine sets of engine modules, at a cost of $213.4 million. All of these contracts were subsidized with loans or grants authorized by the Foreign Military Sales Act. America's military assistance program supports the defense of Israel and a few other friendly nations by allowing them to buy U.S.-made jet engines and other military hardware and then subsidizing the purchase with U.S. funds.

Very shortly after Wallace's arrival in Tel Aviv, it became apparent to him that there were irregularities in certain aspects of these contracts. In a far-reaching collaboration directed by Steindler in the United States and Dotan in Israel, representatives of GE and the Israeli air force were creating false records and submitting bills for project funds to which they were not entitled. While most of the GE transactions with the air force were legitimate, Dotan arranged deals with GE officials in which Israel "bought" engine testing facilities that were never built, as well as support software that was never created. Dotan and GE also padded the sales price for engines.

As far as Wallace knew at the time, Dotan was using this scheme to divert money to other priorities of the Israeli Air Force, such as upgrading power stations at air defense facilities, projects that were not permitted under the Foreign Military Sales Act. He was not alone in that assumption. Within GE, the rationalization for the false record-keeping was that Israel was an ally, and that it was just part of the game to turn a blind eye when money was diverted to other Israeli defense projects not covered under the Foreign Military Sales Act program. Wallace didn't know how much was being misused or that anyone was gaining personally from the scam, but he recognized instantly that the fraudulent reassignment of these funds violated U.S. laws, and he found himself a reluctant participant in the conspiracy. He and his colleagues could all wind up in jail.

On the face of it, the scheme impressed Phillips with its similarities to the recent Iran-Contra scandal, with Dotan in a role like the one played by marine Lt. Col. Oliver North. During the Reagan administration, North and other White House officials secretly violated a U.S. arms embargo by selling weapons to Iran, to the same extremist government that had attacked the American embassy in Tehran and held the embassy staff hostage for 444 days, until the end of Jimmy Carter's presidency. North's covert deal was an attempt to gain the release of more recent American hostages held by pro-Iranian terrorists in Beirut. He and his colleagues then compounded the felony by using the proceeds from that arms sale to support the Nicaraguan Contras, which was illegal as well. No one suspected Israel of redirecting the American subsidy to programs that would in any way harm the United States. Nonetheless, taking American money for an authorized purpose and then using it for something else was a serious breach of trust, and it was against the law.

Phillips accepted the case on that premise. Mindful of the national outcry of just a few years before, including congressional hearings and criminal investigations, when the Iran-Contra scandal was finally exposed, the attorneys proceeded with extreme caution. They lined up evidence and built a careful, solid case to prove that GE and Israeli officials were defrauding the U.S. government. Given the international ramifications of Wallace's accusations, they knew that even the smallest misstep on their part could have enormous consequences.

The most immediate consequence, of course, would likely be to the relator. From the start, Wallace had been uncertain how far the corruption extended. He was sure the key players could not carry off such a scheme without the knowledge and acquiescence of high-level GE officials. Even if he leapfrogged his own superiors in raising these issues at the next echelon of management, there was no way to be sure he wouldn't be talking to another member of the conspiracy. He had documents that would prove the funds were being misused, but he was afraid of what might happen if he was caught trying to take them out of Israel. The incriminating evidence had implications for Israel's security, and because he and his wife were living in Tel Aviv, he had to consider the possibility that bringing charges through the available channels could cost him his job, and perhaps even both of their lives.

Eventually, to get out of this untenable position, he asked for reassignment. In early 1989 he was transferred to Switzerland. Up to then, even though he traveled frequently between Israel and the United States, he had never attempted to bring out any of the incriminating paperwork. He feared that if the papers were recognized by Israeli border officials, his intentions could be revealed at the same time, a situation in which the concept of shooting the messenger might easily rise above the level of metaphor. The move to Switzerland provided him with the cover he needed, and the

incriminating papers left the country hidden among his household furnish-
ings and personal effects.

Mary Louise Cohen became the lead lawyer on the case, and shortly
after the move, she and John Phillips met with Wallace to receive and review the smuggled documents. At the start of the meeting, their client said
he wanted to clarify one other matter. The name he had given them two
years before was an alias, a form of insurance against the kind of leak that
could lead to disastrous preemption or reprisal. John Wallace revealed that
his real name was Chet Walsh.

Over the next several months, lawyers at the firm meticulously
combed through the smuggled paperwork, some three thousand documents, extracting evidence and building a strong legal case of massive fraud.
They pieced together the paper trail connecting both Dotan and GE to
the scheme, and tried to verify all of Walsh's information. They were particularly mindful of the implications his charges might have for America's
policy toward Israel, and took pains to ensure that everything that might
be used in their filing was subject to exacting rules of proof.

Once they determined that the *qui tam* lawsuit should be filed in Cin-
cinnati, where GE's jet engine plant was located, they decided to retain
James B. Helmer, Jr., a local attorney, as cocounsel. Helmer was the lawyer who had successfully represented whistle-blower Jack Gravitt in a False
Claims Act case against the company in 1984, before the law was amended.
Phillips first met Helmer during Grassley's hearings in Washington, where
Helmer had testified to just how vindictive GE could be to a whistle-
blower; in retaliation for Gravitt's suit, the lawyer had said, his client was
given poor performance reviews and later fired.

Meanwhile, Walsh had decided on his own to gather additional incriminating evidence of the fraud. On one of his regular visits to the
division's headquarters in Evendale, he put a small recorder in his pocket
and secretly taped conversations with other GE officials, some of them
longtime friends. Over several years, he had secretly taped conversations
with colleagues in Cincinnati and elsewhere.

Later, as Cohen listened to those tapes to ensure the accuracy of tran-
scriptions that were made for the FBI, there was a quality to the conversations that seemed out of place, even vaguely disturbing. She knew that
Walsh had built his entire life around GE, that he depended on the com-

pany for his paycheck, his sense of self-worth, his social life, and virtually all of his friendships. Like many other relators, he found himself suddenly torn between a lifetime habit of loyalty and a bitter sense of betrayal. By doing what GE had done, the company—and his coworkers—had forced him into a decision he never wanted to make, a choice that led away from the comfort of the familiar, into exile and an unknowable future. What took Cohen by surprise was how committed he now seemed to separating totally from his past.

Many of the voices on the tapes belonged to colleagues who were longtimers like himself and who clearly regarded him as an old friend. One after another, with remorseless conviviality, Walsh steered them into revelations that had the potential for damaging or ending their careers. It was clear from the conversations that at least two of the officials knew that Dotan was involved in questionable dealings and that GE could eventually face questions from Israel.

One of them even went so far as to talk about a planned cover-up. "We are all moving to Building 90 [at Evendale]," he told Walsh. "All these files that's, uh, been locked up back here—will get lost, conveniently. And I've got a great excuse. I don't know nothing."

The following year, in the summer of 1990, Walsh was transferred again, this time to Madrid, to head GE's aircraft engine marketing programs for Spain. That November, as he was flipping through an aviation magazine, Walsh suddenly froze. There was a story on Dotan. He had been arrested in Israel for shaking people down for kickbacks and bribes. It was apparent from the article that the charges against Dotan were unrelated to Walsh's allegations.

Later, the Israeli investigation of the GE contracts would find that both Dotan and Steindler had deposited millions of dollars from the contracts into their personal bank accounts. They also learned that Dotan had paid someone $50,000 to kidnap, hurt, and threaten a former official who had tipped off the Ministry of Defense about Dotan's illegal schemes. These disclosures supported Walsh's contention that his life was in danger, vindicating his use of an alias when first pursuing his *qui tam* lawsuit and his waiting to turn over evidence until he was out of Israel and out of harm's way. Dotan had wrapped himself in the flag of his country to justify the juggling of defense accounts, but in the end he was just another crook who had stolen to get rich. Israeli defense minister Ezer Weizman told the *Jerusalem Post,* "If it was possible we could tar and feather Dotan, like they used to do in the U.S., I would do it myself."

Days after Dotan's arrest, Walsh's attorneys quickly put the finishing touches on his *qui tam* lawsuit and filed it, under seal, with the United States District Court for the Southern District of Ohio in Cincinnati. The defendant was General Electric Company, the largest corporation on earth.

Four days later, in the office of the United States attorney in Cincinnati, Helmer and Cohen met with lawyers from both the civil and criminal divisions of the Justice Department, along with agents from the Federal Bureau of Investigation. The agent in charge of the investigation was named Stephen Kosky. Cohen assessed Kosky throughout the meeting. He was in his early forties, and she learned that he was a lawyer and native Ohioan who had just been assigned to the Cincinnati white-collar crime squad after sixteen years in the FBI's Chicago office. He was straightforward and professional, showed a quick grasp of the issues, and seemed unencumbered by any biases or preconceptions about the role of whistle-blowers. She was reassured by the choice.

Cohen supplied Kosky with a ten-page chronology of the allegations she had assembled with Walsh, along with the smuggled records, organized in a way that laid out the entire fraud.

On December 3, she flew to Boston to meet with Walsh, who had just arrived from Spain. The next day, they flew to Cincinnati. Joined by Helmer, they met with a large group of civil and criminal prosecutors from Washington and Cincinnati, along with Kosky and other government investigators. Cohen and Kosky caucused privately to discuss the agent's plans for the remainder of Walsh's visit. The FBI wanted Walsh to record conversations, Kosky said, with colleagues at GE who had any knowledge of what was going on in Israel. The pretext for such conversations would be the recent arrest of General Dotan. The case was still under seal, so no one at GE or in Israel was yet aware of Walsh's lawsuit.

Because those conversations could require Walsh to act as if he had a role in the illegal transactions, Cohen asked that her client be immunized against prosecution for the crimes he had reported. This was a standard procedure with cooperating witnesses, and the FBI immediately agreed to seek approval from the criminal prosecutors. Walsh also turned over the secret recordings he had made on his own of conversations with colleagues about Dotan and GE.

It took a day for Kosky to line up the support team. On December 7, Chet Walsh walked into the GE facility in Crescentville, Ohio, wearing a wire for the FBI. The FBI had given him a specific list of the people he was supposed to talk with and a script of what he was to say. Outside, on International Boulevard, Cohen and Kosky sat in the agent's car, listening in and following his progress as he ambled down the familiar hallways, engaging the targeted employees in conversations and following the script. After work, they listened in again as he unwound with old friends at the Bombay Bicycle Club, a popular GE gathering place on Chester Road, and continued the recording.

In one of those conversations, a colleague told Walsh a chilling story about a recent incident in Israel. A GE executive had been visiting the country on business around the time of Dotan's arrest. In the middle of the night, Israeli agents woke him up at his hotel and took him away for questioning. He had no idea what they would do to him. He cooperated and was released, but the ordeal left him badly shaken.

Ten days after the tapings in Evendale, following discussions between attorneys for GE and the general counsel for the Defense Department, the company turned over several dozen boxes of requested records to Kosky. Meanwhile, other FBI agents in New Jersey executed a search warrant on a front organization consisting of little more than a telephone and a fax machine which had been set up to shuffle papers and siphon money from the Israeli projects.

At the end of February 1991, Kosky and a group of government lawyers met in Washington with four high-ranking officers from the Israeli Air Force, including two generals. The U.S. team spent the entire week interviewing the Israelis on what they knew about the case. A few days later, two other agencies joined the FBI in the investigation. The Defense Contract Audit Agency and the Defense Criminal Investigative Service were brought in to help sort through the paperwork, working in parallel but separate tracks under Kosky's leadership over the following year.

A month after the meeting in Washington, the Israeli government brought Dotan to a speedy trial. He was charged with fraud, theft, and accepting kickbacks from GE and other contractors that netted him an illegal fortune of some $10 million, and with plotting against his colleague in the Ministry of Defense. Disgraced, the general started a thirteen-year sentence in an Israeli prison.

In August, Walsh's *qui tam* case was unsealed, and his role as the whistle-blower became public. GE immediately put Walsh on administrative leave. But the company didn't stop there. Officials cried foul over the lawsuit and began attacking Walsh's actions and character. The company threatened to sue him for breach of contract and vowed, in effect, to remain his nemesis forever. The unrepentant tough talk went all the way to the top. In an interview with *Corporate Crime Reporter*, GE chairman Jack Welch reiterated the same hard company line, dismissing Walsh as "a money-grubbing guy who sat back and waited in the weeds so the damages would mount."

In a barrage of stories and interviews, GE repeatedly cited an ethics statement that Walsh had signed, and pointed to supposedly anonymous hot lines they said he could have used to report the thefts within both GE and the Department of Defense. The ethics statement, which had to be signed by all GE employees annually, certified that he was unaware of any company wrongdoing. Walsh had tried to avoid signing it, but when pushed he had no choice. A refusal would have carried the same perils as telling his superiors what he knew. Either move could have jeopardized his safety, and risked his becoming the scapegoat in a GE cover-up. GE used the same line of attack in settlement negotiations and in the courtroom.

Phillips responded that members of management were the perpetrators, and that the telephone lines were widely suspected as being anything but anonymous. Besides, even if the system did protect an informant's identity from government investigators or the GE security people, Walsh's knowledge was so specific that anyone who was involved in the conspiracy would have no trouble at all in recognizing that he was the source of the complaint.

The stress of the case was taking a physical and mental toll on Walsh. Before he and his family left Israel, he had confided in no one besides his attorney about the fraud. His wife, Birgitta, knew he was seeing a lawyer, but in the two years between his first contact and the filing of his *qui tam* case, he shared virtually none of the details. While agonizing in Israel over whether to blow the whistle, he came down with shingles, which is often stress-related, and the illness caused him pain for years. His adult daughter, Christina, later told a reporter, "I have to remember when I see him not to hug him because it hurts him." After the unsealing, every attack seemed to add worry lines to his face and age him visibly.

During the depositions, he would frequently break down and weep. He appeared to be ashamed that he was physically afraid of Dotan. Throughout the long ordeal, he never departed from his standard uniform of light suits and white shirts. During one four-day deposition in Washington, Cohen learned it was Chet's sixty-seventh birthday, and in the hope of cheering him up she bought him several new shirts. If the surprise gift brought any relief from the stress, it was only momentary.

GE acted swiftly to contain the political and legal damage that followed Dotan's arrest and the filing of Walsh's *qui tam* suit. The company hired a Washington law firm headed by Lloyd Cutler, a former adviser to President Carter, to conduct an internal investigation. Walsh's former American boss, Herb Steindler, was fired, and some twenty employees who had known of the thefts but did nothing to stop them were demoted, transferred, or forced to retire. The latter included most of the friends whose conversations Walsh had recorded.

But even as the company was closing that door to the corporate stable, new doors were being opened by others. The scandal gave rise to a congressional investigation. Representative John Dingell, a Michigan Democrat, held hearings and publicly blasted GE officials for failing to catch the fraud and stop it. In June, the Defense Department did the unimaginable, stunning GE with the suspension of its jet engine unit from future military contracts. The sanction lasted only four days. All of the government attention forced some major changes. The company agreed to create an independent oversight board for monitoring its foreign military sales, to reimburse the government for any funds misspent as a result of the fraud, and to give federal investigators access to its records and facilities.

Revelations of Dotan's theft also created a brief crisis in the relationship between the United States and Israel. Citing reasons of security, Israel refused Justice Department investigators access to the general or any other Israeli officials involved in the scandal. In response, the U.S. threatened to withhold critical military aid. Dingell questioned whether any of the diverted funds were used for covert operations, which the Israeli government strongly denied.

Despite its admission of wrongdoing and the heat from the congressional and federal investigations, GE continued to act toward Chet Walsh as if the real villain in the story was not the thieves or their accomplices, but the man who had turned them in. They harried him relentlessly, attacking his motives and his character and repeatedly threatening to sue. "They're doing it to send a message to other GE employees," John Phillips told the *New York Times*, "that they shouldn't think they can file a False Claims Act suit and win a recovery and then walk off into the sunset and live happily ever after."

It was equally obvious to the presiding judge on the case, Carl Rubin, that GE intended to use Walsh as a cautionary model. Appointed by Nixon in the early 1970s, Rubin had seen what the company did in the Gravitt case, and he knew that no other whistle-blower had ever caused the company as much embarrassment or elicited such a potentially devastating sanction from the government as Chet Walsh. With GE's dependency on government contracts, employees who might be considering a similar course had to be discouraged at almost any cost.

Settlement negotiations among GE, the Justice Department, and Walsh's attorneys dragged on for many months. Finally, the government asked Walsh's lawyers what they would consider a reasonable settlement figure. Based on their best estimates of how much had been stolen and the precedents up to that time for enforcing the statutory penalties, the lawyers and Walsh calculated the minimum value of the case at $60 million. A major factor in that estimate was the fact that Judge Rubin had presided in Helmer's earlier *qui tam* case, finding against GE and coming down almost as hard on the government for not supporting the whistle-blower. The next day Phillips told the Justice Department that $60 million was as low as he and his team were willing to go without objecting in court that it would be inadequate.

In July 1992, three months after GE's opening offer of $4 million, the company, the whistle-blower's attorneys, and the Department of Justice announced that they had settled the civil case, under the False Claims Act, for $59.5 million. The company also pled guilty to four federal charges of criminal fraud and paid an additional fine of $9.5 million.

Toward the end of the settlement discussions, Walsh's attorneys had made it clear that they would not approve a final resolution unless it included a written guarantee that GE would not go after their client. Rubin agreed. He even threatened to require that CEO Welch appear before him to accept the guilty plea in court. "I know what you're trying to do here, and I'm not going to let it happen. You can spit on each other's graves after you're dead," he told them, "but you will give this man a release."

In response, GE promised in writing that the company would leave Chet Walsh alone.

Even with the signing of the waiver and then the settlement, Chet Walsh's odyssey was still a long way from a happy ending. As soon as his attorneys and the government achieved this landmark civil settlement, the prosecutors wasted no time in letting Walsh know the honeymoon was over. By law, he was entitled to a minimum of 15 percent of anything recovered through his False Claims lawsuit, so his attorneys calculated the reward to be at least $9 million. Instead, at a meeting in Washington following the settlement, the Justice Department offered $7.5 million. It looked as though the government had decided to switch sides and, waiver or not, was now helping GE to deliver on its threat to deny Walsh a share in the recovery.

Walsh and his attorneys rejected the government's offer. The federal attorneys appeared stunned at their decision. "If you're going to turn this down," a Justice Department official later told Phillips, "we have no reservations about going after your client."

Phillips and Cohen were resigned to the inevitability of a courtroom battle to collect their client's due reward, as well as their own fees and expenses from GE, as mandated by the law. For them, it was to be the hardest-fought part of the entire process.

GE and the Justice Department appeared to be putting more energy into this phase of the contest than they had spent on the case itself. Company representatives insisted Walsh could have and should have stopped the fraud. The Justice Department now picked up on GE's argument as a justification for denying Walsh's reward altogether. Under the False Claims Act, no matter how much money the government recovers, any whistle-blower who is guilty of planning and initiating the fraud gets nothing.

The judge refused GE's request to participate in the phase determining Walsh's share since it had no financial interest in the outcome. Despite that refusal, the company's lawyers and executives regularly showed up in the courtroom audience every day of the hearing on the relator's share. Whispering and passing notes, they made no secret of their collaboration with their former adversary, the Justice Department, in a continuation of their campaign against the whistle-blower.

To prepare for the hearing on Walsh's reward, Cohen asked to depose the agent in charge, Steve Kosky, as a witness to the indispensable role of Chet Walsh as a relator. The Justice Department then threw up a novel and unexpected barrier. It argued that because the case involved classified information vital to the nation's security, and in addition was the subject of an ongoing criminal investigation, it was "too sensitive" for Kosky to testify in the presence of the relator's civilian attorneys. The Justice Department had to know that preventing the FBI agent's testimony would seriously undermine Walsh's ability to make his case.

Phillips and Cohen knew their client's best hope lay with Carl Rubin, the federal district judge in whose court the FBI agent would have testified. In the earlier false claims case brought by Helmer, Rubin had taken the Justice Department to task for its "antagonism" toward the whistle-blower. Now, rather than argue the merits of the Justice Department's claims, Walsh's lawyers approached Rubin with a unique proposition. If they weren't allowed to take Kosky's testimony, maybe the judge could do it instead, using questions they would supply him in advance. "We don't have to be present," Phillips said, "because we're confident he'll tell the truth."

It was a calculated risk. They were certain of Kosky's integrity, and they had good reasons to be equally confident in the judge. Rubin made no secret of his distrust of GE, insisting on a transcriber even when he met with the company's attorneys in chambers. In one such meeting, the judge listened as Phillips and Cohen, their client, and attorneys from GE and the Justice Department exchanged arguments about whether Walsh himself was culpable for the crimes he had reported. At the very least, a GE lawyer said, he had an obligation to report these misdeeds to the head of the company's compliance program for the Israeli contract, rather than increasing his potential reward under the False Claims Act by remaining silent until the fraud had become much larger. Walsh pointed out that the head of compliance was himself instrumental in the theft. After listening to this exchange, Rubin commented that he had sat on previous cases involving the company and whistle-blowers, and it was his experience that "the whistle-blower always gets screwed." Cohen was confident that the judge wasn't about to let it happen again. GE tried to disqualify him, but it couldn't get the judge off its case.

Phillips glanced around the room as Rubin pondered the proposal to take Kosky's testimony. It was obvious the suggestion was an unwelcome surprise to the other attorneys, not only because it could demolish their artificial barricade but because it would be difficult for DOJ to object to it without its appearing that the government too was challenging the judge. When Rubin commented that he had never done anything like that before, Cohen may have seen a few, fleeting expressions of guarded hope on the opponents' faces, but the optimism quickly vanished when the judge finished the thought by saying he was willing to make this case a first. The Justice Department replied by objecting anyway.

Agent Kosky gave his deposition before Judge Rubin and two government attorneys in a closed session in Cincinnati on October 2, 1992. In his opening remarks, Rubin said he was surprised by the government's objections to Kosky's testifying, and promptly overruled them. He said he was going to ask the questions prepared by Walsh's attorneys, and that he would consider any unanswered question to be unfavorable to the position of the United States.

He needn't have worried that Kosky would try to minimize Walsh's role or hold back on anything. After answering no to a question about whether he had opened a file on GE in this matter before Walsh filed his suit, the agent volunteered that the United States government had had no information of any kind about any of this problem.

Kosky was equally emphatic about the importance to the case of Walsh's principal attorney. He said Cohen had helped organize the evidence in such an effective format that the FBI had used it without any changes for the entire two years of the investigation. In general, he said, Cohen had been his sounding board for new ideas and strategy during the entire investigation. He said he had learned to trust her advice more than the Justice Department's.

Judge Rubin asked the agent about the timing and motivation of Walsh's charges. Was there any evidence, he asked, that the FBI investigation would have been easier if, instead of filing a false claims action, Mr. Walsh had reported the fraud directly to the government when he left Israel in March 1989?

If Walsh had come to the FBI with what he knew about the fraud when he left Israel, Kosky responded, the case would not have been as strong because many aspects of the scheme had not yet been implemented. He said the evidence of fraud would not have been as clear-cut as it was later.

Kosky said he considered it to be "of no consequence" that Walsh had failed to report the thefts on the forms GE provided for that purpose, in accord with the disclosure pledge that employees were required to sign annually. More important, he said, was that Walsh never withheld information or lied to him. He agreed with Walsh that he might have put his own safety at risk if he had reported his allegations while still in Israel. There were plenty of clear models for the negative career consequences of bringing up improprieties within GE.

In early 1989, a GE employee named Alaric Fine began asking questions suggesting the company had been paid for a $7 million piece of aircraft engine testing equipment that did not exist. The company's legal staff took a halfhearted look at the allegations, then filed a weak report which management simply ignored. The only firm action to result from the exercise occurred when Fine's questions came to the attention of General Dotan, who quickly made a phone call to his friends within the company. Fine was called on the carpet and then reassigned out of the Israeli programs. GE never bothered to advise the United States government of the issues Fine had raised. Chet Walsh hardly needed to wonder what would happen to his own career in military sales, Kosky told the court, if he were to bring the subject up again.

Judge Rubin asked Kosky if there was any evidence that Walsh had profited personally from the false claims described in the complaint or that he assisted in any way in setting up the scam. Kosky replied that Walsh had gotten nothing out of it at all.

The same could not be said for those who had devised the scheme. Kosky told the judge that of the $40 million of misused money, Steindler and Dotan skimmed $12 million for their personal bank accounts.

At the end of the deposition, Judge Rubin asked one last question, clearly not from the list that had been prepared by Walsh's attorneys. Whatever happened to Steindler?

Kosky replied that he was fired in March 1991, and that he had moved around under difficult circumstances before enrolling at Ohio State to become an emergency medical technician. But if Kosky had personally lost track of him, he told the court, he was certain the Defense Criminal Investigative Service had not. And indeed, Steindler was eventually sent to jail.

In December 1993, after a two-day hearing in which Helmer presented the case for the relator's share, Judge Rubin awarded Walsh 22.5 percent of the recovered money for his key role in the case. The Justice Department appealed Rubin's decision. To end the process, Walsh and his attorneys agreed to settle with the government for a relator's share of 19 percent so that Walsh, then in his late sixties, could put it all behind him. It was over a quarter higher than the statutory minimum but more than $2 million below the amount ordered by Judge Rubin.

It had been a costly battle. Between Judge Rubin's decision against GE and the final settlement in favor of the relator's attorneys, both GE and the Justice Department fought so fiercely against rewarding either Chet Walsh or his counsel, the law firm was forced to spend another $750,000 on witnesses and legal fees.

After the last appeal was settled, Walsh split the relator's share with coplaintiff Taxpayers Against Fraud, a nonprofit foundation started by Phillips to support *qui tam* cases and funded in the beginning by fees that otherwise would have gone to his firm and his co-counsels. When Chet Walsh had cashed the government's check, and finally did take that long-awaited walk into the sunset, he had no job, no career, and hardly a friend remaining from the life he left behind.

What Chet Walsh did have, for what it was worth, was the satisfaction of having told the truth and prevailed, not only against the largest company on earth but against his erstwhile allies in the Justice Department of the United States. He also had a promise in writing that GE would leave him alone, that it would not pursue him, as it had threatened, with its endless resources or continue to use the courts to seek revenge. He had two lawyers who knew his every wart and foible but believed in him anyway, and who had stood the course with him.

And he had $6 million.

THIRTEEN

UNJUST REWARDS

With the steady growth in both the number of false claim cases and the size of recoveries, the amount and variety of media coverage increased as well. Even though the stories were uniformly positive, perhaps because the subject touched on deep, complicated issues in the social contract, the still-few members of the public who'd ever heard of the False Claims Act seemed to have a hard time deciding whether the law was good or bad.

Even before the revised act gave relators new protections and strengthened the provisions for reward, whistle-blowers occupied a nebulous, uncertain claim on the public imagination. But it was clear that the new law would entice some people who had knowledge of serious financial fraud against the government to blow the whistle, offering them the opportunity to get rich and maybe to get even.

In reality, especially for those early relators who would blaze the trail, they often got neither.

David Navarette was a mechanical designer and illustrator at Rocky Flats, a nuclear weapons plant managed by Rockwell International under a contract with the Department of Energy, eight miles south of Boulder, Colorado. In this small, secret city, 7,600 employees designed arms and produced plutonium triggers and other warhead components for the military. Navarette was employed by the Future Systems Department, basically a model shop for making mock-ups of high-security weapons systems and devices, nuclear bombs, and components for the Strategic Defense Initiative, Reagan's "Star Wars" antimissile program. The department was equipped with the most advanced tools and materials available, and housed in a building so secure that everyone who worked there required a high-level "Q" clearance; even the Rockwell vice president in charge of the plant couldn't enter without an appointment. Also for security reasons, the department was exempt from normal accounting and management controls. These circumstances created a temptation as irresistible to Navarette's boss, the appropriately named Warren Rooker, as the "Eat me" sign spelled out in currants on Alice's cake in Wonderland.

Navarette knew that Rooker had been stealing goods and services from the government, while being protected from federal inspectors by the facility's security blanket, for seventeen years. He used the shop's equipment, and a virtually unlimited supply of platinum, gold, silver, and rare woods, to create unauthorized objects of all kinds. The illegal output included ornate gifts, trophies, and awards for Rockwell executives, government officials, and favored suppliers, created at the request of Rooker's superiors for corporate use but entirely at government expense. It was not uncommon for some of the shop's artisans to labor over individual items for months, billing their time to the Department of Energy at $56 an hour.

But the company wasn't the only beneficiary of Rooker's misdirected creativity. A lot of what he stole was for himself. Navarette resented the assignments from further up the hierarchy because he knew they were illegal, but at least they supported the company's relationships with its suppliers, sponsors, customers, and employees. But when Navarette was told to drop everything in order to work on the plans for Rooker's $800,000 retirement home in the mountains of New Mexico, it was the straw that broke the camel's back.

Navarette had traveled this road before. The first time was in the mid-1960s, when he'd worked for Rooker at American Car and Foundry in Albuquerque and was ordered to design a three-bedroom ranch-style home on company time. Those kinds of abuses drove him to find another job, but he found himself working for Rooker again a decade later, and one of his first assignments was to design his boss another house. This time, the cost of the plans was $17,000, all of which Navarette was ordered to bill to Rockwell's government contracts.

Except for the illegal assignments, Navarette loved his job. He delighted in the craftsmanship and creativity, and he knew the models he built were viewed by the most powerful decision makers in government, sometimes including presidents and kings. But even though there was even some of that same satisfaction in creating the corporate contraband, he became progressively more resentful about the way in which he was coerced into complicity in the fraud by having to fill out false time reports. "Every time Rooker decides to steal," he complained to his wife, Sonja, "it means we all have to steal. I don't like being a part of it."

He didn't get much sympathy. Sonja had been a janitor at Rocky Flats when Navarette first joined the company, and after working her way up the ladder to product manager, she was a staunch company loyalist. By 1985 they had been married five years, and had a combined annual income of $70,000. She wasn't about to encourage her husband to jeopardize their hard-earned security by rocking the boat.

Maybe it would have been easier if they had faced it together, but Sonja's attitude really had nothing to do with the basic dilemma. Navarette was middle-aged, and despite his skills he had never gone further with his education than high school. Even if he decided to approach management, what would he be telling them that they didn't know already? Rooker had boasted in the office that if the company ever came after him for stealing, he'd take a lot of the top leadership with him. "If all the thieves at Rocky Flats go," he said, "nobody will be left." Instead of seeing Rooker as the problem, there was a good chance that management would decide it was easier and safer to get rid of the complainer.

That spring, Sonja left home on a business trip during a week when Rooker also happened to be out of town. Without his wife to talk him out of it, and without having to face his boss directly, Navarette took his complaint to Rooker's assistant. He said he was "burning out" from all the unauthorized work and asked for a transfer to another department. The assistant denied the request and told him to get back to work on the house plans. On Rooker's return, Navarette was moved to an isolated drawing board, stripped of his supervisory duties, and ordered to work on nothing else until the house plans were finished.

A week later, Navarette had had enough. He went to the personnel department to repeat his request for a transfer, and wound up telling his story to the director of employee relations. All he really wanted was another assignment. But someone in the company recognized the much larger implications of his complaint and decided that the risk of remaining silent was greater than the potential fallout from disclosure. Once the process had begun, his complaint traveled upward through the system, and in due course Rockwell notified the Department of Energy that something was awry in the model shop.

If the company did the right thing in reporting the problem all the way back to its client, it soon became apparent that the same sensitivity did not extend in the other direction. Navarette was reduced to the status of a temporary employee, moving around the plant from one menial job to another, no longer allowed anywhere near a drawing board and relegated to manual labor. The FBI arrived in early June. The model shop was closed for the collection of evidence and its other employees were furloughed during an audit by the Department of Energy. Navarette, who was widely recognized as the source of all this chaos, was shunned and sometimes openly cursed by his former colleagues, and he began to get threatening phone calls at work and at home. Like Samson, he had shaken the temple, and now he felt himself being buried in the descending debris.

But he wasn't alone.

Rooker was sent out of town on business, and while he was gone the FBI searched his home, his garage, and an antique Greyhound bus he had converted into a mobile home with materials stolen from Rocky Flats and labor falsely billed to the government. When he got back he was suspended without pay, and later he was fired.

With the help of detailed drawings created by Navarette from memory, the FBI was able to assemble a list of stolen treasure equal in value to the contents of a pirate argosy. An $11,480 walnut plaque had been built for Edward Teller, father of the hydrogen bomb, inset with jewel-quality medallion logos of every lab or university where Teller had ever worked. Gemlike neodymium glass, meant for models of lasers for the Strategic Defense Initiative, were converted to jewelry. Nearly two hundred pounds of silver were diverted from their intended purpose in the making of model nuclear bombs and turned into countless other medallions. Many of these gifts were used to bribe scientists, particularly at Lawrence Livermore Labs in Berkeley, who like Teller were in a position to influence the choice of Rockwell as a Star Wars vendor. One associate director at Lawrence Livermore received a gift of a hundred sapphirelike neodymium gems valued at $20,000. Another was given a custom-built, finely crafted distillation system and separate fruit press for making liqueurs at home, at a combined cost of $68,000.

For $5,300, the shop created two dozen wooden foot massagers exactly comparable to items sold through a catalog for $10 each. Another $15,000 was spent on a hundred tie tacks, $25,000 for half again that many pairs of earrings, and $34,000 on the same number of cuff links. One elegantly rendered gift was a sensitive carving that appeared to be a monk in shroud and cowl when viewed from the front, but that when seen at another angle became a phallus.

The greatest single recipient of all this largesse was Rooker himself. He spent at least $46,000 of the government's money on customized accessories for his three personal vehicles, another $20,000 for three walnut grandfather clocks, and $15,000 for a suspended spiral staircase in his home, and he even had his employees use stolen materials and company time to create customized plastic toys for his dog. When confronted with these excesses, Rooker denied them all. He denied having profited personally. He denied any knowledge of the $68,000 gift to the executive at Lawrence Livermore. (So, at first, did the executive, but in a second interview he changed his mind, acknowledging the gifts and estimating their value at $150. By the third meeting, the number had risen to $1,500—still only about 2 percent of the actual cost charged to the government.)

About the only thing Rooker was willing to admit to was that he was a borderline diabetic, and he described associated symptoms of tightness in his chest and occasional faintness. He even went so far as to fall down on a sidewalk outside his home, but after being examined by two EMTs from a local ambulance service, he drew the line at being taken to the hospital for tests. Not surprisingly, the FBI saw these health claims as a bid for sympathy.

In January 1986, David Navarette appeared before a federal grand jury in Denver. He showed the drawings he had made for the FBI, and again described the unauthorized items that Rooker had ordered built in the model shop. The FBI agent in charge of the case was watching the jurors for their reactions. He knew that the assistant United States attorney was considering the prosecution of seventeen people on charges ranging from theft to bribery, and at the end of Navarette's testimony the agent was certain the jury was going to return some of those indictments.

It never got the chance to vote. The government attorney told the agent that the Justice Department had been contacted by the CIA. Taking this any further would compromise too many people at the highest levels of the Star Wars program, he said, and the country couldn't afford to lose them. Justice agreed to bury the case, and the jury was sent home. It was obvious the government was handing out free passes, but the agent didn't believe that the CIA had anything to do with it. He told the Justice Department attorney he planned to keep on digging and would try again later with another grand jury. But the following March, the U.S. attorney shut down the investigation and the FBI agent was pulled off the case.

Later that spring, in 1987, an investigative reporter from Boulder named Martin Connolly went fishing with a friend who was a city detective. Over the campfire, the policeman told him that the FBI had been trying to make a fraud case in a highly secured area of Rocky Flats, and he happened to know that the agent in charge was mad as hell about the way it had been swept under the rug. The detective wouldn't tell him anything else, not even the name of the agent. But Connolly knew he had been set on a scent, and that the rest was up to him.

The FBI didn't have that many agents in Boulder, so it wasn't hard to identify the one who had been in charge of the Rocky Flats investigation. Because the story involved so many sensitive issues, from national security, politics, big business, and potential libel to the sometimes fratricidal hierarchy of the justice system, Connolly didn't expect to be greeted with open arms and a torrent of inside information. The agent proved to be almost as cryptic as the detective had been. He told Connolly the informant's last name was Hispanic, that it began with an "N," and that he had worked in Future Systems. In fact, by then Navarette had been transferred to the plutonium recovery unit, a frightening, *Silkwood*-like setting where radioactive materials were extracted from old warheads. The reporter finally tracked him down by telephone and, although Navarette said later that the call had "scared the hell" out of him, they agreed to meet in person on the following day.

As he had been for the FBI, Navarette turned out to be an almost ideal source for the reporter, retelling the story in precise detail and sharing with Connolly all the drawings he had produced for use with the grand jury. Everywhere else Connolly turned, however, he was met with a stone wall. With Rooker, Rockwell, Lawrence Livermore, and the Energy Department all uniformly unresponsive, Navarette's continued cooperation was all the more essential to the story. But as they continued to meet, it was apparent to the reporter that his witness was becoming increasingly edgy and ill at ease.

A big part of the reason for this turned out to be Sonja. It became obvious she was unhappy with how her husband's actions had stirred up so many problems for their employer. Now here he was again, talking to a reporter while they were still trying to recover from the way his earlier disclosures had changed their lives. By now the FBI was out of the picture, and the Navarettes didn't even have a lawyer. Connolly had a year of legal training after college, and he realized that if he didn't help them build some kind of safety net to ease their worries, the story could go up in smoke. His first thought was to check the Internet. He found the False Claims Act, and then he called John Phillips. It was agreed the reporter would bring the Navarettes to Los Angeles.

Connolly convinced his newspaper to fund the trip. While the commitment was barely enough to pay for three air tickets and a single cheap motel room (Connolly in one double bed, the Navarettes in the other), it was an enormous testament to the publisher's faith in the importance of the story and in its reporter's nose for news. After a long night of gunshots, wailing cats, and howling dogs, the bleary-eyed trio arrived at the law office as soon as it opened the following morning. When Phillips heard where they had stayed, he shook his head and said he was amazed they'd made it safely through the night.

Sonja chain-smoked through the next twelve hours, remaining noncommittal and mostly silent while the attorney listened to her husband's story and explained to them both how the False Claims Act was designed to work, detailing the steps involved in preparing a suit. So far, only one case had ever been brought under the recently amended law, by an ophthalmologist in San Diego. A few days later, David Navarette's suit against Rockwell International, Lawrence Livermore Labs, and Rooker, filed under a sixty-day seal in federal court, became the second case filed by John Phillips and the Center for Law in the Public Interest. There was no expectation of a large recovery; the damage to the Treasury would not be measured in millions, but in hundreds of thousands. For Phillips, as for Navarette, the case's appeal lay in the prospect of redressing outrageous misconduct.

Navarette was a determined but apprehensive pioneer. At the outset, two years before, he had not for a moment anticipated the profound consequences of his request for a simple job transfer. It had never crossed his mind that by trying to get out from between a rock and a hard place he would be seen by his friends and coworkers as any kind of troublemaker, let alone a whistle-blower. But events had taken on a life of their own, and he and Sonja had been swept reluctantly along. Now all the secrecy and uncertainty were about to end. Navarette realized that when the seal was lifted in sixty days, the case would finally become public, there would be a settlement, and, for good or bad, their lives would take a totally new direction.

He was right about the effect on their lives, but wrong on the timing. The process would drag on for the next six years.

Fueled by national publicity, popular anger against the excesses described in the lawsuit provided the ideal platform, by December, for congressional hearings. They were chaired by Representative Mike Synar, an Oklahoma Democrat sympathetic to whistle-blowers and friendly to the False Claims Act. But despite careful preparation by John Phillips, under the intense scrutiny of a wall of Rockwell officials the event became yet another ordeal for the already nervous Navarette. He was trembling badly when he picked up a glass of water, and when Phillips saw that the contents were spilling onto the table he reached over and took Navarette's arm to reassure him. But as painful as the process was for him, Navarette was the star of the show.

The hearings opened to rave reviews. ("Scandalous," said one lawmaker, while others on the network news clucked in dutiful disparagement over "Santa's workshop.") It was exactly the kind of leverage Phillips had been hoping would move a dilatory and intransigent Justice Department into joining the case against Rockwell. For six months he had been encouraging Michael Hertz, a top official in the Civil Division, to get involved, and now his pleas were being supported by congressional zeal and public outrage. But the Justice Department still wouldn't budge; it assigned an attorney to monitor Navarette's suit, stressing that its role was absolutely neutral.

Phillips wasn't alone in trying to rally Justice to its duty. An equally unrelenting nemesis was John Layton, a former FBI agent who became the Department of Energy's inspector general after the fiasco at Rocky Flats and who persuaded his own management to reverse its passive acceptance of the wrongdoing there. But it wasn't until after another two years of steady insistence that Rockwell and Lawrence Livermore be held accountable for their misdeeds that the holdout came to an end. In August 1990, five and a half years after David Navarette complained to the personnel department and two and a half years after he filed his lawsuit, the Justice Department finally decided to enter the case.

Meanwhile, Rockwell and Lawrence Livermore had gone to the battlements in defense of their right to steal. They challenged the constitutionality of the False Claims Act. They said it couldn't apply to events that occurred before it was passed. Lawrence Livermore claimed "sovereign immunity," as a part of the University of California, from suits by private citizens or the federal government. Rockwell took the position that its contract with the government gave it immunity against being sued, including being sued for stealing from the government. None of the claims prevailed in courts, but the process ate up years.

Fairly early in the aftermath of Navarette's revelations, Rooker realized that his problems were not likely to end simply with the loss of his job. In the next five years, however, he found hopeful refuge under the same umbrella of obfuscation, arrogance, and denial that protected those he had served. When the Justice Department finally entered the case, he could see that the umbrella was at risk of blowing inside out. Through his lawyer, Rooker made overtures to John Phillips. Perhaps a deal could be struck. He was willing to testify against his fellow defendants—those who had ordered the gifts and those who had received them—in return for being dropped from the suit. Phillips was wary, but knowing that Rooker didn't have money to pay any judgment against him, he was willing to fly to Denver just before Christmas to hear what Navarette's former boss had to say.

It wasn't much. He argued that he had only done what he was told to do. When questioned about the work and materials he had stolen for himself, his answers were evasive, partial, and self-serving. It seemed to Phillips that a larger part of what he was trying to convey was through body language—the same theatrical displays of respiratory distress and clutching at his chest that had been observed in earlier interviews with the FBI, and just as transparent to Phillips as they had been to the Bureau. But as it turned out, the body language may have been the most honest part of the interview. A month later Warren Rooker had a heart attack, and on January 22, 1990, he died.

His old boss's death didn't make life any easier for David Navarette. They had both been out of the model shop for years, and for most of that time Rooker had been out of the company, but the rancor of his coworkers continued unabated and their sneering, harassing reminders of what he had set in motion were with him every working day. Realizing that this situation was unlikely to improve as long as the company struggled against the truth and his lawsuit remained unresolved, he finally threw in the towel. He was ready for more than a change of employment; quitting Rockwell could mean a whole new life.

He moved to Houston but couldn't connect with the right job, so after a few months of looking he came back to Denver and got a position as a model designer. Sonja chose not to follow him through any further changes, and they divorced. The following year, in 1991, he had open-heart surgery but soon recovered and was able to continue working. The judge on his case retired and was replaced. The two principal recipients of illegal largesse at Lawrence Livermore both retired. By then, the Department of Energy's multibillion-dollar Rocky Flats management contract had been taken away from Rockwell.

With the possible exception of the divorce, none of these changes was a consequence of Navarette's lawsuit. Rockwell lost its contract after allegations were made that for years the company had been illegally burning hazardous wastes in incinerators and dumping toxic materials into Colorado's famously pristine mountain streams. In 1992 the company pled guilty to criminal violations of ten waste storage laws at the nuclear weapons plant and paid a fine of $18.5 million. By then the Soviet Union had collapsed and Star Wars, which had weathered endless controversy about its technical feasibility and political appropriateness, seemed likely to die of irrelevance.

Still, neither Rockwell nor Lawrence Livermore was willing to give an inch, and it was clear they were prepared to spend far more for their defense than they would ever have to pay in an adverse judgment. Both organizations were determined to avoid a dangerous precedent in allowing a whistle-blower to escape without consequence, and even though the dollar amounts were trifling compared with those that had been involved in the pollution case, an outcome that included paying Navarette any kind of reward was unthinkable. Phillips had assigned Lauren Saunders to the case, and she found the defense attorneys so openly disdainful, and often insulting, that at first she wondered if the reason was her youth and gender. But when she saw they were at least as abrasive with John Phillips, she realized it was because of their attitude toward the law.

The case finally settled on July 16, 1993, eight years after Navarette took his story to the personnel department and six years after the start of his lawsuit. Although it had been filed the same year as the Michelson suit against Scripps, the resistance from Rockwell and Lawrence Livermore had been so fierce, and until recently the Department of Justice had abetted that resistance in so many ways, that the process had dragged on five years longer. In the end, Rockwell and Lawrence Livermore agreed to pay a total of $450,000 in damages. For the defendants and the government, it was a drop in the bucket.

It was hardly more than that for David Navarette. The court awarded him a maximum relator's share of 25 percent. A third of that share was pledged on contingency to Taxpayers Against Fraud, and 40 percent of what was left went to Navarette's ex-wife as part of their divorce agreement. The balance, $44,273, averaged out to $15.37 a day for eight of the hardest years of his life. But even with all it had cost him, he was satisfied, because he knew he had done the right thing.

By the time the case ended, suits under the False Claims Act were no longer a rarity: By the end of 1993, some six hundred such actions had been filed since the passage of the amended law. Most of those were still in the pipeline, but recoveries by the government were already approaching the billion-dollar mark.

FOURTEEN

SOLOMON

One of the still-unresolved cases at the time was Emil Stache's and Al Muehlhausen's suit against Teledyne. The FBI raid had taken place the previous October. For months beforehand, Emil and Al had worked closely with their new Phillips & Cohen lawyer, Ann Carlson, a young, self-assured, magna cum laude graduate of Harvard Law School who had taken a prominent role as the Teledyne case heated up. Carlson had quickly mastered government contracting regulations, along with all the details of Teledyne production, and worked closely with Emil and Al in cooperation with the investigating task force. Controlled by the United States Attorney's Office, it included the air force's Office of Special Investigation, the army's Criminal Investigation Department, the navy's Naval Investigative Service, and NASA's Office of the Inspector General, as well as the FBI. When twenty-two federal agents had descended on the company, they were equipped with far more than a search warrant. Emil and Al had painstakingly tutored them on the government specifications for the failed switches, identifying all the known areas of deficiency, and prepared detailed maps of the plant, along with people's names, where to find incriminating files, and even lists of what questions to ask of individual employees.

The director of quality, who was usually late for work, walked into his office and discovered a stranger at his desk, sealing the office files in preparation for their removal.

"Who the hell are you?" he asked.

"FBI," the agent said, continuing with his task.

Stunned, the director backed out of the room and sat down heavily in a chair in the reception area. He looked into his office for a moment, his expression of disbelief quickly giving way to annoyance and then contempt. He began to laugh, not with humor but with arrogance, as though to tell the agent that he was wasting his time, that the company couldn't be touched.

Down the hall in Human Resources, agents were already removing employment records when the director of the department walked in and viewed the turmoil with an expression of incredulity and resignation. He turned to the manager, the Vietnam veteran who had interviewed Emil Stache several months earlier, and shook his head in disgust. "Look!" he said, gesturing theatrically toward the sudden chaos. "Look what your friend has done to us now."

Emil had known at the time of his departure that several of the technicians were sympathetic to his position, even if they had been unwilling to add their own voices when he took the complaint to management. Before the raid, he had given the agents names of employees he thought were most likely to be helpful, but when the FBI held interviews that morning at the plant, it was obvious that the sympathy had disappeared and they were all for Teledyne. It wasn't hard to figure out why. When they had talked with Emil months before, he was one of their own. None of them liked what the company was doing, and what it was making them do, but it was one thing to be on Emil's side when he was taking all the chances, and quite another when the jobs at stake were their own.

On the other hand, not all the surprises in the raid were disappointments. One of the main targets on the list of names Emil and Al had given the FBI was the engineer who designed the equipment and was now in charge of the Qualified Products List lab. He was not one of the old friends Emil or Al thought might be cooperative, but it was important that the agents single him out, because his job was central to the process by which Teledyne had been cheating the government.

A camera was set up, and one by one the principal players in the scam were interviewed on videotape. The process created a legal record for possible use in court, but the presence of the camera also provided a major disincentive to making statements that might later be proven false, or to subsequent denials by the interviewees themselves. But when Emil later saw this particular videotaped interview with the FBI, he felt the engineer talked about the equipment and the failure rates with amazing candor. It wasn't because he was trying to be helpful, Emil sensed, but because he thought it didn't matter.

Some of the other witnesses had been almost as open, but many of them showed the same attitude as the director who'd merely laughed at finding the FBI in his office; they viewed the company as so powerful—

and their superiority to government oversight so long-standing and absolute—that they felt immune to consequence. In several such interviews,
the agents had to stop the subjects in mid-sentence and read them their
rights, because the speakers were incriminating themselves. But with the
engineer, there didn't seem to be any arrogance at all. It was as though
he had come to see his job as nothing more than the certification of products, faulty or otherwise, and as if the original purpose of quality control
had long ago been subverted to that process. Emil shook his head in
wonder.

Shortly before the raid, Emil had landed the job with another component manufacturing company, this one in Van Nuys, a recent acquisition of Data Electronics in Nebraska. He knew that the division had been
through a similar situation of its own, though on a lesser scale than
Teledyne's, and he soon learned that the company was still in serious
trouble. At that point, however, his new employer knew nothing of the circumstances behind Emil's departure from his previous job. The night before the raid he called his new boss at home in Nebraska and said, "You're
going to hear something tomorrow about Teledyne, and I'm part of it. Do
you have a problem with that?"

His boss immediately guessed what kind of news Emil was referring
to, and he said, "No, but I have a question for you: Are you personally in
any kind of trouble?"

It was a warmer response than anything Emil had hoped for. He told
him he was not. His boss thanked him for the heads up, and asked that Emil
call him the following day after it was out in the open and they could talk
about it.

Even after the raid was announced and was all over the news, Emil's
name was still not publicly connected to the story. But he knew that his
forthrightness had won him respect and credibility at the new company,
and more than once he wondered about how different everything would
have been if Teledyne management had reacted with the same openness
when he'd first reported its testing failures.

Ironically, he would not have to wonder for long. The new company
had been badly hurt by the earlier cover-up in quality control, and there
was a major backlog in testing, plus a lag in processing the results. Because
of the division's recent history, when Data Electronics made the acquisition it was decided that quality control managers would be made directly

responsible to corporate headquarters in Nebraska, so it fell to Emil to report previously undisclosed high failure rates. The company was trying
to do everything by the book, but it seemed that whatever he did now just
made matters worse. The company had a failure, he would report it, and
virtually on the way back to his office he would encounter people packing
up their personal belongings because they'd been laid off. He was doing
his job, but he felt like the grim reaper.

At the time of the raid, nobody at Teledyne knew that there had been more
than one whistle-blower. Like the personnel manager, Al Muehlhausen
encountered considerable distrust from his colleagues based on his longtime friendship with the prime suspect, Emil Stache, but as far as anyone
then knew, his only guilt was by association. A rumor quickly circulated
within the company: The case against Teledyne couldn't go on without
Emil Stache, and any day now someone was going to give him a lethal
injection and everyone's problems would be over.

Al's relative immunity vanished when the case was unsealed and it
became known that he too was a party to the suit. The company saw that
the government was reacting almost immediately to new moves within the
division after the raid, and it wasn't hard to figure out it was getting its
information from someone still inside. First, Al was demoted, based on the
claim that he was not effective. He immediately notified his lawyer. Ann
Carlson called Teledyne, and he was back on his old job the following day.
But now it was out in the open. There were new death threats, all the more
serious because this time the target of rage was still within the company.
He encountered resentment at every turn, and frequent menace. On one
occasion he sensed he was being followed in a shopping center near the
plant, and when he went back out to the mall parking lot he found that all
the lug nuts had been loosened on the wheels of his car, an old, easily recognized, blue and white Suburban. He got in and wobbled down the road.
Some of his coworkers repeated the earlier talk about a lethal injection,
and this time the threat was clearly pointed at Al and spoken within his
hearing. Despite the enormous pressure, Al continued in his old position,
working as before with the people whose lives had been changed by the
action he and Emil had initiated.

The negative reactions were mainly on the job, but he also ran into them in less likely places. On one occasion Al was at a social gathering, talking with a stranger who happened to ask where he worked. When he told him Teledyne, the man shook his head sympathetically and asked with jovial contempt, "Do you know Al Muehlhausen?" There is a natural impulse to spare even the worst social offender from his own gaffe, and for a moment Al hesitated. Then he said, "As a matter of fact, I *am* Al Muehlhausen." The conversation ended.

After two years in this unrelenting vise, Al's situation at work deteriorated to the point where Teledyne told him it felt it could no longer guarantee his safety on the job. A separation settlement was worked out, and he left the company. But even then, both Emil and he frequently had to return, literally, to the scene of the crime. The FBI had set up a trailer on company property just outside the plant, and the two relators spent hour after hour sifting through records and other evidence delivered there in cardboard cartons. By then neither of them was allowed inside the plant, but a lot of the employees had to come out to the trailer, and often the bad feelings they brought with them were palpable.

The investigation dragged on. The QPL testing area had been locked down after the raid, under an armed guard, and the Defense Electronics Supply Center took over the testing function. The company was required to pull samples from production, DESC ran them through the certification procedures, and time after time the switches failed. At first the failures were explained away, but even if DESC accepted the alibis, the problem still had to be fixed, and eventually production was shut down in order for Teledyne to make adjustments in its equipment. Despite the dramatically changed circumstances after the raid, the attitude of the DESC inspectors remained pretty much the same as before. "Do whatever you have to do," they seemed to be saying to Teledyne, "and tell us when you are ready." So they allowed the company to modify everything, and when Teledyne said the problem had been fixed the government dutifully recommenced the testing. The samples failed again.

Up to then, the feeling among division employees was that they were going to get through this and still come out on top. The raid had been a surprise and a huge pain in the neck, but they still knew more about their product line than the FBI, government inspectors, their clients, or anyone else in the switch business; it was just a matter of time before they got this crap behind them and were back to business as usual. But with this latest set of failures, it finally started to sink in: They just couldn't pass the test. They wrote the specification, and still they couldn't make it work.

By then, not even the hugely accommodating DESC could stop what happened next. The plant was told to quit shipping relays, and a dreaded GIDEP (Government Industry Data Exchange Program) alert was sent to every manufacturer in the defense sector, including the sub-industries. All the trade papers carried the story that Teledyne Relays was shut down and not permitted to sell military products. If the sanction was taken one step further, it would essentially put corporate Teledyne out of the defense business. The parent company moved into full-scale damage control.

One of the first results was the decision to centralize all of Teledyne's quality management. Until then, the department had been bullied and ignored by the people whose work it was intended to oversee, and production managers were often more willing to replace the testers than to fix the cause of failures. A centralized quality department would bring new disciplines and integrity to a process that had run amok.

It wasn't going to be a quick fix. Along with its credibility, the division lost the certification criteria it had developed over the course of millions of now-suspect testing cycles. That meant it could no longer offer certain products in the high-reliability government market without accumulating comparable new data to justify the higher price of a Mil-Spec circuit. So it not only lost its ability to ship, but had to requalify as a government contractor at a much lower level, if it qualified at all, because a lot of its products were still failing.

By the time the process had dragged on for more than a year, Emil's new company was experiencing problems with its own failure rate, and the whole division was cut back to a four-day week. On his off day and weekends, he worked with the FBI. By the end of the second year, at about the same time Al left Teledyne, Emil finally quit his job in order to keep up with all the travel. The case had become a full-time job in its own right, and by then they were both beginning to see it as an investment in a future that held very little other promise.

The FBI set up an office in Redondo Beach with rooms full of documents seized in the raid. Emil worked there with his attorney and the FBI, helping them make sense of what they had collected. With seemingly end-less forbearance, he provided detailed information about how relays were made, how they were tested, what the government expected of relay manu-facturers, how the Mil-Specs worked, how the relays were marketed and shipped to customers, how they were used, and how Teledyne was orga-nized. Over and over again, he illuminated details of the tests the relays had failed, and the technical implications of those failures.

Without his patient explanations, the documents would have been close to meaningless. He knew Teledyne inside out, and he knew how to convey his knowledge to nonexperts. He could explain the operation of a relay to his lawyer, who had no background or training in electronics, in a way that allowed her to understand and speak technically about the case. He performed the same role for the lead criminal prosecutor and the count-less agents from all the involved agencies.

Along with attorney Carlson, Emil and Al made trips to the proving grounds near Albuquerque and to the testing facility contracted by the FBI in New Hampshire. Although the latter was located in a Victorian office in a rural setting, it was highly regarded throughout the industry for the sophistication and integrity of its relay testing, and government experts clearly held the man in charge of the testing facility in the highest esteem. When he was introduced to Emil, he hailed him as a hero. It sounded to Carlson as though he might have suspected previously that Teledyne was engaged in fraudulent testing but could never prove it.

In the throes of intense litigation that seemed as though it would never end, it was easy to wonder whether the whole effort would ever result in anything. The New Hampshire relay tester made Emil feel that no matter what happened in the case, his actions were truly moral and heroic.

Once the civil litigation began, Teledyne scheduled numerous depo-sitions of people who had been involved in the testing of its relays—within the company, at Sandia National Laboratory, in New Hampshire, and with university experts in Ohio. The company's aim, it appeared, was to dis-credit the testing that had revealed its products as defective, or at the very least to suggest that the failures were not all that meaningful. The lawyers from the Department of Justice had failed to hire an expert witness of their own on relay testing, and to Emil they seemed to have spent little time if any in anticipating the impact of those depositions or in controlling their potential damage to the credibility of the evidence. As *qui tam* plaintiffs,

Emil and Al had the right to participate in those depositions, so Ann Carlson attended all of them as their attorney. Throughout this process, Emil continued to serve as her full-time, unpaid expert. He explained how electromagnetic relays worked, what each of the government procedures was intended to test, and anticipated potential Teledyne tactics for dismissing or minimizing test failures.

Thanks to Emil's coaching, when Teledyne attempted to shift the blame to the testing equipment, suggesting that a failure in the lab would not lead to failure in the field, Carlson was ready for them. She objected to questions from Teledyne that seemed designed to mislead or were otherwise problematical, and asked carefully planned questions of her own. By contrast, the unprepared DOJ lawyer who attended the depositions appeared to have no idea what was going on. The government attorney followed up Teledyne's interrogatories with a series of questions that ignored the company's attempts to discredit the evidence, and that were largely meaningless. When it was Carlson's turn, drawing from Emil's expert technical advice, she systematically established on the record that the independent testing was done properly, that the equipment was accurate, and that there were indeed significant problems with Teledyne's relays.

The lawsuit stretched out to a full four years. Another *qui tam* case had been filed against Teledyne by a relator in a separate division, and because the two cases were proceeding together the judge recommended one settlement conference for both of them. Finally, in late 1994, a group of some two dozen attorneys representing the plaintiffs, the Department of Justice, and Teledyne met in the chambers of the special settlement judge, William Matthew Byrne, Jr., in the United States District Court in Los Angeles, to try to bring the case to an end.

Emil and Al's attorneys were pleased with the choice. Byrne was widely regarded as one of the smartest, most effective judges in Los Angeles. More than twenty years earlier, he had presided over the trial following the break-in at the office of the psychiatrist for Daniel Ellsberg, the Defense Department analyst who had released the Pentagon Papers to the press, fueling the protest then raging against the Vietnam War. The attempt to use Ellsberg's therapist's files to discredit him was one of the so-called dirty tricks engineered by the Nixon administration, and the chicanery didn't stop with the break-in. During the trial, Byrne had been approached by John Ehrlichman, domestic affairs advisor to President Nixon, who met him at a park bench in Santa Monica to explore Byrne's interest in becoming the new director of the FBI. Just the year before, Byrne had headed up Nixon's Commission on Campus Unrest, which had been his springboard to the federal bench. Later, when information about the Santa Monica meeting became public at the Watergate hearings, it was interpreted as an apparent try by Nixon's staff to influence the judge's decision in the Ellsberg case. Even though Byrne didn't bite on the job offer—in fact, he ultimately ruled against the administration and threw out the case against Ellsberg—his reputation suffered anyway, not for anything he had done or not done, but for the bad luck of his proximity to the national scandal.

The *qui tam* attorneys' expectations for Byrne in the Teledyne case were warranted. He proved to be an extremely able and creative judge.

He didn't have an easy job. The lawyers for the Justice Department had come to the negotiation with two great deficits. The first was their orders from headquarters in Washington to stand firm for a settlement—not including the relators' expenses and legal fees—of at least $220 million. Emil's lawyers considered that amount to be extraordinarily unrealistic; it was nearly twenty times higher than Teledyne's equally fanciful tender of $12 million. A damage analysis by Emil's attorneys and their experts had concluded that a good settlement would be $80 to 90 million, which would represent the premium the government had paid for relays that didn't meet the testing specifications, times a substantial multiplier. Second, the local Department of Justice attorneys didn't have the ability to negotiate on the government's behalf, and their Civil Division bosses who made decisions about the amount were on the other side of the country. It didn't take Byrne long to realize these surrogates were operating under instructions that they were powerless to modify, or that the Teledyne attorneys were prepared to be equally intransigent. The two sides were so far apart, any compromise would be orders of magnitude larger or smaller than their stated expectations.

Byrne told the gathering, which comprised eleven lawyers, that the polarity in their expectations was "outrageous." He then met separately with each of the three groups, listening to attorneys for the government, the two *qui tam* plaintiffs, and Teledyne. The Justice Department and Teledyne attorneys didn't move from their starting points, but the relators' attorneys told him that their idea of a realistic settlement was only half the amount that had been named by the government.

Byrne then brought all three groups back together and handed out pieces of blank paper. "I want each one of you to write down what you think these cases could settle for—not what you want them to settle for," he said. Everyone was quiet. There was no caucusing or discussion. Each of the attorneys wrote down a number, folded the piece of paper, and handed it back to the judge.

It was apparent that at first some of the government attorneys were uncomfortable with the exercise, perhaps because of the risk that they could later be accused of breaking with their mandate from Washington. On the other hand, they quickly realized that whatever they wrote was protected by the parlor-game rules of anonymity, and after a few moments of what might have been interpreted as thoughtful deliberation, each of them appeared happy—even relieved—to comply with Byrne's request. The judge collected the eleven pieces of paper, held them close to his chest as he read them, then folded them up and tucked them into a folder where they couldn't be seen by anyone else. "Okay," he announced to the lawyers as he left the room, "I think I can settle this case."

A few minutes later, he met with the Teledyne defense attorneys. Meanwhile, Phillips looked around as his colleagues and the Justice Department lawyers traded speculations on the likely quality of the response from the opposition. The mood in the room was far from hopeful; a number of the attorneys saw the exercise as frivolous, and it seemed likely that the Teledyne lawyers would respond in kind, perhaps even by lowering their earlier proposal. A few minutes later, Judge Byrne returned to the room.

"I think we can settle this case for between a hundred ten and a hundred fifteen million dollars," he said. "I suggest that a realistic figure would be a hundred twelve-five."

It was an astonishing result. Although his proposed figure was just about half of what the government said it wanted, it was nearly ten times higher than Teledyne's last offer and almost exactly where John Phillips had hoped it would be, in the middle of the two extremes that had polarized the negotiations for so long. The Department of Justice subsequently agreed to that outcome, and so did the relators.

Out of the $112.5 million settlement, Teledyne paid $85 million to settle the case brought by Emil Stache and Al Muehlhausen, and $27.5 million on the other whistle-blower's case against the company's Systems

Division. Previously, Teledyne had paid a criminal fine of $17.5 million—by far the largest ever paid in connection with defense contractor theft—and pled guilty to thirty-five counts of criminal fraud. The size of the criminal fine shocked the defense industry, which had come to expect its wrongdoing to be answered with little more than a slap on the wrist. The vice president of quality pled guilty to two additional counts of fraud. The manager who had laughed at the FBI wound up selling real estate.

Based on the degree of Emil and Al's cooperation in helping government investigators and attorneys build the case over three and a half years, the cost to their careers and personal lives, and the substantial contributions made by their counsel, Phillips and his clients believed the relators' share should be near the maximum of 25 percent. But when the settlement approached the $100 million level, Phillips warned, it was reasonable to expect resistance from the Justice Department, which, despite clear congressional intent to the contrary, still viewed rewards as public money which it was mandated to hold to the lowest amount possible. The investigators they had worked with for so long had nothing but good to say about the cooperation and technical expertise both Emil and Al had brought to the case. When the department offered a relators' share of 21.5 percent, it was accepted with minimal negotiation. Their attorneys were disappointed with the offer; but after years of working with the government, Emil and Al didn't want to become adversaries of the same people who had been their allies, especially in a battle they knew could last indefinitely.

That came out to $9,137,500 each. They paid a 20 percent share to Taxpayers Against Fraud and a contingency fee to their attorneys, which had been reduced in exchange for the agreement with TAF.

When Emil got his check, he went shopping for a lawn tractor. The new ones listed for about $1,200. He settled on a demonstrator for $300 less.

FIFTEEN

WHERE THE MONEY IS

I n the middle of the last century, a reporter who apparently had run
out of sensible questions asked Willie Sutton why he robbed banks.
Sutton's answer, "Because that's where the money is," made him an
instant icon in the country's business schools, especially among students
planning careers in investment banking. Today, it isn't uncommon for a
specialist in that field to make as much in a single transaction—sometimes
honestly and sometimes not—as Sutton was able to steal in his lifetime.

Investment banking is a heavily regulated and closely scrutinized
industry. In a field based on personal relationships and investor confidence,
despite frequent reports of outrageous excess, it has carefully cultivated
an image of probity and decorum. Its very language—trust, bond, pledge,
and redemption—is less the lexicon of commerce than of sacred ministry.
Yet, in almost every division of any Wall Street firm, there are specialists
whose mission is to figure out how close to the border of the law the company can operate without getting into trouble.

Like the giant accounting firms with which they frequently collabo-
rate, these corporate craftsmen are rewarded for their creativity, whether
in the formulation of profitable new financial products and services or
in the weaving of impenetrably opaque fiduciary tapestries to protect
schemes on the wrong side of that border from discovery by regulators.
On Wall Street as elsewhere, fraud and complexity go hand in hand. The
more difficult it is to understand, the smaller the likelihood that an elaborate financial scam will ever be detected. Occasionally an educated guide
steps forward from within the ranks of the offenders and blows the
whistle.

One of the most successful and widespread scams in the history of
Wall Street was the practice known as "yield burning." Investment banks
were secretly pocketing profits they made by overpricing U.S. Treasury

bonds sold to state and local government clients—profits of which their clients were unaware and which should have been given to the federal government. No one outside of Wall Street knew of the fraud because it was buried within incredibly complex municipal bond refinancing transactions. The whistle-blower, up to then a rising star in the firm of Smith Barney, was a witty, edgy, young banker named Michael Lissack. He turned out to be a prosecutor's dream: an insider with the courage and integrity to report on the wrongdoing, and a brilliant explainer whose crisp, creative insights would help turn the darkness into daylight.

Lissack grew up in Marblehead, Massachusetts. At Williams College, which he chose because he "liked the idea of being a big fish in a small pond," he majored in American civilization and political economy, participated in student government, helped with fund-raising, and graduated magna cum laude and Phi Beta Kappa in 1979. The next stop was Yale, where he received the equivalent of an MBA and graduated owing $50,000 in student loans. From Yale, he was recruited to work for Smith Barney as a banker in the public finance division.

He threw himself into his new career. For the first couple of years on the job he had no life outside the office and was working over a hundred hours a week. One morning in 1983 he got out of bed and found he could barely move. He thought of making his usual cup of coffee, but he didn't even have the energy to cross the kitchen.

He sat on the edge of his bed and analyzed what was happening. He had been pushing himself relentlessly, and now, he realized, his mind was telling his body to shut down. He dragged himself to the telephone and told his boss he would be taking off the next couple of weeks—he wasn't sure whether he'd be staying with his parents or if he'd just check into a hospital. He wound up doing both.

The experience didn't prompt him to reduce the hours in his workweek, but it did result in a resolution to take a solid month of vacation time each year to recharge himself physically and spiritually. Back on the job, he drove himself as hard as ever. In short order he was promoted to second vice president, then vice president. Billion-dollar financings became routine—to build roads, bridges, and schools across the nation. He put together deals in New Jersey, Florida, North Carolina, and Ohio, and was involved in public financing projects in nearly every state in the union. He became a managing director at the age of thirty—the second youngest in Smith Barney's history—in the firm's public finance department. Over time his salary and bonuses came to more than $600,000 a year.

In his seventh year on the job, a bond attorney introduced Michael to a mergers and acquisitions lawyer from Los Angeles named Merrill Bernstein. She was smart, like him, seemed to be as driven as he was, and was financially successful. They were married in 1989 and moved into an opulent midtown Manhattan penthouse on which he had signed a purchase contract two years before.

Early in his career, Michael read an article in a business magazine about how some companies deliberately encouraged top producers to spend on the basis of their expectations, a strategy designed to make employees dependent on lifestyles that could be supported only through continued high performance. From the start, Michael was determined not to fall into that trap. With their two incomes, he and his wife were living extremely well on less than $300,000 a year. The rest of their take-home pay was going into the bank.

In December 1993, the couple went to the Florida Keys on a vacation. Their relationship was in trouble, although at least up to the time of that trip Michael didn't feel that the marriage had actually started to unravel. Both he and Merrill were highly focused on their careers. For Michael, and perhaps for both of them, the mutual independence that had seemed such a virtue in their courtship had started to give way to loneliness and a sense of unfulfillment. His job also had him down. He knew the industry's practice of secretly skimming profits off municipal bond refinancings through yield burning was wrong. For the past few months he had been having a hard time keeping his mouth shut and going along with the fraud. It was one thing to find loopholes; it was another to steal outright. Feeling he had no one he could really talk with during the vacation, he passed his days in long, solitary walks along the beach.

Often on those walks he brought along papers that had been faxed to him by his secretary, and he would read through them in his favorite Key West coffee shop, catching up on the office news. One morning a particular story brought him bolt upright in his chair. The United States Attorney's Office in Boston was investigating Merrill Lynch and Lazard Freres on allegations the two firms had been illegally collaborating with each other and their competitors, splitting fees and markets in public finance transactions. The particular focus of their investigation had been a bond issue by the Los Angeles Metropolitan Transit Authority, LAMTA. Michael knew that both banking firms were still under investigation for similar charges on bond issues in Massachusetts and the District of Columbia.

What galvanized his attention was not the possibility that two of his biggest rivals were involved in fee and market splitting. What astonished him was that in the course of chasing after this relatively penny-ante offense, the government had stuck its nose into one of the biggest swindles in history—and had no idea what it was looking at. He put down the article and pondered his options.

His first impulse was to turn his rivals in. But could he do it in a way that wouldn't ring down the curtain on his career in investment banking? The practice of yield burning was protected by a far-reaching network of secrecy and quid pro quo, and an attack on a single perpetrator would be universally regarded as an attack on the industry as a whole. If it ever came out that he had given up one of his own—even though it was a competitor—his life on Wall Street would be finished.

Yield burning was rampant throughout the industry, and Michael himself was as deeply into it as most of his colleagues. Indeed, one of the reasons he had become unhappy with his job was that he didn't like where it was taking him.

One of Lissack's particular talents was risk assessment, and now he weighed the choices before him. Even if he pointed to the fraud, it was apparent the investigators would need someone to explain it. He knew there were ways he could do the pointing without giving away his identity. After all, he was turning the government on to a fraud of enormous proportions. How much explaining would it take before the government saw the light and his revelation took on a life of its own?

He found a pay phone near the beach and called the United States Attorney's Office mentioned in the story. Moments later, he was speaking with a government investigator in Boston.

Michael wasn't going to give his name, he said, because what he had to say could stand on its own. (Even though the phone number had been set up to encourage anonymous tips, he suspected the subject of his identity might arise later in the conversation.) Instead of objecting, the voice on the phone asked him if he'd be willing to call back in a half hour. It would take that long, he explained, to round up the other people in the office who needed to hear whatever it was Michael had to say. Dutifully, Michael hung up and passed an almost endless thirty minutes before dialing again.

This time, the call was put on a speakerphone in the office of Assistant United States Attorney Brian O'Connor, who introduced a number of FBI agents on the Boston end of the conversation.

Lissack wasted no time in getting down to business. The reason for the call, he said, was that the government was on the wrong track. The big secret at Merrill Lynch and Lazard Freres was only marginally related to fee or market splitting. For years, the two investment banks had been working in illegal collaboration with each other even while they worked hard on the appearance of being competitors. They were stealing the socks off the government, he said, through a practice known as yield burning. The voices at the other end of the telephone line were silent, and Michael asked if the investigators were familiar with the term. Someone in the room told him to keep talking, which Michael took as an admission that none of them had ever heard of it.

The trouble with this kind of a call, Michael realized, was that there was a limit to how much the government agents were willing to learn. This wasn't like a tip on a drug deal or a ring of car thieves, where once a veneer of secrecy was removed the wrongdoing was immediately obvious. This crime was protected by its fundamental complexity, which made it inaccessible to all but a handful of specialists. Most of the time, even the agencies issuing the bonds had no idea that a theft had occurred. The challenge in this telephone call would be to not only point to the fraud, but to explain it—and in language that the prosecutor and the agents would be able to understand.

The agents listened as he laid out the basics of the scheme, and they even asked occasional questions, but it was hard to tell how much they were really able to take in. Lissack was worried that they might be attempting to trace the call back to the coffee shop's pay phone, and when he sensed they were approaching saturation, he decided it was time to end the call. He promised to contact them again—he would identify himself as "your friend from Florida"—after the investigators had a chance to discuss the conversation. Michael hung up and continued his walk along the beach, sorting through emotions that ranged from depression to exhilaration, from anxiety to delight. But they did not include regret. He was glad he had made the call. Now it was someone else's problem, and he would watch from the sidelines as the drama played itself out.

Back at the hotel, he told Merrill he had seen the story in the paper, and that he had telephoned the United States Attorney's Office. She looked at him with disbelief. "You called who . . . ?" she said. "You *what*!?"

He started to describe his conversation, offering his wife the same assurances he had given himself before and after the call, stressing that it had been anonymous. But even as he recaptured the details, he sensed that he was paddling against a fast-turning tide; his wife's incredulity was quickly ripening into outrage. Merrill seemed certain that his call would have terrible consequence for both of their careers. He shifted the focus to why he had done it—that he couldn't keep on working in a job that rewarded him for breaking the law, and that this seemed like a relatively risk-free way of bringing the illegal practice to an end—but Merrill was unmoved. When he paused, she angrily terminated the conversation. "Thank you," she said, "for ruining both of our lives." Feeling more isolated and lonely than ever, he left their room and went for another long walk.

In the weeks following their return to New York, despite his wife's intransigence, Michael made several more calls to a steadily growing audience in Boston. As the government's "friend from Florida," he laid out the basics of the fraud. His listeners now included finance specialists from the United States Attorney's Office and special FBI agents assigned to the ongoing fee- and market-splitting investigation.

Municipal financings had long been a source of tension between federal regulators and Wall Street. Tax exemption for interest payments made to municipal bond holders was supposed to be limited to situations in which bond proceeds were used to further a public purpose, such as building bridges, schools, or public roads. This was a form of federal subsidy for municipalities, because the federal government forgoes taxes on municipal bond interest income it would have otherwise collected. But the differential between the lower interest rate for tax-exempt investments and the higher rates paid for taxable investments created an irresistible temptation. Wall Street bankers set about developing schemes to invest tax-exempt bond proceeds in high-yielding taxable investments, and to capture the difference between the yields—sometimes referred to as "arbitrage"—for their own profit.

The potential for abuse of tax-exempt financings was enormous, and the bankers showed endless creativity in their schemes to skim off the price difference between interest payments on tax-exempt and taxable investments. In the 1970s it was the "invested sinking fund"; in the early 1980s it was the "blind pool funds"; in the late '80s it was "hedge funds." Congress tried to stop Wall Street from abusing tax exemption, but at every turn bankers found a loophole—and slid through it.

In 1986, Congress thought it put an end to the abuse by requiring that whenever tax-exempt bond proceeds were invested in taxable investments, the differential between the nontaxable and taxable yields had to be returned to the U.S. Treasury. Congress repeatedly made clear that it did not provide tax-exempt status for municipal bonds in order for Wall Street to reap the financial benefit.

Lissack explained that the Wall Street of the 1990s was once again circumventing federal law. Yield burning was possibly the biggest fraud yet.

When interest rates decline, state and local governments often refinance their municipal bonds to lower their borrowing costs, not unlike a person refinancing a home mortgage when interest rates drop. These refinancings are known as "advance refundings." As part of the transaction, banks purchase on behalf of municipalities higher-yielding Treasury securities with the proceeds of tax-exempt advance refunding bonds and use the income to retire over time the higher-interest tax-exempt bonds it originally issued. By law, their investments with those proceeds cannot earn higher aggregate yields than the yield earned on the newly issued tax-exempt bonds. Any excess profit must be paid to the federal government.

By adding large price markups to Treasury securities purchased with bond proceeds, Wall Street bankers were making illegal profits by artificially depressing—"burning"—the yield on those securities, so that the yield appeared to be within the allowed limits even though it would have been above the limit had the securities been priced at fair market value.

The practice infected thousands of transactions across the country and touched nearly every public issuer of municipal debt. "Yield burning was costing the Treasury more than a billion dollars," Lissack estimated, far more than the illegal sharing of fees and markets, which the government was pursuing. The fraud was undiscovered, Lissack explained, because it was buried within incredibly complex muni-financing transactions.

But at its heart, it really was nothing more than a garden variety rip-off. Wall Street bankers were overcharging the municipalities for Treasury securities, and nobody noticed because the theft was concealed in the arcana of convoluted bond refinancings, nearly opaque rules, and hundreds of minute details.

The investment bankers, Michael told his listeners, lied for each other, certifying that the outrageously inflated prices being charged for these securities met the requirement of "fair market value." Obviously the certifier, presumed by the issuer to be neutral, was in on the fix, approving prices it knew were inflated, often more than a hundred times over the cost of an honest deal. There was no direct sharing of the secret profits; the participants repaid each other in subsequent deals, when the beneficiary from the last issue might become the certifier for the next one.

In the course of Michael's conversations with the government investigators, it was nearly impossible for him to gauge his listeners' true reactions. They were all trained interrogators, and they weren't about to give anything away or allow a witness to revise the basic inequality in their roles. The fact that he was calling anonymously may have made him appear less reliable than an informant whose identity they knew, but Michael realized their relationship would never approach anything like parity or allow for the possibility of reciprocal candor. However, there was one thing he could do that might enable him, eventually, to monitor how seriously they were taking his calls. In one of their last conversations, Michael gave the FBI the names of ten people to interview about his charges. His own name was on that list.

In anticipation that his initiative would eventually stir up turmoil and probably some personal liability, Michael hired an attorney, a solo practitioner in New York. It was a relief to finally have someone he could talk with, but the expected reaction from the government was slow in coming. Weeks passed, and then months. Michael spoke with the lawyer frequently through the summer, but their conversations seldom led to anything concrete. As a vent to his frustration and impatience, Michael launched a series of college-level pranks, mostly through the Internet, designed to flood a former supervisor's mailbox with unwanted messages. His goal, as he later described it, was to "drive them crazy" at work.

By fall he had still heard nothing at all. Meanwhile, although he and Merrill spent countless hours in therapy and counseling, after their Florida vacation it was apparent that their marriage was dissolving. At the office, with his attorney's cautious approval, he began speaking openly with colleagues about his dissatisfaction with Smith Barney's—and his own—growing involvement in the very practice over which he had anonymously blown the whistle on two of the company's competitors. More than once, he even went so far as to suggest that he ought to drop the dime on Lazard Freres and Merrill Lynch for the LAMTA yield-burning debacle, which he described as daylight robbery. Whenever he brought it up, his colleagues responded with the same comment: If he did make such a call, he'd be dead.

It wasn't said as a threat, because no one in the office seemed to take Michael's rantings literally. Their response to his remarks suggested that reporting a rival—and exposing the scheme—would be tantamount to betraying Smith Barney, which would mean exposing himself as well. If his comments weren't exactly driving people crazy, there was a certain satisfaction in stirring the pot, and he kept speaking up.

If his employers knew what he had already done, Michael thought, there was a possibility that the metaphor of his being dead could become a literal reality.

Although his identity was still unknown to the Justice Department investigators, and despite his own involvement in the very sort of crime he had reported, ever since placing the first phone call from Florida he'd felt as though he were an undercover agent for the federal government. The problem was, because he alone knew the identity of the FBI's "friend from Florida," his sense of mission did not include the comfort and advice that even a James Bond could reliably expect from those he served. There was no one at the office he would be foolish enough to confide in, he had virtually no friends outside of work, and he wasn't getting a lot of comfort at home. In the absence of any other outlet than his lawyer for his frustration and anger, he had to settle for raging at his colleagues and other people in his office. It wasn't enough.

A few weeks later, on a business trip to San Francisco, he found himself contemplating suicide. He called the psychiatrist he had been seeing in New York, who prescribed an antidepressant.

After months of counseling, he and Merrill reached an apparently permanent détente. They were still friends, but they agreed that the marriage had ended. She moved out of their apartment, and once more he was alone. In the hope of getting his feet back under himself and dealing more effectively with his depression, he took a six-month leave of absence from his job. When he learned that Smith Barney wanted to fire him during that leave, he countered that the stress was work-related, and that he would sue for job discrimination.

That summer, while he was on leave, he read an article in the *Wall Street Journal* about a case being prosecuted under the False Claims Act. He spoke with his attorney about it, suggesting the possibility of filing a *qui tam* lawsuit as a way of getting the government to examine his allegations. The lawyer agreed he had the basis for such an action, but he knew nearly nothing about the law and mistakenly thought the legal basis for their case was tax fraud. Neither of them acted on Michael's idea. The conversation occurred during the time when the firm was threatening to fire Lissack, and the lawyer told him they were far better off focusing on an employment lawsuit against Smith Barney.

The firm didn't go through with firing him, but when he returned to work in September 1994, he found that he essentially had lost his job anyway. He learned about it from a memorandum outlining his new assignment. He was required to come to work, and the company provided an office. But that was about it. He was to sit in the office and do virtually nothing. His attorney referred to the document as the "potted plant memo" because he had suddenly become little more than an office decoration.

Finally, in November, he heard from the government attorneys. They didn't contact him directly; the query came through Smith Barney's legal department. Nearly a year after his initial call from Florida, the Bureau wanted permission to depose Michael Lissack in connection with a public finance investigation. Obviously the FBI did not yet know he was their anonymous source, and the method by which it initiated this contact gave the firm no reason to suspect it either. Michael feigned bewilderment when his superiors told him of the request, and because the query appeared to have arrived out of the blue he decided to add a warning, as though the idea had just come to him. If the subject turned out to be yield burning, he told them, he would answer honestly. There was no immediate response, but he knew it was not the kind of assurance they were hoping to hear.

Privately he was elated at this evidence that the government had been working its way down his list and had finally gotten to his name, and he spent the next few days rehearsing his answers to the expected questions.

But when the interview finally took place, that elation quickly vanished. The conversation was held in Lissack's office, but it was done by telephone, and under the watchful eyes of two of Smith Barney's attorneys. To his astonishment, it soon became apparent that the subject was "pay-for-play"—essentially bribes paid by investment banking firms to participate in municipal bond transactions. Yield burning was never even mentioned. The FBI was interviewing him because it was investigating Smith Barney's business practices in Texas; the selection of his name was simply a coincidence, and had nothing to do with his initiatives of the previous December. With the Smith Barney legal counsel watching his every move, there was no way he could bring up the subject on his own. His long, anonymous tutorials had fallen on deaf ears, and a year of waiting had been in vain. He realized then that the government would not act unless he took more deliberate steps.

His new nonstatus in the firm gave him plenty of free time to ponder what those steps might be. One morning shortly after the devastating interview, he was sitting in his office leisurely reading through the *Wall Street Journal* when he came upon a possible source of guidance. This story was about John Phillips and his False Claims Act practice, Phillips & Cohen, which was now based in Washington, D.C. This was just the kind of perspective his situation demanded, and after some coaxing he persuaded his attorney to call Washington.

The lawyer's call was put through to Erika Kelton, a bright, creative, young attorney who had only recently joined Phillips & Cohen, after working on *qui tam* cases in the Washington office of one of New York's largest and most prestigious law firms. Like Phillips, she had graduated from law school at the University of California and had been an editor of the *California Law Review*. Kelton's instincts told her there might be something to the case, even though her caller was a lawyer, not the potential relator, and seemed to be having a hard time describing the nature of the false claim. She encouraged him to put her in direct contact with his client, but he was skittish about revealing Lissack's identity. In a series of subsequent calls over the next few days, the New York lawyer went back and forth between his client and the attorney in Washington, and finally the confidence level was high enough that both he and Lissack agreed to such a conversation. When Kelton heard the explanation direct from Lissack, she understood immediately what the banking firms were doing.

She told Lissack and his lawyer that the False Claims Act had never been applied in a securities case, but that it was the perfect law for the fraud described by Lissack. Under the act, they could be prosecuted for falsely certifying compliance with federal yield restrictions and pocketing the government's money. Lissack estimated the extent of that theft to be in the hundreds of millions.

He signed a contingency contract with Phillips & Cohen, and Kelton immediately set about the long, complicated process of drawing up the complaint. Lissack's New York attorney, who remained focused on the employment lawsuit, proposed holding a press conference to publicize the *qui tam* action as a way to pressure Smith Barney into an early, favorable settlement. Kelton had to explain to him why that couldn't be done, that the case had to remain under seal until the government had investigated the facts and decided whether to join the action. Any public discussion of the case by Lissack or his attorneys, she warned, could automatically end it.

There were other ways to apply pressure, however, and soon Lissack had a powerful new incentive to use them. At the end of January 1995, when the firm distributed its annual bonus checks for the year just ended, he was stunned to discover that his reward was less than half his salary—and nearly $400,000 less than the bonus he had been paid the year before. First Smith Barney had taken away his work, and now it had cut off his income. He knew he was still viable in the banking industry, but considering all the elements that he had already set in motion, he decided his viability wouldn't last long either. He had nothing left to lose. He began liquidating stock options, in preparation for being fired.

On the morning of the first Wednesday of February 1995, anyone passing Lissack's office might have wondered what he was doing to keep himself so busy at his desk. He was putting the finishing touches on a detailed memorandum to senior Smith Barney executives, written with the help of his New York attorney. It identified specific questionable practices in one of the company's bond offerings in Dade County, Florida, and cited "trade-offs" in municipal business with the executive at Lazard Freres who was being investigated by the FBI. Predictably, reactions to the memo were uniformly negative. How dare he raise these issues? Who did he think he was? What on earth did he have in mind?

But there was more to come. The next day, his lawyer filed an employment arbitration complaint, citing his well-known objections to those practices as the reason management had stripped him of all responsibilities and essentially restricted him to sitting in his office.

Michael told his employers he wouldn't be coming in on Friday, allowing some time for everyone to cool off after learning of his complaint. But even though he kept his word, he let them know he was still thinking of them. On Friday morning he faxed Smith Barney's management a six-point memorandum, each point signaled by a typographic bullet, listing the specific practices by which he felt the firm had violated securities laws. At the end of the memo, he put his employers formally on notice that he was no longer going to withhold this information from the authorities. He read the memo to himself after it had been sent, then said to his attorney, with a kind of grim glee, "Bullet, bullet, bullet, bullet, bullet, bullet."

The following Monday, Smith Barney informed his attorney that Michael was no longer welcome to return to the office. Lissack then faxed his memos of the week before to the United States attorney, the SEC, and the FBI, with a note explaining that his bulleted memorandum referred to a bond issue in Florida and suggesting that the agencies might want to call him. A few days later a couple of officials from the SEC's Dade County office called and interviewed him, but they were investigating Smith Barney for other reasons and didn't seem interested in anything Lissack had to say about yield burning.

Unbeknownst to his employers, Michael wasn't even in New York the day his job and his career in investment banking came to an end. He was in the Washington offices of Phillips & Cohen, preparing for the next step in a well-planned strategy.

Three weeks after his termination from Smith Barney, Michael Lissack filed a *qui tam* lawsuit under seal against more than a dozen Wall Street and regional investment banks. Several days later, the story of his allegations of yield burning against the municipal bonding industry appeared on the front financial page of the *New York Times* without any mention of his False Claims Act case. In a self-deprecating reference to his baldness, Lissack described himself as "a Samson—blowing out the industry and pulling down the walls as I leave." He said that everyone in the business knew about the fraud, and that competing firms would help each other get away with it by taking turns as "objective" experts, certifying to issuers that the outrageously inflated prices were reasonable. "We even kept track of whom we did opinions for and who owed us," he told the reporter. No Wall Street insider had ever broken ranks in such a spectacular way, and in quick succession, similar articles appeared throughout the business press.

The response from the accused bankers was complete denial. Smith Barney attempted to dismiss the charges of irregularities by describing Michael Lissack as a disgruntled employee seeking revenge in a salary dispute. Neither alibi got many takers outside the industry. Four months after the story became public, *Fortune* wrote about yield burning in an article entitled "The Big Sleaze," saying that "even if [Lissack] is hell-bent on revenge against Smith Barney, what matters is whether he is telling the truth."

It was only after the filing of his lawsuit and his identity becoming known to the federal government that the government actually began to investigate the charges he had made anonymously from the pay phone in Florida more than a year before. When Michael learned of this, he thought back on the tension, the depression, the strains on his marriage and his career through months of fearful hopes and anxious waiting. The process he thought he had set in motion had been nothing more than a fantasy. Nobody had taken him seriously enough to act. The avenging juggernaut he had so long expected was only in his mind, and justice had remained not only blind but deaf as well. An enormous fraud had been committed, and the system had failed to respond.

If it weren't for the False Claims Act, he realized, he would still be at the mercy of a corrupt system, and all the risks and losses would have been for nothing.

SIXTEEN

AN AMERICAN DREAM, PART II

L issack's charges hit Wall Street at a bad time. Virtually the whole municipal bond industry already was under investigation for a variety of other illegal practices. A particular target was gifts or political contributions made to local and state officials in return for preference in the assignment of underwriting business, a widespread form of bribery known as "pay-to-play." Just a few months earlier, the husband of former Kentucky governor Martha Layne Collins went to prison for regularly demanding and getting payments from Wall Street firms in exchange for a piece of the state's municipal bond business. In New Jersey, a former chief of staff to ex-governor Jim Florio had pled guilty to securities fraud for sharing in $200,000 in kickbacks from a local bank. And several dealers were facing similar charges in the aftermath of a securities fraud that had bankrupted Orange County, California.

But yield burning was by far the biggest, most pervasive fraud in the municipal bond market. The earlier cases were mere firecrackers compared with Lissack's five-hundred-pound bomb. Within the industry, there was a lot of maneuvering to be elsewhere when it went off. That October, the National Association of Bond Lawyers, which represent municipalities on bond deals, was careful to disavow any liability on its part. Its members "do not possess the necessary financial and market expertise to perform these reviews and verifications," the association told the IRS, that its clients purchased securities at fair market prices. Lissack reveled in the uproar, which he saw as evidence of the strength of his lawsuit.

To prove the case, he and his lawyers had to show how extensive yield burning was and how much the government had lost as a result of the fraud. This required analyzing security prices on hundreds of individual escrow transactions. Lissack spent days at the New York Public Library, scanning back issues of the *Wall Street Journal* to gather historical Treasury bond prices. He searched Municipal Securities Regulatory Board filings for more data. By July, preliminary analysis clearly demonstrated the huge markups banks were adding to the prices they charged their government clients for securities.

Working on the case nearly full-time, Lissack set about designing analytical software to draw a more detailed picture of the fraud. Phillips & Cohen bought data files of historical Treasury bond prices for analysis by those programs, and the firm wrote to more than five hundred public agencies around the country requesting the closing documents from advance refundings to get bond prices.

Government officials were eager to get more information from Lissack about fraud in the muni bond industry. His attorneys presented what amounted to a series of informal tutorials to officials of the SEC, Justice Department, and FBI that were designed to bring the government up to speed about fraud in the municipal bond industry. He also testified before a grand jury in Boston. During those sessions, Lissack provided detailed insights into the politics of landing municipal bond deals, such as high-priced lunches, golf outings, and the hiring of politically connected consultants. His audiences couldn't have had a better tutor. It would have been hard to find an expert with a more intimate understanding of the bond market, let alone one who was willing to tell what he knew.

On the inside, Wall Street is a small town, and municipal reinvestment specialists were an exceptionally small and exclusive group. They were zealous competitors, but also close colleagues who migrated constantly among the rival firms. And within their tiny circle, they liked to gossip. In many instances, a refunding transaction could not be accomplished without the participation of another firm, which had to verify that the prices of the Treasury securities were reasonable. That second firm was likely to pass on information about investment pricing practices to others in the circle.

Not all of the federal agencies were equally enthusiastic about the False Claims Act, or about going after Lissack's choice of targets. In one of the first sessions with Justice Department officials from Washington and the Manhattan U.S. Attorney's Office, Lissack and his lawyers got a preview of the obstacles that lay ahead. "I don't get it," said one of the

Washington attorneys. "Usually in *qui tam* cases we sue over something tangible, like widgets. What's tangible in this case? It's just about money."

"It's a billion dollars!" John Phillips stammered in response. He knew this attorney was antagonistic to *qui tam* cases in principle, but he nearly choked in astonishment at her dismissive comment.

This was hardly the way Phillips and his firm had expected the case to be received. At the outset, they had been thrilled at the prospect of working with the famous Southern District of New York. Under the previous U.S. attorney, Rudolph Giuliani, the Justice Department's Manhattan office had taken on Ivan Boesky, Michael Milken, and other so-called Masters of the Universe in the 1980s and sent them to prison.

But times had changed, and so had the Southern District's leadership. The new U.S. attorney in charge was Mary Jo White. Several of the convictions the office had won during the heady 1980s had been overturned, apparently at a high cost to the office's crusading spirit. The team of Justice Department attorneys assigned to Lissack's case, led by the Manhattan office's Civil Division, seemed to have little interest in taking on Wall Street's big names and New York's top law firms. Attorneys from the Southern District and the main Justice Department office in Washington attended meetings with the SEC, IRS, and Lissack's attorneys on the case, but that was about the extent of their involvement. From 1995, when Lissack filed his *qui tam* case, until 2000, when the government settled essentially the last remaining yield-burning charges, the Justice Department never issued a subpoena, deposed a witness, or even calculated the government's losses from the fraud. Whatever leadership and support Lissack's attorneys or the SEC might have expected from the Justice Department in Manhattan and Washington, nothing of the sort ever materialized.

But this time, the Justice Department wasn't the only game in town. By then, California had passed its own False Claims Act, drafted by John Phillips and modeled after the federal statute, allowing *qui tam* lawsuits for recovery of losses to local and state entities. A few months after he had brought his federal case, Lissack sued Lazard Freres & Co. in California, with Phillips's guidance, over the municipal bond deal with the Los Angeles Metropolitan Transit Authority. This second litigation front was entirely independent of the federal government. With the newspaper story on the LAMTA offering he had read while in Key West the starting point for his long crusade, Lissack knew this was a particularly blatant case of yield burning.

Lazard had risen to prominence under investment banker Felix Rohatyn, when the firm helped New York City out of a huge financial crisis in the 1970s. But as LAMTA's financial adviser in Los Angeles in 1993, the firm was nowhere nearly as public-spirited. Lazard bankers convinced the agency to use their firm rather than a competitor to purchase the Treasury escrow securities for a $560 million municipal bond refunding transaction. The agreement didn't come without conditions. Lazard had promised it would sell the Treasury securities to LAMTA at the lowest possible cost, and that the prices were at fair market value. When the numbers were fed to Lissack's new software for the analysis of muni bond refinancing transactions, however, it was obvious that neither promise had been kept. Lissack was intimately familiar with the Lazard deal because he had competed for the business for Smith Barney, and after it was awarded to Lazard he still followed the transaction closely. His lawsuit charged that Lazard secretly and illegally overcharged LAMTA by more than $3 million.

When the California lawsuit was unsealed in April 1996, LAMTA joined the action and hired Phillips & Cohen as its attorney. By representing both Lissack and the state agency, the firm became, in effect, both the private and public attorneys general. The firm added new claims on behalf of LAMTA for breach of fiduciary duty, and sought punitive damages.

It was the kind of story the media love to get mad about, and there was no shortage of sound bites from obliging public officials. Zev Yaroslavsky, a Los Angeles County supervisor who sat on the LAMTA board, said Lazard Freres had "set out to cheat and steal money that was rightly the taxpayers'." Yaroslavsky also had some encouraging thoughts about the punitive damages. "While it's important for us to recover our money, it is just as important for us to send a clear message to the financial and investment banking community that they can't and won't get away with manipulating and defrauding their public agency clients and the taxpayers."

Lazard offered a few bites in return, but they were not nearly as tasty. "We continue to believe that our markup for the securities sold was fair and consistent with accepted market practice," a company spokesman told the *Los Angeles Times*. It was a familiar line. Other investment banks had likewise defended the markups with the claim that the prices reflected the risks. If the deals fell through, they said, the banks would be stuck with the bonds that they held in escrow for their clients. The problem with that argument, Lissack and the attorneys pointed out, was that the deals never fell through. And even if they ever did, the banks were more than likely to make money than to lose it.

Based on what they had learned from Lissack's groundwork, Phillips & Cohen hired an exceptionally bright economic analyst, Steven Feinstein, a young professor of finance at Babson College, near Boston, to measure the extent of the theft. Kelton worked closely with Lissack and Feinstein to gather detailed information about hundreds of advance-refunding deals and to analyze each one—something no one, apparently, had done before. They debated and critically examined their findings to ensure they held up against any argument Wall Street could muster. Their analysis torpedoed the banks' argument that the amount they charged clients for securities was based on risk by showing that a Wall Street bank would charge one client substantially more than it charged another on the same day for the very same securities. The only explanation was the amount of arbitrage the banks could rip out of the deal. They analyzed the price difference between sole-source refunding deals like the Lazard-LAMTA transaction, and deals in which there had been open competition. Nothing like it had ever been done before—one reason why bond dealers got away with yield burning for so long. The economists analyzed more than three hundred muni bond refinancing transactions based on responses to the earlier query by Phillips & Cohen. They looked at big deals and small ones, competitive and noncompetitive, those involving Lazard and those involving other firms. The hard numbers proved the offense and showed its scope. The Wall Street bankers didn't have a leg to stand on.

The analysis demonstrated that widespread yield-burning abuses in municipal bond transactions in the early 1990s had cost the federal government and state and local governments hundreds of millions of dollars. It demonstrated that no-bid refunding deals present identical risks to those associated with competitive bidding deals, and that they should have been priced in exactly the same way. Instead, while competitive deals were indeed priced close to their fair market value, noncompetitve deals were on average twenty times higher. The average markup of bonds on competitive deals was only about four cents per

$1,000 worth of bonds; in sole-source deals, the markup was a breath-taking hundred times as much.

The analysis showed how opportunistic Wall Street firms would routinely charge different markups on securities sold to different issuers on the same dates. They would settle for modest profits of five cents per $1,000 worth of bonds in a competitive offering, then charge another issuer $5 per $1,000 for the same thing when the fix was in. Except in a few cases where the greed was even more outrageous, the local and state agencies issuing the bonds weren't the ones who suffered from these enormous pricing differences. By law, the excess profits didn't belong to them but to the federal government, and by inflating their commissions the bankers were stealing money that actually belonged to the United States Treasury. The issuing agencies had little incentive to question whether the banks' charges were really at fair market price.

There was another reason public agencies were often so willing to forgo competitive bidding. Banks encouraged their clients to view bond refinancing as a complicated juggling act that was best left to the professionals. They frequently claimed to know more about the issuer's needs than the agency did, and would promise to tailor a mix of securities accordingly. The economic analysis revealed that lie as well, demonstrating that noncompetitive bidding was always for the benefit of the banks, never for the issuers.

In the LAMTA offering, Phillips & Cohen's experts showed that the bonds had been priced at least fourteen times higher than the prevailing market rate. Lazard had told its client that the bank would make only $200,000 to $300,000 in profit from the securities sale; in fact, it made $3 million. The SEC relied in large part on the economic analysis from Phillips & Cohen to determine what the U.S. Treasury's losses were for yield burning in each bond transaction, and used those numbers as a basis for settlement negotiations.

While the Justice Department continued to sit out the game, the Internal Revenue Service decided to act boldly on its own. In July 1996, the IRS gave notice to muni bond issuers that they had one year to pay the government the illegal profits if they didn't want to lose the tax-exempt status of their bonds.

The IRS knew that the investment banks, not the municipalities, had pocketed the forbidden gains, but the agency's enforcement authority in this area is generally limited to bondholders and state and local authorities. Although in certain circumstances the IRS can go after the underwriter as well, it was subject to limitations; the amount of money the IRS would be able to collect from the banks wouldn't be anywhere close to what they had stolen from the Treasury. Right on cue, local and state officials across the country picked up the phone and called their bond underwriters and investment advisers. If this isn't settled, they said, forget about any more underwriting deals from us.

With equal predictability, the state and local issuers and their lobbyists urged the IRS, SEC, Congress, and the White House to redirect the attack and go after just the investment banks. They argued that pulling the tax-exempt status of so many issues would drain them of any value and throw the entire municipal bond market into turmoil. The IRS yielded slightly in September 1996 by removing the one-year deadline. But the municipalities continued to feel the pressure from the tax agency. IRS officials made clear in public speeches that they would pursue bond issuers until the matter was resolved. Leading the charge at the IRS was a thin, gangly manager in the agency's tax-exempt bond division named Charles Anderson. Known as a straight shooter with a slow drawl and a fast, deliberate mind, Anderson became a symbol of rectitude and of the agency's resolve.

Soon after the IRS announcement, Treasury Secretary Robert Rubin said his department and the IRS would work with all parties affected by the ruling, including the bond dealers. But it was immediately apparent that Rubin himself was touched by the controversy. Before assuming the top job at Treasury, which oversees the IRS, he had been cochairman of Goldman, Sachs & Co., the first firm named in Lissack's lawsuit and now under investigation for yield burning. The Treasury Department delivered on his promise, but Rubin recused himself from all discussions of the IRS notice.

The SEC responded to the pressure as well by going directly after the investment banks. Like the IRS, the commission had never been involved in a False Claims Act case. Created during the Great Depression after the stock market scandals of the 1920s, the SEC had always focused on protecting the investing public and the markets, rather than the interests of the federal government. In this case, it was up to the SEC to protect the government's interest too, since the Justice Department continued to play a passive role. The SEC, working with Phillips & Cohen, took on the burden of proving the fraud and negotiating settlements.

A key player was Lawrence West, a skilled and innovative lawyer who had come to the SEC only a few years earlier from a private Washington law firm. Along with another SEC enforcement attorney, David Battan, and their boss, William R. Baker, West led the SEC's strategy in tackling the massive case. One of the SEC's first steps was to send out questionnaires on refunding escrows to more than a dozen major Wall Street banks. Then it began to focus on building evidence against the largest offenders, issuing subpoenas, taking depositions, and gathering documents. The SEC didn't have the resources to go after all of the violators, so it targeted a couple of the worst to serve as a warning to others.

Baker then made a series of presentations to various industry groups about the SEC's thinking on the case, all designed to move the offenders' feet closer to the fire. At one trade group meeting, he described to bond lawyers the securities law violations that might result from yield-burning abuses. At another, he warned securities dealers that financial advisers who sold escrow securities to their clients could be viewed by the SEC as having violated federal adviser laws.

In early 1997, the Government Finance Officers Association, whose members handled municipal bond transactions throughout the United States, invited Phillips & Cohen to present its economic analysis at the GFOA annual meeting in Washington, D.C. The Babson consultant, Feinstein, explained the firm's methodology and then, one by one, stripped away the veils that had been woven to hide this theft from the officials' view. The audience listened attentively as he led them toward the light, demonstrating how investment banks had cheated their government clients out of hundreds of millions of dollars. For many, it was like watching the film from a surveillance camera that had recorded a massive daylight robbery.

As soon as the presentation ended, a member of the audience jumped to his feet. Unlike most of the others in the room, he was not a government finance officer but an official of the Public Securities Association, a bond dealers trade group. His voice quaking with outrage, he railed against Lissack, his attorneys, and the consultant who had just presented the evidence against his industry. They're just lawyers, he shouted. They just want to tear things down and attack people. We build things; they destroy them. The impromptu tirade was an impressive codicil to what had come before, but for most of the audience it achieved just the opposite of its intended effect. The last nail in the coffin of yield burning, like the scam itself, had been driven from inside.

Although such public displays of emotion were rare, there obviously was a lot at stake. If the bonds lost their tax-exempt status, bondholders could be held liable to the IRS for billions of dollars in back taxes and interest on income they had received over the years that they thought was tax-exempt. A class action on behalf of bondholders, in turn, could make bond dealers liable for billions of dollars for fraud. And for the municipalities that had issued the bonds, the result could be skyrocketing costs in the financing of schools and other construction projects.

Michael Lissack, meanwhile, was keeping busy. In the first year after being fired, he had a hard time separating himself from Smith Barney. A workaholic who didn't know how to relax, he continued trying to stir the pot at his former firm by using the Internet to pull pranks on former superiors. He posted a plaintive request asking readers to send teddy bears to his former boss, whom he described as an eight-year-old boy suffering from a fatal kidney disease. Many people did as they were asked, and his boss was soon inundated with stuffed bears. The firm eventually traced the pranks to their source, and took Lissack to court for using the Internet to anonymously encourage people to indirectly hassle his ex-boss. He pled guilty to second-degree harassment.

Eventually, he was able to put Smith Barney behind him and focus on starting a new life. He had done what he could to help build his case, and it was time to leave the rest to his attorneys. He enrolled in the doctoral program in business at Henley Management College. He continued operating at his same high energy level, but now in academic research, organizing conferences on complex issues of management.

In February 1998, his old life came back to haunt him. Three years earlier, he had written in an op-ed piece for the *New York Times*, "... I got sucked into a pattern of doing whatever it took to make money for the firm and, I admit, for myself." Now, to settle allegations that he had misrepresented how much money Dade County, Florida, would save in a municipal bond transaction, he agreed to pay $30,000 and accept a ban of at least five years from the securities business.

Two months later, his lawyers called to tell him of the first breakthrough in his *qui tam* lawsuit. CoreStates Financial Corp. of Philadelphia agreed to pay $3.7 million to settle Lissack's case and all other related federal charges against Meridian Capital Markets, which it had acquired two years earlier. The lawsuit said Meridian defrauded the federal government through yield burning in more than a hundred transactions involving advance refundings totaling approximately $357 million between 1992 and 1995.

The news was particularly encouraging because the Justice Department, the SEC, and the IRS had all agreed to the settlement. Lissack wasn't the only one who was glad at the outcome—the issuers of those bonds were relieved to learn that the resolution included an IRS agreement to not challenge their tax-exempt status. Other investment banks pored over the settlement documents, trying to decide whether it would be cheaper to continue the fight or to try for a similar result. But the answer wasn't all that obvious. The settlement did not say what the federal agencies had determined was a "fair" markup on the Treasuries. It gave no hint of how much the government might consider enough to settle similar charges against other banks.

What the CoreStates settlement made crystal clear was that the time had come for the investment banks to take Lissack's lawsuit seriously. The major dealers in the muni bond market formed a joint defense group. They each had different attorneys, but all were from New York's top law firms, and they agreed to share information in support of their common goal. The lineup facing Phillips & Cohen and the firm's understaffed government allies comprised an all-star team of legal talent: former prosecutors, former Supreme Court clerks, even a onetime head of enforcement for the SEC.

Meanwhile, in California, Lazard had used similar resources to drag out its fight against Lissack's *qui tam* LAMTA lawsuit for three years. The bank was represented by Wachtell, Lipton, Rosen & Katz, one of Wall Street's most aggressive, successful, and rich law firms. In 1997, Wachtell had sent the LAMTA a long, carefully detailed response to the charges against Lazard. It laid out the complexities of the muni bond transactions, explaining Lazard's profits in seemingly rational terms.

When Lissack read the letter, he scoffed. It was wrong from beginning to end, he said, packaged in jargon that could be translated only by an insider, a classic example of how the banks had been able to get away with their scam for so many years.

Phillips & Cohen spent thousands of hours preparing legal briefings and arguments, taking depositions, reviewing and analyzing hundreds of thousands of pages of documents. It brought in a local firm to help coordinate the case in Los Angeles. It invested nearly half a million dollars on a custom-designed, computerized document retrieval system. Erika Kelton led the effort to assemble a detailed, lucid chronology of every step in one Lazard-LAMTA transaction. Over hundreds of pages, the lawyers laid out the dates and content of all correspondence, phone calls, meetings, contracts, and trades.

A trial date was set, but six weeks before it was to begin, Lazard requested that both sides meet with a mediator in San Francisco. LAMTA delegates attended along with Phillips & Cohen attorneys. The mediator asked each side to send him a statement of the case and documents supporting its position, setting a limit of just one day for the negotiation. If no settlement was agreed to by five o'clock that afternoon, the case would go to trial as scheduled.

The opposing teams were assigned to separate rooms in the downtown office building. The mediator went back and forth between the two, telling each side the weaknesses of its case and the amount its opponent considered to be an acceptable settlement. He wasn't above using florid theatrics to bring the two sides together, sometimes appearing calm one minute, then the next abruptly interrupting an attorney with a dismissive, "I know that." In another change-up, he would berate an attorney for a legal argument, then suddenly reverse his tone in a show of sympathy. It was a long day. As it crept along toward night, past the five o'clock deadline, the bank's attorneys offered to settle for $3 million, which was roughly the amount that Lazard had made on the transaction.

They all knew that if the case went to trial and a jury found the bank liable for yield burning, Lazard would be required by law to pay three times what it had stolen. In addition, LAMTA had damage claims because Lazard had breached its duties as LAMTA's financial advisor. The LAMTA team was aiming for the triple damages, and counting on the bank's uncertainty over the additional punitive liability, which was potentially massive, to tip the mediation in its favor. "My lawyers tell me I have an excellent case," the LAMTA representative told the mediator. "We won't take one penny less than nine million."

The endless rounds continued up and down the hall. Finally, just before eight o'clock that night, the LAMTA representative told the mediator there was no point in dragging this out any longer. If LAMTA couldn't get what it had come for through mediation, it could do even better with a jury. It was time to pack up and head to court. The mediator made one more circuit. This time he returned with Lazard's agreement to pay $9 million.

Phillips, Kelton, and the LAMTA officials were ecstatic. Not only had they won a major recovery, but they felt that this victory might provide a template and a new motive strong enough to persuade the Justice Department to at last join Lissack's much larger federal *qui tam* case and to take an active role.

They would never get all they hoped for. After Kelton and Phillips returned to Washington, the firm sent numerous formal requests to the U.S. Attorney's Office in Manhattan, asking it to request materials from the banks in order to develop evidence. But rather than seizing on the momentum of the Lazard settlement, the Justice Department was trapped in its own inertia. Despite repeated urgings to be as aggressive against the other investment banks as Phillips & Cohen had been against Lazard in California, Justice continued to look the other way. The requests were ignored.

Kelton expressed the firm's frustration in a letter to the U.S. Attorney's Office. "We understand that the Justice Department has received documents collected and developed by the SEC in the course of its investigation," she wrote. "We believe, however, that it is not sufficient to rely entirely on those materials for the False Claims Act matter. It is, therefore, up to the Justice Department and relator to investigate each defendant's yield-burning practices." Still there was no response.

So it was left to the SEC to bring the case to its conclusion. One by one, the commission pressured the investment banks to come to the negotiating table to settle the yield-burning charges and put the case behind them, but without anywhere near the leverage it would have had if Justice had participated as well. The banks all balked and grumbled, but when they dutifully fell in line it was likely with a secret sense of relief. In April 1999, Lazard paid $11 million to settle Lissack's lawsuit and related federal charges. Seven months later BT Alex. Brown paid $15.3 million. The biggest settlement came in April 2000, when seventeen banks paid a total of $140 million to the federal government. Included were the best-known names on Wall Street: Salomon Smith Barney, PaineWebber, Goldman Sachs, Merrill Lynch, Lehman Brothers, Morgan Stanley Dean Witter.

By the end of that year, after the final defendants in the case settled, yield-burning recoveries by the federal and some state governments totaled more than $200 million.

Using money from his multimillion-dollar reward, Lissack endowed an academic chair in social responsibility and personal ethics at his alma mater, Williams College. Except for a certain pride in being known as "the man Wall Street loves to hate," he was glad to shut the door on the past and get on with his new life.

On balance, Lissack and his attorneys had good reason to be pleased with the results. But they all knew—and so did the Department of Justice—that if the banks had settled on the same terms that the law firm had achieved in California, the amount would have been nearer to a billion.

When Congress amended the False Claims Act in 1986, many opponents predicted that whistle-blowers and their attorneys would be freeloaders who would seek rewards for little more than the filing of a lawsuit. In this case, it was Lissack and his attorneys who had done the heavy lifting, and the Department of Justice that had been the easy rider.

SEVENTEEN

LET ME COUNT THE WAYS

I n the decade following enactment of the False Claims Act amendments, government contractors—initially the defense industry and
then joined by the health care industry—constantly tried to weaken
or kill the law through Congress and the courts. Almost from the filing of
the first case, *qui tam* attorneys had been aware of the ultimate threat to
the law. If the Supreme Court found the whistle-blower provisions of the
act to be unconstitutional, *qui tam* cases could no longer be brought and all
of the enormous investment by whistle-blowers and their lawyers in ongoing cases would be lost in an instant. The defense industry had recognized that same possibility, and had been working overtime to challenge
the law on constitutional grounds in cases around the country. The Justice
Department was quick to offer moral support to the attackers.

In 1989, as head of DOJ's Office of Legal Counsel, William Barr wrote
a memo arguing that the *qui tam* provisions were indeed unconstitutional
because they violated the constitutional separation of powers. According
to Barr, Congress could not authorize a *qui tam* relator to perform a function reserved for the executive branch. In addition, Barr said, relators lacked
the legal standing necessary to bring lawsuits. Two years later President
George H. W. Bush appointed Barr attorney general. As a result, the Justice Department would not defend the law in court.

Qui tam attorneys around the country worked together to spot the
brushfires, sharing legal briefs and research to win all of the early challenges brought before federal district courts. However, in 1993, one such
attack threatened to become a conflagration.

A motion filed by Boeing, and joined by such other industry giants
as Hughes, Lockheed, Rockwell, Litton, Northrop, and the Aerospace In-
dustries Association of America, raised Barr's arguments in a Los Angeles
court. The lower court ruled in favor of the law, but when the Ninth Circuit

U.S. Court of Appeals agreed to review that ruling, the stakes were suddenly raised. The Ninth Circuit covered a huge part of the country, including California, where many defense contractors had plants. The court's decision would directly affect all other cases in that area and would influence decisions by other circuit courts on *qui tam* cases nationwide. A victory by the defense industry would encourage further challenges to the law and would greatly increase the chance that the Supreme Court would agree to rule on its constitutionality. Because the Supreme Court had a track record of limiting the ability of Congress to empower individuals to bring lawsuits for the public benefit, there was real concern that the *qui tam* provisions could be struck down.

Phillips and other *qui tam* lawyers scrambled to help marshal the legal forces to answer the attack. Phillips's firm drafted a brief on the background of the law to aid the court's deliberations. After the Justice Department refused to defend the act, Senator Grassley persuaded the U.S. Senate, in an unusual move, to submit a brief in support of the law. By the time the case actually reached the Ninth Circuit, Bill Clinton had been elected president and Barr had been replaced as attorney general. His successor, Janet Reno, wrote a letter to the court refuting Barr's memo and making clear that it did not reflect the department's views.

That September, the Ninth Circuit ruled against Boeing and in favor of the relator, specifically declaring the *qui tam* provisions to be constitutional. One of the reasons that whistle-blowers do have standing to sue under the law, the judges said, was the "stress, anxiety, and mental anguish" they face from fear of being fired or otherwise punished by their employers.

It was an important victory, but the battle was not over. Predictably, Boeing appealed that decision as well, and so the case was headed to the Supreme Court after all.

The wait for the court's decision on whether to review Boeing's appeal dragged on for a long, nervous year. If such a review was granted, it would mean that a majority of the justices felt the *qui tam* provisions probably were unconstitutional, which would cast a black cloud over all such cases during the many months before there could be any ruling on the case itself. No defendants would want to settle any cases while there was a chance the Supreme Court would throw out the law. And whistle-blowers and their attorneys would be reluctant to risk wasting time and money in bringing new lawsuits.

Phillips had focused for the past ten years on this law, and all of his firm's pending cases would be affected. Predictably, he was anxious about the outcome. On the first Tuesday of every October, the Supreme Court commences its new term with an announcement of which cases it will review of the hundreds of petitions received since the end of the previous term in June. On that morning in October 1994, thirteen months after the decision by the Ninth Circuit, John Phillips and Mary Louise Cohen happened to be on Capitol Hill, attempting to counteract the latest lobbying efforts by industry to weaken the law. The Supreme Court clerk would not accept calls before ten o'clock. On the stroke of the hour, just after leaving one of those meetings, Phillips picked up a telephone. He could feel his heart pounding as he punched in the number, and he spoke with careful precision when he identified the case to the clerk. There was a moment's delay, and then the clerk replied, "Cert denied."

"Yes!" Phillips shouted, startling Cohen and several passersby in the hallway. People from surrounding offices came rushing out to see what the excitement was about. The clerk's response meant that the Supreme Court had decided not to review the case. The circuit court ruling stood. For the moment, at least, the cloud had passed.

Later, when Phillips and Cohen left the Senate Judiciary Committee office after meeting with staff members in support of the act, they happened to intersect with a group of lobbyists for GE who were on their way in to pitch amendments to weaken the law's *qui tam* provisions. The lobbyists apparently were not yet aware of the Supreme Court's decision, and there was no exchange of information as the opponents went their separate ways. Phillips knew the outcome was only a temporary reprieve, that until the highest court in the land clearly stated whether or not the *qui tam* provisions were constitutional, industry attacks on the law would continue. But beneath his calm demeanor, he was exultant.

The Supreme Court wasn't the only avenue of attack on the law. Through the years, industry had tried to convince Congress to weaken or repeal the whistle-blower parts of the act. Perhaps the strongest attack launched on Capitol Hill came in 1998. After extensive lobbying by the American Hospital Association, Representative Bill McCollum, a Republican from Florida, introduced a bill that would create exemptions for fraud by health care providers. It had bipartisan support, with 201 members signing on as cosponsors. A parallel bill was introduced in the Senate by Senators Thad Cochran, a Republican from Mississippi, and Ernest "Fritz" Hollings, a Democrat from South Carolina.

In an attempt to garner congressional support for the bill, McCollum and the AHA related stories from legislators' respective states and districts about the heavy-handed and often clumsy enforcement of the False Claims Act by the Justice Department. "But the horror stories," Grassley later said, ". . . had no bearing on what the AHA peddled as the solution—gutting the False Claims Act."

McCollum and the association characterized the proposed changes in the law as innocuous. In reality, the bill would have greatly limited the use of the False Claims Act against the health care industry for Medicare fraud. Providers would have faced no liability if the government loss from the fraud was 10 percent or less of the provider's total billings or if they were in "substantial compliance" with their compliance plan, even if they were defrauding Medicare of millions. One provision would have deleted the 1986 standards of deliberate ignorance and/or reckless disregard of the falsity of information submitted to the government, and substituted the requirement that the defendant have actual knowledge. Because actual knowledge is much harder to prove, the change would have opened the door to the "ostrich defense," in which the pretense of ignorance can become a license to steal. The biggest change the legislation proposed was to make it more difficult for the government and whistle-blower to prove fraud by raising the standard of proof from the "preponderance of evidence," as is required in all civil cases, to the much more difficult to prove "clear and convincing" evidence, which is required in criminal cases.

Grassley was outraged by the proposed legislation and the AHA's tactics. "The issue," he said, "is the integrity of the government's present and future efforts to stop widespread fraud, waste, and abuse against taxpayer-funded programs."

With Grassley and Congressman Howard Berman leading the fight on Capitol Hill, Taxpayers Against Fraud helped organize grassroots opposition and sent information to the media. It banded together with various nonprofit organizations that cared strongly about stopping Medicare fraud, such as the National Council of Senior Citizens, to run newspaper and magazine ads about the attack on the law. ("Remember when Congress used to be against Medicare fraud?" asked one.) Dozens of newspapers around the country ran editorials opposing the legislation.

Once legislators began to understand that the supposedly innocuous bill would actually neutralize the False Claims Act as a weapon against fraud by health care providers, support for the bill dropped and it died. Grassley called it an "unconscionable assault" on the law and warned that "future attacks on the False Claims Act are undoubtedly around the corner."

The case that actually produced a long-awaited opinion on the matter reached the Supreme Court the following year. In 1999, the court agreed to review a *qui tam* lawsuit brought by a former employee of the Vermont Agency of Natural Resources. Jonathan Stevens accused the agency of exaggerating the time its workers spent on federally funded environmental projects in order to get more money for the state. The agency's potential liability in the case was $25 million, more than its annual budget. Vermont argued that states cannot be sued under the False Claims Act because of the sovereignty granted them in the Constitution.

The case had wide ramifications. At the time there were several outstanding *qui tam* cases in which whistle-blowers were suing state hospitals for defrauding Medicare. If the justices ruled against Stevens, those cases would be thrown out, and whistle-blowers could not bring any new ones against state hospitals, no matter how egregious the fraud.

With so much riding on the outcome, the law—and Stevens—needed a litigator with a good track record at arguing cases before the Supreme Court. The job called for a highly sophisticated legal mind capable of retaining vast amounts of legal research in order to respond to whatever questions the justices might raise. The lawyer would have to think quickly and be a thorough student of every opinion and argument of the court. The Supreme Court is the most closely watched stage in the legal world; the nine justices routinely intimidate any attorneys approaching the bench with stars in their eyes, and quickly make fools of those who arrive improperly prepared. Stevens's Vermont counsel agreed to forgo the rare opportunity to appear before the Supreme Court. Phillips persuaded Taxpayers Against Fraud to hire Theodore B. Olson, an experienced, highly respected lawyer who had successfully argued many cases before the Supreme Court, and who met all the required criteria to the letter.

At first it seemed that the outcome would affect only *qui tam* cases brought against state agencies. Then, in a surprise move ten days before oral arguments were scheduled, the Supreme Court expanded the scope of the case by ordering the parties to file briefs responding to this question: Does a private person have standing under Article III of the Constitution to sue for fraud against the government? At last, the long-sidestepped issue was on the table.

With the court itself questioning the constitutionality of *qui tam* lawsuits, Phillips again faced the very real possibility that his practice would be destroyed in an instant. The millions of dollars the firm had invested in existing cases would be worthless. The government would be able to continue pursuing the suits, but any money recovered would go only to the U.S. Treasury. The whistle-blowers would not get a dime, and neither would their attorneys. Careers would be ensured or ruined, fortunes preserved or destroyed—all with one court decision. And the government would retain or lose its strongest weapon for fighting fraud.

There were two legal issues involved in the Vermont case. One was whether states were protected by their sovereignty from federal lawsuits. The other issue was "standing," or the question of who has the right to go to court to sue. Justice Antonin Scalia had already authored a series of decisions on cases involving so-called citizen lawsuits, based on laws allowing private individuals to sue a company on behalf of the public for violating environmental laws. Those earlier decisions had narrowed the definition to allow citizen lawsuits only in instances where the person's interest was different from that of the public at large. An individual could sue a company for violating the Clean Water Act if it was polluting a creek in that individual's backyard, for example, but it couldn't sue the company for polluting the city's drinking water. Those decisions had made clear that protecting the public's interest was the job of the government. Opponents of the False Claims Act now argued that the same narrow definition should apply to *qui tam* lawsuits.

Scalia and the more conservative justices, however, had often indicated strong support for the doctrine of original intent, or what the founding fathers meant for the Constitution to cover. The concept of allowing a private citizen to sue on behalf of the government extended back to English common law. That history offered a solid, legal basis for a convincing argument in support of the law.

The First Continental Congress incorporated the concept in at least six *qui tam* statutes it enacted to collect penalties and/or forfeitures for certain illegal acts, such as avoidance of liquor import duties. All of those laws authorized private individuals, then called informers, to bring lawsuits and to share in the recovery with the government. The *qui tam* provisions of the False Claims Act were in effect a modern version of laws far older than the country and that had been practiced by signers of the Constitution.

The judges held oral arguments on November 29, 1999. "I guess we've had some form of *qui tam* suits authorized by Congress since the earliest days, haven't we?" asked Justice Sandra Day O'Connor. A few minutes later, Chief Justice William Rehnquist spoke. Given that the First Congress, which had a number of members from the Constitutional Convention, enacted a *qui tam* law, he asked, wouldn't that mean it thought the law was constitutional? The questions suggested the two justices thought that the *qui tam* provisions met the criteria for "original intent."

Six months of uncertainly slowly drifted by. On May 22, 2000, Phillips got a call in his office from Olson. His tone was subdued. He told Phillips, with whom he had earlier discussed the case, that he had just gotten the Supreme Court's decision. They had lost the case. The state's sovereign immunity had prevailed; Stevens was not allowed to sue a Vermont agency in a federal court. The ruling ended strong cases Phillips's firm had brought against state hospitals that had defrauded Medicare of tens of millions of dollars. The money the firm had invested in those lawsuits was lost as well. Phillips held his breath, waiting for the second shoe to drop.

On the far more important issue, Olson went on, the court upheld the constitutionality of the *qui tam* provisions of the False Claims Act. Relieved and grateful, Phillips slowly exhaled. This outcome was as good as whistle-blowers and their attorneys could have hoped for: The Supreme Court had shut the door on the arguments that had dogged the law for over a decade. The False Claims Act was stronger than ever.

For Phillips, it also meant that the biggest false claims case in history—a giant, complex, high-risk lawsuit in which his firm had already invested millions—was still in play.

EIGHTEEN

ROCKY MOUNTAIN LOW

I n the late 1960s, a young surgeon from Tennessee named Tommy Frist, Jr., found himself at a crossroad. Just out of the air force, he had returned to his hometown of Nashville and was trying to decide what to do next with his life. He came from a medical family, but he was also powerfully attracted to the world of big business. His cardiologist father was associated with a hospital that was for sale, so Tommy suggested that they use it to start a profit-making chain, based on the model of the Holiday Inn hotels. A group of hospitals, he reasoned, would have greater purchasing power and would be able to share resources, lowering costs. His father agreed. In 1968, Thomas Frist Junior and Senior joined with Kentucky Fried Chicken cofounder Jack Massey and another local entrepreneur, Henry Hooker, to form Hospital Corporation of America (HCA).

At the time, for-profit hospitals were a relative rarity. Most hospitals were tax-exempt entities owned by churches and civic organizations and were designed to serve their communities rather than private investors. The idea of a hospital's being in it for the money was anathema to the nonprofit majority. Besides violating a long tradition of selflessness, it was feared by some critics that investor-owned hospitals would skim the cream of potential patients, treating the affluent ones who could pay the bills while turning away the poor.

Wall Street, by contrast, liked the concept from the start. When the Frists' company went public the following year, the stock price jumped from $18 per share to $46 on opening day. The company grew fast, acquiring old hospitals and building new ones in response to shifting population needs, primarily in the South. For a fee, HCA also managed hospitals owned by others. The concept grew as well. By 1971, there were thirty-eight investor-owned hospital chains, all hoping to cash in on the model of the Frists' success.

Even before Tommy Frist's brainstorm, a crisis had been brewing in American health care. In 1965, the federal government had created two new programs: Medicare assured health care for the elderly, and Medicaid shared the cost of care for low-income patients with the states. Because Medicare reimbursed hospitals for their costs of treating Americans over sixty-five, health care providers soon came to view the program as a blank check. Hospitals and doctors had an incentive to develop all sorts of schemes that would increase costs, because their own incomes rose in direct proportion. The American Medical Association had strongly opposed creation of Medicare, saying it would lead to "socialized medicine." Instead, it proved to be a gold mine. Hospitals and doctors soon became the largest single customer of the Medicare program.

Medicare expenditures escalated rapidly throughout the 1970s, boosted by rapid inflation in the economy, increases in hospital expenses, and advances in medical care that relied on greater use of technology and medications. President Nixon and then President Carter each proposed measures to control the spiral, but it wasn't until President Reagan's first term, in 1983, that the federal government finally took decisive steps to curb the double-digit inflation in health care costs. The solution was a complete revision in the way Medicare and Medicaid paid health care providers for treating elderly patients. The programs shifted to a prospective payment system for most inpatient services and created the concept of diagnosis-related groups (DRGs) to determine fees. For each diagnosis, providers were paid a predetermined, fixed amount, no matter what the actual cost of treatment or length of hospital stay. This was done to encourage providers to figure out ways to cut their costs and treat Medicare and Medicaid patients in the most economically effective way. If the treatment cost less than the payment, the provider could keep the difference. Private health insurers quickly followed suit and instituted similar payment systems.

The new payment plan brought the runaway system under control. But it also raised concerns about the quality of care for hospitalized Medicare patients, because it contained incentives for hospitals to shorten stays and choose the least expensive—rather than the best—methods of treatment.

Some hospitals expanded into other health care–related businesses, consolidating control and improving economies of scale. But that wasn't the only way to increase revenue. Another was to game the system, maximizing claims in the few areas that Medicare and Medicaid reimbursed them for their actual costs, such as the direct costs of outpatient services to Medicare patients. The program would pay hospitals a percentage of the capital expenses associated with the treatment of Medicare patients, like the cost of a new hospital wing or the purchase of X-ray equipment. Claims for billions of dollars of these allowable expenses were contained in complex, often arcane "cost reports" prepared by accountants and filed with Medicare and Medicaid annually.

By the mid-1980s, HCA had become a giant in the industry. It owned or managed 366 acute-care hospitals, 28 psychiatric hospitals, and 27 hospitals overseas. But it too was beginning to feel the impact of new cost constraints imposed by the federal government and private insurers. The company's 1986 earnings were just half those of the previous year, and in early 1987 the company reported its first quarterly loss since 1970. With its stock price languishing, the family-run company was ripe for a takeover.

In April 1987, a health care lawyer named Richard Scott and two former industry executives made a friendly takeover offer, which CEO Tommy Frist and the HCA board quickly rejected. Two months later, in an effort to make a future takeover more difficult, Frist spun off 104 small, rural hospitals, generally regarded as HCA's least profitable, to form the independent HealthTrust Inc. The reorganization gave HCA a substantial new fund of cash to buy back stock and reduce debt, which helped boost its market value. A year later, HCA made another defensive move: Frist took the company private through a $5.1 billion leveraged buyout. To help pay the debt from the LBO, the hospital management side was sold as well, becoming Quorum Health Group. The new entity's CEO was a former HCA executive. Overnight, Quorum became the nation's largest hospital management company.

A year after Quorum was formed, the company was approached by North Valley Hospital in the town of Whitefish, in the northeast corner of Montana. The hospital's administrator had decided to move on, and the board was considering a change to a management company.

The director of fiscal services at North Valley was named Jim Alderson. Both he and his wife, Connie, had grown up in Montana, and Jim had graduated from the state university in 1969. After six months of active duty in the National Guard, Jim had gone to work with the accounting firm of Arthur Anderson in Denver. It was a good job, but after three years and a new baby he and Connie decided Colorado was just too far from home. In January 1973, the three Aldersons moved back to Montana.

A promised job didn't materialize, but Jim was a certified public accountant, so he decided to open his own firm. He worked alone for two years, then took in a partner in 1975. Five years later, he sold out the tax and bookkeeping part of his business and reduced his focus to financial statement audits. Three of his clients were hospitals, and he developed a particular expertise in the auditing of health care accounting.

In early 1984, the director of fiscal services at North Valley Hospital in Whitefish died after a brief illness. The hospital was one of Jim's audit clients, and a director asked if he would take the position and work for North Valley full-time. Jim and Connie talked it over. They wouldn't have to move. The job would require less travel and would provide a good, stable income and a retirement plan, as well as a number of other things that didn't come with being self-employed. They agreed he should accept the offer. He started that February.

It turned out to be the right move for both Jim and his employer. North Valley became known as one of the most successful small hospitals in the state, with good profitability, high-quality care, and a positive image in the community. When Jim was hired, North Valley was run by Brim & Associates, a hospital management company, but in 1987 the board decided to switch to an on-staff administrator. Three years later, early in the summer of 1990, the administrator left for another job, and the board decided to once again hire a management company to run the hospital. It interviewed a number of prospects, including Quorum Health Resources out of Tennessee.

Jim's first glimpse of the future came just before the sales pitch to the board, when three Quorum executives were brought briefly to his office. They were introduced as Eric Fox, district vice president; Will Fahlberg in marketing; and Clyde Eder, another district vice president in charge of seven regional hospitals. Dropping into Jim's office for a kind of courtesy preview of what they were going to present, one of them commented that Quorum would save the hospital 30 percent on its purchasing. Jim asked, "Is that thirty percent off retail or off what we are already paying? Because we're already paying wholesale." None of them replied, but the cordiality disappeared in an instant from all three faces. The expression that took its place said clearly enough that their stop in his office was a formality, and that Jim was definitely off on the wrong foot with that kind of challenge.

In the boardroom, on the hospital's lower level, the three pitchmen were seated at the same long, horseshoe table as their audience, which included about eighteen of the hospital's directors and managers. Looking around the windowless, well-lighted room, Jim thought how easy it would have been for an outsider to tell the two sides apart. The Quorum executives were poised, self-assured, and—the phrase went through Jim's mind more than once during their pitch—dressed for the kill. Their attitude suggested that they viewed the contract with North Valley Hospital as already in the bag.

The presentation was well rehearsed and professional. Still uneasy after the exchange in his office, Jim checked frequently on the reactions of the others in the room. Clearly the board was favorably impressed by the same slickness that Jim was beginning to find off-putting, even alarming.

Jim fought his rush to an early judgment. Perhaps his apprehension was based on nothing more than style. But just as he was making a silent resolution to hear the three pitchmen out and be objective, he was astonished to hear the same Quorum executive repeat the very claim that Jim had questioned just an hour earlier: "We'll save you thirty percent on your purchasing."

It couldn't possibly be true. North Valley was already on a national purchasing contract, and the difference between that and Quorum's leverage couldn't have been more than 1 or 2 percent. It was also apparent that this false argument was central to the Quorum strategy for selling the contract to the board. The management fee alone was $190,000 per year, and the salaries of the CEO and CFO were passed through on top of that. But what the three men were saying was that it really wouldn't cost North Valley anything. First, they were experts at Medicare reimbursement and knew ways to make the hospital a lot of money in that area. And second, they could save 30 percent on purchasing.

It was obvious the board was enamored with the presentation, which culminated with a tape of W. Edwards Deming, the guru of total quality management who had helped Japan rebuild after World War II. Copies of Deming's book were distributed, and one of the speakers said it reflected exactly the Quorum philosophy.

As the North Valley CFO, Jim realized that the repetition of the claim of a 30 percent savings placed him in a potentially disastrous conflict between the hospital's interests and his own. If he remained silent, both he and the Quorum visitors would know that he was going along with the lie. If he spoke up and Quorum got the contract anyway, which seemed a near certainty, he wouldn't be going anywhere; the new management would see to it that his career at North Valley came to an abrupt end.

The hospital's trustees were all outsiders. The eclectic mix included a banker, a school principal, an attorney, a logger, a county commissioner, and a district judge. But the member the pitchmen focused on was the board chairman, a retired pharmacist who had been a client of Jim's in his CPA practice. Eder would call him "Mister Chairman" and say to him, "Hey, Boss." Jim looked around the room. He was friendly with all the board members, particularly the prior administrator and the district judge, and he could tell that most of the others also saw what was happening.

But they had to make a decision. None of them wanted to go back to Brim & Associates, and Quorum was the only candidate they ever really interviewed. Jim did his best to be objective. If he hadn't known any of the underlying facts and had just sat there at the presentation as a board member, he'd have to admit Quorum was impressive. The three officials said their company was the nation's biggest and best, and that with its purchasing and reimbursement expertise Quorum would increase hospital revenues to more than pay for its management fee. In the end, that was all the board really wanted to look at.

Quorum took over management of North Valley Hospital on August 1, 1984. Jim didn't know exactly what to expect from the new hierarchy, but neither did he feel threatened by the change. He had been at the hospital six and a half years, and had been assured the board wanted him to stay. The CEO and CFO would be Quorum employees, and he knew there would be a new administrator. In the interim the former job was filled by Quorum's regional vice president, Clyde Eder. On the day the new higher-ups began, a Quorum manager came into Jim's office and told him they would give him a ninety-day evaluation to see if he met standards as a CFO. This evaluation period was to start on September 1, 1990.

As director of fiscal services and chief financial officer during the previous administration, Jim was responsibile for cost reporting, among many other things. After each fiscal year, hospitals submitted cost reports to Medicare that laid out the hospitals' capital expenses and the proportion of those costs that were attributable to treating Medicare patients. The federal program then reimbursed the hospitals for that amount, which was a major source of their revenue. The system depended on providers to be accurate and honest, since the government, with its limited resources, could audit only a small percentage of the filings.

Back in July it had been apparent the Quorum team had been using its implicit criticisms of the work done by Alderson and Brim on cost reports as a lever to gain the account. But two months later, no one at North Valley had yet heard how Quorum planned to improve on the previous cost-reporting system. Jim had his suspicions. For one thing, he was sure that one way Quorum was going to contain costs was through layoffs. Typically, 50 percent of a hospital's overhead is salary and benefits. He was also beginning to suspect that the ninety-day evaluation was a setup—that one of the first jobs Quorum planned to eliminate would be his own.

Jim's evaluation period started September 1, the Friday before the Labor Day weekend. The day passed like any other. Despite the holiday, Jim came in the following Monday to get together the numbers for Jack Schisel, the consultant from Brim, who was due in on Tuesday to prepare the cost report for the year ended June 30, the end of Brim's tenure. Clyde Eder was still the acting administrator, but he also managed seven other hospitals. He was living in Roseville, California, near the Quorum regional office, and would fly up to Whitefish a couple of times a month. One of his visits was on that Tuesday, September 5. Jim and Jack were working downstairs on the report, in a windowless room just a few doors away from Jim's office. That afternoon Eder poked his head in the door, then walked into the room as though his visit there were just a happenstance. He had never met Jack, so Jim introduced him and explained what they were doing. Clyde was friendly and started off with small talk. Then, almost as an afterthought, he asked Jim, "Do you guys do just one cost report?"

Jim thought he was asking if they did one for Medicare and one for Medicaid—although that was the kind of thing he would have expected Eder to know. "Yes, we just do the one. Medicaid actually does theirs off the Medicare report; they just plug in their own numbers."

"No, I mean for going into Medicare," Eder said. "Do you prepare just one cost report?"

Jim looked at Jack for help, but it was obvious that he was equally at a loss. Shaking his head, Jim asked, "What do you mean?"

"Well," Eder said, "Quorum always does two." He was still friendly, but there was a hint of patronage in his tone. He explained that Quorum did one that it called an "aggressive" report that was designed to maximize Medicare reimbursement to the client hospital; that was the one it sent in to the government. And then it did a "reserve" one that was more conservative in its claims and calculated reimbursement based on a closer adherence to the regulations. That way, if the government audited a Quorum client, the company and the hospital had an idea of how much they would owe. The amount of the differential was accounted for in a reserve fund.

It was as simple as that. There had been nothing casual about this visit after all. Eder had come to Whitefish at the start of Jim's evaluation for no other purpose than to initiate him into the mysteries of how Quorum earned its money. Eder was telling Jim that Quorum's accounting system involved what amounted to two sets of books. Clearly, Jim was being invited to join his new employers on the other side of the abyss.

For a moment the situation reminded Jim of the days when he was practicing as a tax accountant. Whitefish was a small town, and sometimes he learned more than he wanted to know about his clients' secrets. One time, a small businessman asked him to do a Schedule C without showing the depreciation expense. The client had looked slightly embarrassed, explaining that he wanted to take it to the bank to borrow money. Jim told him that he wouldn't be a party to it and to leave his office. Other times clients would ask him to evaluate a business they were thinking of purchasing, and he would insist on seeing the seller's tax returns. "See what they paid a tax on," he'd say. "They can tell you anything on a financial statement. A tax return has to be the truth."

But there was nothing hesitant or tentative about Eder's comments. He was simply letting Jim and Jack know how the big guys played the game. He looked like an ex–football player, stocky but fit, with slicked-back hair and a cocksure self-confidence that he frequently used to intimidate those around him.

"Look," Jim answered, "June 30, 1990 is the end of Brim's management contract, and I'm not going to do two cost reports for that period. You guys, however you do it, go ahead. But I will not do it for my year."

Eder didn't appear to have expected that response. He glowered at Jim, muttered a couple of remarks about team players, then quickly shifted the topic to the small talk that had opened their exchange and left without arguing the point. Despite his initial reaction, he didn't act as though it were a real problem.

The moment he was gone, Jack Schisel turned to Jim with an expression of open astonishment. "Boy," he said "that sounds like fraud to me."

Jim nodded, staring at the empty doorway. After a moment he looked back at his colleague. "Me too," he said.

Back in August, shortly after Quorum had taken over at North Valley, Jim Alderson had been told to make his accounting system conform to the management company's bookkeeping system. He asked why all Quorum's accounting manuals had another firm's name on them. The first few times he asked, the question was brushed aside, but eventually Eric Fox, one of the triad who had pitched the account, offered an explanation. The other company, HCA, had started in 1968 as Hospital Corporation of America. It had two divisions: the "owned side," which ran HCA hospitals, and the "managed side," HCA Management Services, which ran hospitals owned by others. The divisions worked in tandem, and utilized the same accounting software, which was run through the HCA accounting system. In 1989 the company spun off HCA Management Services as an independent company, and it became Quorum.

When Fox was finished, Jim had asked, "So, it's all the same employees?"

Fox had nodded. "One day we were HCA Management employees. The next day we're Quorum employees. So that's why Quorum doesn't have its own accounting manuals."

Jim and Jack Schisel continued their work on the cost report for the rest of Tuesday afternoon. Neither of them saw Clyde again before he flew back to California the following day. Two days later, Jim, Clyde Eder, Eric Fox, and the Quorum controllers, chief financial officers, and directors of financial services in Clyde's division flew to Juneau, Alaska, for a conference that included people from Quorum-managed hospitals in Idaho, California, Oregon, and Alaska. The event seemed designed in part to give everyone a chance to interact with their counterparts in the Quorum family and to develop a sense of community. There were work sessions on Friday at Bartlett Memorial Hospital, followed by a tour of the facilities. On Saturday they all went out on a chartered fishing boat for salmon.

Despite the doubts and premonition he brought with him, Jim was surprised to find himself having a good time. He liked most of the people he met, and he was glad for the chance to visit Alaska for the first time. He was especially pleased on the fishing trip to try his hand at something he had never done before. To his delight, he caught an enormous fish, weighing somewhere around forty pounds. He knew it was pure luck—out of twenty people, all fishing with identical equipment in the same place, he'd reeled in the whopper. Others congratulated him, and some even talked about skill and a "natural fisherman's touch." Jim would gladly have agreed with them, but he knew better.

While they were still at sea, Eric Fox came up and asked Jim how things were going. Jim grinned and answered, "Pretty good." He knew Fox was referring to more than just the fishing trip. Jim told him he was working hard to get everything done to close out the June 30 cost report and at the same time get everything hooked into the new Quorum accounting system. Fox seemed genuinely interested, and it was an encouraging, friendly exchange. But, for all the fun he was having, their conversation reminded him of the work that was waiting for him when he got back home.

They returned from the fishing trip on a bus that delivered them all to the Red Dog Saloon, a Juneau landmark that Jim had been anxious to say he had visited. But when Clyde invited everyone inside for a drink, some warning alarm went off and Jim had a powerful sense that he shouldn't accept. Everyone had had a couple of beers on the boat, and now there was something telling him to stay away. He had met an administrator from another Quorum hospital, and remembering that he hadn't seen him drinking with the others on the fishing trip, he asked him if he wanted to just walk around Juneau instead. It was a pleasant evening, and after a couple of hours of sightseeing, they wound up back in the Best Western at about nine o'clock.

Some of the others had already returned, but the same instinct that had kept Jim out of the saloon now urged him to the safety of his hotel room. He made it across the lobby, but Clyde Eder caught up with him just as he was getting onto the elevator. "I need to get together with you," Eder said.

He wasn't drunk, but it was clear he had been drinking. Even without Jim's other misgivings, he knew enough to stay out of job discussions under those circumstances. For an instant, it looked as though Eder wanted to talk that night, but Jim was enormously relieved when he said, "How about tomorrow morning for breakfast at eight? You and Eric and me."

Jim arrived at the dining room promptly at the appointed hour, and neither of the Quorum executives was there. Just as he was beginning to wonder if they had forgotten, Eric Fox showed up. Clyde Eder didn't arrive until eight-fifteen. "Sorry," he said, seating himself and snapping open the menu. "I was meeting with somebody else and got tied up."

Everybody ordered. In the time he had been alone with Eric, Jim had decided on a crab omelet. "You don't get seafood in Montana," he told the others.

Fox smiled encouragingly. Eder seemed distracted, and either didn't hear or didn't care. The waiter returned with their orders, and Jim had taken only a couple of bites when Eder's mood changed and his focus visibly returned to the present. "Well, Jim, there's no real easy way to say this, but we are going to be terminating your services. Things aren't working out, and we just feel it's in our best interests that we end the relationship."

At first, Jim said nothing. He looked at Eder until he had finished talking, then turned to Eric Fox, who must have known that this was coming. Jim sensed that unlike Eder, Fox felt bad about what was happening. They had gotten to know each other in the short time they had worked together, and Jim felt they had a good relationship. Fox returned Jim's look, but with an expression of careful neutrality; he never said a word through the whole exchange.

Eder seemed intent on carrying the conversation forward. "So," he said, with almost jovial curiosity, "what do you think you're going to do?"

In a way, the question was more surprising to Jim than being fired. "Jesus Christ, Clyde," he answered, "I don't know. Are you asking because you have something in mind?"

Eder pulled back, as though he hadn't expected his own question to be answered by another. "Well, would you consider any other Quorum openings?"

Suspecting this was just conversation, Jim questioned him again. "Do you have any other openings now?"

"No," Eder answered quickly. "We really don't."

"What kind of time frame are you looking at?" They all knew Jim was referring to his termination and not to some phantom future hope for another job with Quorum.

"Well, we want to get this done in sixty days. But I'll tell you what: You work up a severance package and give it to me, and I'll take it to the board for you. Just don't tell anybody. We've both got to keep this confidential, for the good of the hospital."

Jim only half listened to the rest of what Eder told him. After the comment about "the good of the hospital" to which Jim had given the past seven years of his life, all he could think was "What a great, slick, all-American guy." He looked down at the crab omelet that had been so delicious just a moment earlier. Now he was going to have to pay $8.25 for it, and if he took another bite he'd throw up. But he also knew it was going to make everything worse if he begged or tried to strike a deal. Instead, he said, "So what do you think is a typical severance? What are we looking at?"

Eder was back in his element. "I've seen them anywhere from two weeks to two months," he said. "You decide and give it to me and I'll take it to the board." This last was said with finality. This had been an exit interview, and now he was letting Jim know it was over.

After leaving the dining room, Jim stopped at the front desk for a piece of hotel stationery, to document where he was, then went up to his room and wrote down what had happened. He read it over a couple of times, put it in his briefcase, and then went outside for a walk. He felt half a world away from home and more alone than he had ever been in his life.

His flight was not scheduled to leave until one that afternoon. The salmon he had caught the day before was in a freezer at the hotel. After he packed he went down to retrieve it, then took the shuttle by himself out to the airport. When Eder arrived, Jim was surprised, in a detached, curious way, to find that his former boss had apparently decided they were no longer speaking. Fox was distant, but at least offered a courteous "Hi." The third Quorum executive was standoffish as well. Will Fahlberg was the marketing member of the team. Although Jim didn't know him as well as he did Fox, in the short time they had worked together he had gotten to like him, too. Now he realized that everyone had known he was going to get fired but him.

Jim walked over to the counter and asked the Delta agent for a box to in which pack his fish. When he held it up for her she raised her eyebrows and told him it wouldn't fit.

"Please say that louder," he asked. When she looked at him questioningly, he added, "I want everyone to know that my fish is so big it doesn't fit into the box."

She laughed. "Boy, your fish is so BIG it doesn't fit in the box!" Her voice carried all over the lounge. Some of the other fishermen from yesterday's trip laughed, and a couple even cheered. Clearly, not everyone had known after all.

After he had checked in for his flight, he found a pay telephone and called home. Connie had been sick, and he knew the news wouldn't make her feel any better, but he couldn't keep it from her. He told her he didn't know how it was all going to come out. Connie assured him that together they could handle it.

Later, when they all got off the airplane in Seattle to disperse to their various connecting flights, Jim noticed Clyde Eder talking on a pay telephone. He passed close enough to determine that it was business. Why would he be calling someone about work on a Sunday? It seemed incongruous, and the incident stuck in his mind.

When Jim got to Whitefish he was glad to see that Connie had sent the kids to pick him up at the airport. His daughter Jennifer, eighteen, had just started the University of Montana the week before, and his fourteen-year old son Justin had begun his freshman year of high school. Their mother had told them what had happened, and as they drove into town they asked what he was going to do. Jim said he didn't know. "We'll figure something out. I'm not above taking *anything*, but I can't tell you right now." A few minutes later, when they passed a Pizza Hut with a "Help Wanted" sign, Justin said, "Dad, you could be a deliveryman for Pizza Hut."

Back at the house, Jim sat down with the kids and laid out his income and living expenses. His job at North Valley had paid $48,000, which was pretty good for Whitefish. "Let's say I could make twenty thousand being a deliveryman. That's less than half what I make now, so it would mean cutting way back in our lifestyle." He also explained that he had been out of his CPA practice for six years and had not kept up with all the tax laws, so it would be tough to get back into that business. "Maybe the delivery job isn't all that bad an idea," he said. He wanted them to know how serious the situation was, because soon they would all be living in a new reality. But he also wanted to reassure them that they were all adaptable and could cope with whatever came their way.

Unknowingly, the incident had created a kind of family motto, a metaphor for taking life as it comes, even at its worst. Over the coming months and years, his children would face the family's disappointments and reversals with the same response, which he would hear again and again. "Dad," they would remind him, "there's always Pizza Hut."

Connie was still sick, but after the kids had gone to bed she stayed up with Jim, and they talked until two o'clock in the morning. When he told her that he had promised Clyde Eder that he would keep the news a secret, she responded, "You can't tell anyone you've been fired? That doesn't make sense."

"No, I guess it doesn't, but I gave my word."

Connie didn't say anything further on the subject, but she looked at her husband as though he had made a bad bargain for them all.

After they finally turned off the light, Jim still couldn't stop thinking about that promise. Why had he made it? Every doubt he ever had about himself came flooding in with the dark. Was he really that naive that he had willingly made an agreement to protect the very people who were now undoing his life? And was it a promise that served some legitimate purpose, or had it simply been a way of recruiting him as an unwilling passenger on Clyde Eder's power trip?

On Monday morning, he forced himself to get up and go to work. One of the first visitors to his office was the hospital chairman, the retired pharmacist whom Eder had played so successfully during the Quorum sales pitch. Jim was still his personal accountant, and although he had given up his private practice he had continued doing the chairman's tax returns and tax planning. He knew the man was still getting the VIP treatment from Quorum, including an invitation to corporate headquarters in Nashville.

"Hey, Jim," he said, all joviality, "I hear you caught a big fish up there in Juneau."

Jim had assumed from his manner that he didn't know about the firing, but this remark suggested something different. He smiled back and asked, "How did you hear that?"

"Clyde told me." Jim knew that Clyde was in California, and when he looked confused the chairman added, "He called me yesterday. From Seattle."

There was more talk about the fish, but it was hard for Jim to focus. He was far more concerned with what they *didn't* talk about. After all the years they had known each other, there was not a word about his being fired, not a hint of sympathy or regret. Jim tried his best to hold up his end of the conversation, but he had a hard time looking at his visitor. "You son of a bitch," he thought; "it's started."

Later that day, Jim decided the promise had been too one-sided. He called an old friend, the district judge who also served on the hospital board. "I just want you to know that while we were up in Juneau, I got fired as chief financial officer of the hospital. I guess I'm out of here in sixty days. I think the board should know that."

The judge listened, taking it in. His only comment came when Jim was finished. "Wow, that's a different version from what I heard."

The judge said the chairman had called him that morning, and although he'd said Jim was leaving, nothing at all had been mentioned about his being fired. Jim didn't want to ask a friend to compromise a confidence, so he didn't push for details. But it was starting to make sense. Eder was telling people that Jim had decided to quit, that he couldn't come up to Quorum standards and expectations and realized he was in over his head. Jim will leave, Eder was telling them, and we can bring in a Quorum person to make this thing work. But Jim wants some kind of a severance payout, and here's what he came up with.

Jim and Connie once more talked far into the night. The bottom line was that Eder had broken his end of the bargain, and now all bets were off. Eder had promised to keep the firing a confidence, but then he'd turned around and told the chairman Jim had quit before they'd even gotten all the way home, and the chairman in turn had told everyone else. On Tuesday morning, Jim called a meeting with all the hospital personnel with whom he had direct contact and told them the truth of what had happened in Alaska: He had been fired. It didn't take long for the phone calls to go down to Roseville. Clyde Eder was on a plane to Whitefish the following morning, and when he arrived in Jim's doorway, he was livid. "I need to see you in my office immediately."

They walked together down the hallway, and as soon as the door was shut Eder turned on Jim in a show of rage. "You said you would keep this confidential," he yelled, "and you broke that promise." He lowered his voice. "So you know what? You probably kissed off any chance of a severance."

Jim stood his ground. He said he knew that Eder had called the chairman while Jim had remained silent and that all the board members had been told a story that was totally different from what had happened.

Eder didn't seem at all fazed that Jim knew what he had done. "There are certain things that an administrator in my position has to keep the board chairman apprised of." But beyond this, he didn't appear to have anything left to say.

Jim went back to his office.

Two days later, he was summoned again, this time for a meeting with the executive committee of the board. Eder and the chairman were seated at the conference table, along with the vice chairman, the head of the finance committee, the personnel director, and the hospital's outside attorney. Someone shut the door, and Eder opened the meeting with a question. "Why are you telling people that I fired you?"

"Because you fired me."

"Jim, I did not say 'I fired you.'"

"No, you said you were terminating my services and it would take place within sixty days, and that I was to prepare a severance package, and that you had no other openings within Quorum where I could relocate. I interpret that as being fired."

This conversation didn't go much further than the earlier one. Jim was outnumbered six to one, and the hospital was represented by an attorney, while he was not. He went back and forth with Eder for a few minutes, but it began to sound like, "Did so," "Did not," and he decided to back away. "I have a totally different version of what happened, so I think I need to get representation." The hospital's attorney nodded in what appeared to be a combination of agreement and regret. "You're probably right."

"Clyde asked me to prepare a severance proposal and give it to him. Should I give it to you instead?" he asked the lawyer.

The head of the executive committee said, "Yes, why don't you give it directly to me."

Jim retained an attorney from a town fifteen miles away, and together they drafted the severance package. A local aluminum company had just gone through a leveraged buyout, and in its aftermath had reduced its workforce from eleven hundred to seven hundred employees. Using that as a guideline, Jim asked for five years of salary, or nearly $250,000, as his compensation for being fired. The board members' response was to invite him to discuss it in a formal meeting. There was some initial resistance to his bringing along his new attorney, but they finally agreed.

The day after he made his presentation of the facts, he received a letter. The board and Quorum were both reviewing his situation. He was not terminated. He could stay in his position until further notice. He would be informed as soon as a decision was made. It was signed by "Clyde Eder, Acting Administrator." When he finished reading the letter, Jim called Connie. "The guy who fired me has now written on behalf of the board to say he didn't fire me after all, and that I should keep right on working until they make up their minds about what they're going to do." They both laughed. Maybe there was some hope after all.

On the other hand, "maybe" wouldn't pay the mortgage or the new college tuition, and it promised nothing. Jim needed a little insurance. He called his friend Jack Schisel to ask if he knew of openings at any of the other Brim-managed hospitals. Even if there was a chance things could work out at Whitefish, Jack had told him he'd always considered Jim one of his best CFOs, and it would be good to have some options.

Jack sounded glad to hear from him, and said he thought the hospital in Dillon might be looking. The very next day, Jim got a call from the Dillon hospital's administrator. Could he come right down for an interview?

The exchange was encouraging, but Jim was suddenly overwhelmed with second thoughts. Whitefish was a kind of recreational and social Mecca, with mountains, a lake, golf courses, and all the amenities of the good life. Dillon, by comparison, was an agricultural town of cowboys and ranchers down in the southwestern corner of the state, sixty-five miles from Butte. There were no stoplights in the entire town. The closest McDonald's were sixty-five miles in one direction and a hundred fifty miles in the other.

"The worst time to look is when you're out of work," a friend told him. "You're on top, you're well thought of, so go down to Dillon and if they offer you the job, take it."

Jim wrestled with it for a day and a night, and then went down to Dillon for the interview. Paradoxically, he was a little disappointed that he liked what he saw. He really hit it off with the administrator, the people were friendly and intelligent, and the town had the same class of sports as Whitefish, Class A, so Justin could probably play on the high school teams. The hospital was in pretty good shape financially, with a building project that was backed by a bond issue. It looked like a good opportunity. Both sides agreed that the next step, if Jim decided to go ahead, would be a second interview, and this time he would bring along his wife so she could see the town.

Nearly half the drive from Whitefish was through the mountains, and the stretch from Missoula to Butte crossed a hundred fifty miles of wide-open prairies. About a hundred miles after that they turned south for the last fifty-eight miles to Dillon. On this second trip, that last leg felt like the longest fifty-eight miles of Jim's life. There was almost nothing there, just mile after mile of bare ranch land, not even any trees, with only an occasional car to break the monotony. Jim knew that the first Dillon exit off the interstate was bordered by sales lots and dismal industrial buildings containing farm equipment and agricultural supplies. He chose the second one, because it offered a more promising introduction to the town, running by the college and the hospital. They drove to the motel, then went out to dinner.

The next morning, when Connie dropped him off at the hospital, she said, "I don't know whether to wish you luck or not." But again, the interviews went well. The hospital plant seemed run-down, but his interview gave him more details about the bond issue and he was impressed by their ambitious plans. They had a good medical staff. Jim had let Jack Schisel fill them in on what had been going on at North Valley in Whitefish, so he didn't have to say anything himself about why he might be leaving.

Jim knew the hospital had five candidates, but the day after he got back to Whitefish he got a call from the administrator in Dillon. "You're the one I want. The job has been open for a while, and we're at the point where we need to make a decision. I'd like to have your answer within a week."

Jim managed to hold him off for twice that long before he finally said yes. Jim would take the job and commute back to Whitefish on weekends, with the plan to move his family to Dillon the following spring. He set a starting date of November 5, and then gave Quorum notice that he would be leaving North Valley on November 1. It wasn't going to be easy. The new job meant a $5,000 salary cut to $43,000, which would have to cover the cost of maintaining two households and the expense of the long and arduous commute.

His last day at North Valley was October 23. The hospital's new administrator had started three weeks earlier, and Jim's final workday was like walking on eggshells, with everyone wondering what was going on but no one willing to talk about it. He took his final week as vacation time, and used it to get ready for the move. Through an ad, he and Connie found an apartment that turned out to be in an old building. It was owned by the vice principal of the local high school, and when they arrived, the landlord took one look at them and said, "I'm sure you don't want this."

The apartment was one long, narrow room with space for a desk at one end, a bed at the other, and a couch in the middle. There was a small kitchen, and a bathroom with an old claw-foot tub, but no shower. The rent was $150 a month. Jim said, "I'll take it."

"Are you sure?"

"Yes, it's perfect."

They unloaded the trailer and Connie drove back to Whitefish. However fitfully, Jim realized he had started his new life.

Jim set up a schedule at Dillon by which he would work longer hours during the week and try to leave Friday at noon, which in good weather could get him into Whitefish at suppertime. Sometimes, when there was a basketball game between Dillon and Whitefish, he was able to meet up with Justin and take him back to Whitefish afterward. But as the days shortened, the snow started to get deeper, and there were nights when the temperature would drop to 40 degrees below zero. On Sunday afternoons, it got harder and harder to go back to Dillon, especially after Christmas. But they were all trying to tough it out.

One weekend in January, Jim was supposed to meet Justin in Whitefish for a basketball game. He had traded cars with his daughter because hers got better mileage. It was cold, and Jim's apartment did not come with a garage. On that day, it was 38 below, with a forty-mile-an-hour wind and a chill factor of 80 below. When he turned the key in the ignition, it didn't even click. He walked down the street to get a new battery. As he was putting it in, the nuts on the support bar snapped in the cold. He was able to replace them. But if the battery terminals broke, the trip would be off and he would be trapped in Dillon, in the cold and away from his family, for the weekend. He could work only about five minutes at a stretch before the cold would force him inside to warm up. It was painful, grueling work. After a long struggle he finally got back into the car and sat behind the wheel warming up the motor. He thought about where his life had brought him. Six months ago, he had been on top of the world: His daughter had graduated from high school as president of her class, his son was starting high school, his family knew everybody in town. Now he was barely existing in a $150-a-month apartment, changing the battery on a '77 Volkswagen Rabbit that he was driving to save gas. He put the car into gear and pulled out into the frozen blackness. He talked to himself for most of the long trip home.

In March, Connie and Justin moved down to Dillon. Jim had found a nice, older home in an established neighborhood for only $68,000, which they remodeled before moving in that April. In the meantime they all managed to squeeze into his small apartment. He bought a foldout hide-a-bed. It took up so much of the space, the only way they could manage was for everyone to go to bed at the same time.

Neither Connie nor the kids had ever questioned his decisions or suggested that any of them doubted his version of events, but it was obvious that they all wished everything had never happened. Connie, in particular, had a hard time letting it go. Often, with no provocation, she would ask how they could have fired Jim just nine days into a ninety-day review. Jim had recurrent thoughts of his own: They'd never even offered him five cents of severance. They'd hung him out to dry.

That spring, he called Jim Bartlett, a local attorney, and told him he felt that some of what had been done to him was really wrong. Bartlett agreed, and filed a wrongful discharge action on Jim Alderson's behalf against Quorum and the hospital. The suit listed two complaints: wrongful termination of employment and infliction of emotional distress.

It was a confusing period. During the long, solitary winter, even as his resentment grew, so did his uncertainty about why any of it had happened. One thing that particularly rankled was the accusation that he couldn't get along with people, in particular that he had conflicts with North Valley's director of nursing. In any hospital, the chief financial officer will not always see eye-to-eye with everyone. Jack Schisel was still telling him he was the best CFO in all of the ten Brim hospitals in Montana, and he seemed to mean it. He had always had a perfectly clean personnel file, and three weeks before he left he got a copy from the records department so he would be able to prove it. But when Bartlett subpoenaed that same file from the hospital as an exhibit in the lawsuit, there were a few surprises.

In the space of only ten days during Jim's final three weeks at the hospital, three negative reports—the only ones Jim had ever gotten in six and a half years—had been added to his file by Quorum's new administrator. One was about his request to attend a meeting for hospital CFOs put on by the government agency in charge of reimbursement policy. The administrator denied the request, saying Jim had too much work to do in becoming familiar with the Quorum method of doing things. Another write-up questioned his commitment because Jim had gone to one of Justin's freshman football games on a Friday afternoon—neglecting to mention that he had prepared for the event by working all day on Labor Day, or that he routinely put in many hours of uncompensated overtime. The third write-up was equally trivial and unfair. In none of these negative reports had the administrator ever sent a copy to Jim or advised him that anything new had been added to his file.

Jim frequently commuted to Whitefish to work on his wrongful termination case, but it left him physically exhausted. He would drive at night and early in the morning. Sometimes he would get back to Dillon after midnight, get a short night's sleep, and go to work the next day. Other times he would take vacation time to account for missed work, although he was able to work ten or twelve hours a day in some instances to make it up.

In the course of the lawsuit, Jim's lawyer asked Quorum to produce documents related to cost-report reserve practices. Up to that time, Jim's action against North Valley Hospital and Quorum had made no reference to the discussion with Eder about the two methods of accounting Quorum used in reporting on cases that were reimbursed by the government. But Jim and Bartlett both believed that the whole history of his problems with Quorum began with that meeting. When it came time for his attorney to depose Eder in July 1992, Bartlett pursued that avenue in his questioning.

Bartlett asked Eder if the hospital had a different liability to Medicare in its books than it showed on its cost reports. Eder measured his response, with the tone of someone who was being asked to explain a matter of great complexity. There could be a difference, he said, because the cost report filed with the government is an "aggressive" report that includes claims in "gray areas" to maximize reimbursement to Quorum's client hospital. Quorum also compiles a "reserve" report, he said. This shows what the hospital would owe Medicare if the government audited the aggressive report and discovered the questionable claims.

In other words, Quorum would file a cost report with the government showing, for example, that Medicare owed its client $400,000 for Medicare-related costs. But then the company put together an internal cost report that would adhere to government regulations about what expenses could be claimed and show that Medicare actually owed the hospital only $100,000. Quorum would then create a reserve on its client's books to account for the difference—in this instance, $300,000—and not include that amount in the hospital's profit calculations in case a Medicare contractor audited the cost report and discovered the fraudulent— or as Quorum called them, "aggressive"—claims. Once the hospital received word from Medicare that the cost report had been approved, indicating that the false claims had not been caught, the amount that had been reserved would then be included in the hospital's profits. The odds were in the hospital's favor that it wouldn't get audited, because Medicare didn't have the resources to audit more than a handful of cost reports. Under the worst case, the hospital would get audited several years later and would have to pay back the undeserved $300,000. Because there was no additional penalty, the hospital would have in effect received an interest-free loan.

In many ways, a cost report is like a tax return. Taxpayers are required to file reports that accurately report their income and expenses. At the end of the year, either the government owes them money because the person paid too much in taxes during the year or the taxpayer owes the government money. But some people, knowing that the likelihood of an IRS audit is low, will claim deductions to which they are not entitled as a way of reducing the amount of money they owe the government or increasing the amount the government owes them. In the case of both tax returns and cost reports, that is fraud.

Apparently Eder had never asked himself whether Quorum's actions were legal. To him, the company's cost-reporting practices were just business as usual; nothing ventured, nothing gained. He was surprisingly forthcoming.

Near the end of the year, Quorum decided that Alderson's request for records was overly burdensome, that it would require the company to go back fifteen years for 180 hospitals. What Quorum offered instead was the same information for the nine hospitals in Clyde Eder's jurisdiction. When Bartlett showed his client the company's response, Jim said, "Man, this takes us all the way back to 1975, well before Quorum's spin-off in 1989. This takes us right back to HCA." He told Bartlett to ask for the software and the complete report so they could see where they had changed the numbers.

Jim Bartlett was a good lawyer, responsive to his client and conscientious about the details. But he had no Medicare experience, and he remained focused almost exclusively on the lawsuit for wrongful discharge. When Quorum produced the requested reports, he sent them on to Jim. It turned out that with each report, Quorum included a cover letter saying in effect, "Since you don't understand the Quorum method of reimbursement, we've also given you an analysis which explains the difference between the filed cost report and the reserve cost report."

Jim fell on the new material with fresh zeal. The disparities between what Quorum claimed for reimbursement and what it was entitled to were astonishing. For instance, the filed cost report would inflate the square footage used for treatment of Medicare patients, which would increase reimbursements; the "reserve" one would use the actual square footage and show the effect of the deceit in dollars and cents. Quorum must have assumed that the path was too crooked for an outsider to follow. But Jim was no outsider, and he saw immediately what the company had done. It went all the way back to Quorum's former parent, HCA. The company had been stealing millions from Medicare for years. Now, instead of continuing to hide the evidence, the dumb, arrogant bastards had delivered up the mother lode.

NINETEEN

FLATLANDS

One thing was sure: What Jim Alderson was now looking at—the evidence of a massive fraud extending back many years throughout the entire parent company—was the reason Clyde Eder and Quorum had gone to so much trouble to get rid of him. His lawyer saw it as the clincher in his wrongful termination case. Alderson saw it as far more.

As grateful as he was for Bartlett's continued support of the lawsuit, Jim knew it would be useless to try enlisting him, even with this evidence, to a larger cause. If he planned to take this any further than a simple recovery related to his being fired from North Valley Hospital, he would have to hire a lawyer experienced in this new field, or he would have to make the case on his own. He pondered his next move.

One of the potential witnesses in his suit had been an old friend, Nick Bourdeau. A CPA, Nick had spent the last several years as an audit reimbursement manager for Medicare in Montana—including North Valley Hospital—and was likely to have a better appreciation for the new evidence than anyone else Jim could think of. Jim called to say he had something to show him, and made a date to meet at Nick's office.

Documents in the files that Quorum had provided in response to the litigation bore the rubber-stamped warning, "CONFIDENTIAL—DO NOT DISCUSS OR RELEASE TO MEDICARE AUDITORS." It didn't take Nick any longer to recognize what he was looking at than it had Jim. "This is just unbelievable," he said, shaking his head. "They're secretly keeping track of what they've stolen, so if they get caught they'll know how much they will have to give back. They can't do that!"

With Nick at his side, Jim felt a lot stronger about the pending suit over his termination. He also couldn't help thinking what a help Nick would be if Jim indeed did go ahead with a larger action.

He contacted Dale Jessup, the administrator at North Valley Hospital whose leaving had precipitated Quorum's arrival. Jessup was a potential witness in the wrongful discharge suit, but Jim thought he should also tell him what he had learned in the interim about what Quorum had been doing.

Jessup looked at the evidence and asked Jim what he knew about the False Claims Act and *qui tam* lawsuits. Jim replied that he didn't know a thing about either one of them. Jessup was then working for a Catholic hospital group, and one of the medical centers in that group had been sued two years earlier under the act for defrauding Medicare. He urged Jim to look up that case and to familiarize himself with the law.

It was hard to do much serious research from Dillon. The nearest law library, a very limited one, was at the county seat, and it had very little information about the updated False Claims Act. However, on those weekends when he and Connie and Justin went to visit his daughter at the University of Montana, he tapped into the UM law school library. He also found another resource right at work. The hospital had the Commerce Clearing House books with all the Medicare regulations and cases, so he started taking them home and reading every false claims case he could find.

Using the complaint that Bartlett had written for his suit against North Valley, plus guidelines from some of the cases he read about, he began to draft a new complaint against Quorum, HCA, and another HCA spin-off, HealthTrust Inc., under the False Claims Act. He charged that the three companies were defrauding Medicare by filing false claims in their annual Medicare cost reports. It was a slow, laborious effort. He finished in mid-December 1992 and typed a cover letter to U.S. Attorney General William Barr. He called directory assistance in Washington, D.C., for the number of the Justice Department, and when he dialed it he got a recorded message telling him how to send something to the attorney general. He typed that address onto his letter and put the thin package in the mail. He knew from what he had read that this was how it was done. Under the law, the government had to be notified before anyone filed a false claim suit, and after the Justice Department had a chance to review it, the complaint could be filed under seal.

In the week after Christmas, Jim got a phone call at work. The voice on the line identified herself as Marie O'Connell, from the Civil Division of the Department of Justice. She asked him where he had filed his complaint.

"I haven't filed it yet," he said. "I thought you had to review it first."

O'Connell told him he had done the right thing, but that now he needed to file it so the Justice Department could start its sixty-day investigation period. O'Connell told him he could file it in Butte. So on January 5, 1993, he got back in his car and once more headed north. Connie came along to do some errands, and waited outside while he went into the courthouse.

When he pushed the papers across the counter to the small, elderly woman in the clerk's office, he said, "This has to be filed *in camera,* under seal," exactly as Marie O'Connell had told him to say.

"Okay," the woman said, reaching for the envelope.

Before Jim let go of it, he added, "That means nobody can look at it."

She glared up at him with her lips pursed in exasperation. "Sir, the judge has to look at it."

He let go. "I just don't want to screw this up."

He wrote a personal check for the filing.

Even his attorney, Jim Bartlett, didn't know about the *qui tam* lawsuit.

Meanwhile, the wrongful termination case dragged on. Bartlett notified Quorum that they planned more depositions, in particular with Nick Bourdeau and with Glenn Cody, who had prepared the cost reports Quorum had turned over to Bartlett and Alderson. Quorum had hired Jeremy Thane, a lawyer in Missoula, to represent the company in the case. Thane scheduled Nick's deposition in Missoula, and Bartlett planned to depose Cody immediately afterward by telephone. When Thane had finished with Nick, however, he told Bartlett and Jim that Quorum was done for the day.

"Wait a minute!" Jim protested. "We're going to take Glenn Cody's deposition."

Thane smiled vaguely and said something about not having Cody's phone number.

"Jeremy, I could find Glenn Cody's number on your desk in ten seconds," Jim countered. "Or we can call Quorum right now and ask for it. What's this all about?"

"Well," Thane said, "I'm not sure he's available."

Jim slumped. "So he's ducking the deposition."

Thane said Cody had hired an attorney and that he didn't want his deposition taken.

Another deposition had been scheduled with a woman in charge of reimbursement for Quorum, and Jim and Bartlett were thwarted there as well. The first excuse was that she was pregnant and couldn't travel. But after they had waited a couple of months, Quorum said the timing was still bad and that if it was done at all it would have to be done at her home office in Dallas. By then Jim had surmised that Quorum figured he was funding all of Bartlett's expenses, and that he couldn't really afford it. He was right, and so was Quorum. Bartlett had taken the case on contingency, but the expenses were separate and were billed to the client. Meanwhile, Jim had been in touch with the Justice Department again about the *qui tam* suit, and had asked if there was any possibility of getting some help from the government for the additional expenses associated with that case. DOJ said there was not. Nearly a year after his filing of the *qui tam* suit, as a result of a series of extensions by the Justice Department, the case was still under seal. At the end of 1993, Jim told Bartlett they would have to settle the wrongful discharge action as soon as possible.

The good news was that the government had made some encouraging progress. Back in June 1993, it had issued subpoenas to Quorum for all its cost reports for the previous six years, which produced some major revelations. The Justice Department called Jim to Washington in August to show him the new evidence. Jim talked to Nick Bourdeau, the Medicare auditor, and convinced him to accompany him on the trip in exchange for Jim's paying his travel expenses. Maybe the government would take Nick more seriously, as one of its own, than it had Jim. Jim had to borrow the money for both their tickets.

Alderson had had a lot of time to assess his motivations in bringing this lawsuit. It had never really occurred to him that he would have a hard time convincing others to see the case as he did. He had a profound sense that a terrible wrong was going unanswered. It was not just the wrong of his being lied to and losing his job, although those things were part of it. Mostly, it was his realization that he or anyone else confronted with the same choices was forced either to violate the principles of a lifetime or to suffer a terrible punishment for crimes he or she chose not to commit. He knew that Quorum's real offense was not in his bungled termination but in the reasons behind it, and those reasons deserved exposure. There was just no way a hospital could claim an expense from Medicare at the same time that it labeled it as a "nonallowable expense" on a "reserve cost report" without realizing that it was against all the rules of honest accounting, it was against common sense, and, most of all, it was against the law.

At the meeting in Washington there were about fourteen people in the room, from the Justice Department, the Office of Inspector General, and the Health Care Financing Administration, known as HCFA. Jim explained the case, and Nick added testimony of his own on the criminal nature of Quorum's actions. But the longer they spoke, the more it became apparent that none of the other people in the room were anywhere near ready to share their view.

Later, when he looked back, it was easy to understand why. HCFA thought his lawsuit made the agency look bad. At a deeper level, even at the time of the meeting, he sensed a fundamental antagonism toward his role as whistle-blower, but not for the predictable reason that he had turned on his colleagues. "It felt more like, well . . . ," he tried to tell Connie later, "it felt like jealousy, as though they were the smart ones, the ones who were going to do all the work, and now here comes this guy with his lawsuit and he's the one who is going to get all the money." (Years later, he spoke at a seminar on the False Claims Act at which a fellow panelist described the feeling exactly: "It was like walking into a bad cocktail party.")

If the trip to Washington was an eye-opener on the government's attitude toward his case, it also provided the basis for a new perspective, which became clearer on his return to Montana, on why his putative allies had come to feel as they did. It seemed that every time the case entered a new phase, he found himself confronting a new host of adversaries. When Quorum changed lawyers, Jim looked up the new firm in Martindale-Hubbell, a directory of lawyers, and discovered that it employed over a thousand attorneys. As the case grew and the defendants multiplied, so did the size of the defending armies. The Department of Justice had only a handful of people to put in the field against these hordes, and the big firms knew it. Every one of them retained attorneys who had worked for the government and were intimately familiar with its limitations. Jim Alderson wasn't even represented by counsel. As for the Justice Department, Marie O'Connell essentially was the only attorney working on the case.

Jim also recognized that he had gone as far as he could with the false claims lawsuit on his own. When he'd started, he had expected that all he had to do was report the fraud to the government and it would take over from there. He had written the complaint himself, thinking at the time that that would be the toughest part of the process. But after the trip to Washington, he knew it had just been the beginning, and that he was standing virtually alone against giants.

He got in touch with Dale Jessup, who gave him the name of a firm in Kansas City. When Jim called, he was heartened to hear that the company was interested, but disappointed when it told him that it had never had a *qui tam* case. On the plus side, the attorney he was dealing with had been a regional counsel for the U.S. Department of Health and Human Services, which administers the Medicare program, in Kansas City for twenty-one years prior to joining the firm—and he was excited about Jim's story. But first they would have to convince his colleagues that the case was worth risking the firm's time and money. In November 1993, Jim flew down to Kansas City to help make the pitch.

The firm, the second largest in Kansas City, was on the twenty-sixth floor of one of the tallest buildings in town. Jim presented the case in the best light possible, but he had to admit that the firm might have to put up several hundred thousand dollars of its own money, plus a lot of time. Even then, the government still might decide to walk away from the case and leave the company on its own. He gave the lawyers a copy of the complaint. For all the work he had put into it, it was only four pages long, and he thought later that it must have looked pathetically thin.

He returned home to Montana to wait for the firm's answer. The settlement on the wrongful termination case was still several weeks away, and the outcome was by no means certain. Connie remained firmly behind him, but he suspected that the money he had borrowed for the trip to Kansas City was disappearing down a sinkhole. A few days later he heard back from the lawyer in Kansas City. The firm had agreed to take the case on a contingency basis, including expenses. It was a terrific Christmas present.

At the end of the year, Bartlett settled the wrongful termination suit, though for only a small fraction of the five years of wages that Jim had initially proposed. They were bound by a confidentiality agreement that said neither side was allowed to disclose the terms. But the day after the settlement, the hospital's attorney called the former administrator, Dale Jessup, and told him the figure was $38,000. It reminded Jim of Eder's call to the board chairman, after promising to tell no one he'd been fired. When he had paid a third to Bartlett and netted out his expenses, Jim cleared about $20,000. He realized that if he were still pursuing the *qui tam* lawsuit on his own, it wouldn't have been enough to keep the case alive for more than another few months.

There were more trips to Washington, and countless hours in meetings and phone calls. By that time Jim had told the government everything he had found in the Quorum reports based on his knowledge as a CPA, and Nick had verified all of it. But then, the government told him he had to find someone else—"someone neutral"—to analyze the reports all over again. Even though Nick was a professional government cost-report analyst, Quorum might say that he was speaking as Jim Alderson's friend and that they were too close for Nick's testimony to be credible. So Jim and his new lawyers hired a CPA firm in Philadelphia.

It turned out to be a good choice. The accountants had a lot of experience in cost reporting, and they had just the right combination of expertise and detachment. As he had come to expect, when he first explained the case he found them skeptical, but the doubts vanished as soon as they looked at the documents; they shook their heads in amazement at what Quorum had produced. They told Jim they were amazed at how clearly Quorum had documented the claims they had deliberately overcharged to Medicare.

But even the new experts were not enough to move the Department of Justice. For the next two years, Jim and his lawyers worked to convince the government to join his case against Quorum, HCA, and HealthTrust, but with no result. Jim's lawyers were spending hundreds of hours and enormous amounts of money going through a mountain of reports the health care providers produced in response to new subpoenas. Jim would review the files first, then forward them with his commentary to Kansas City. Connie reminded him that the government received the same documents he did, and would be reviewing them as well. But Jim wasn't as sure as she was that this was the case, and he was even more doubtful that it would be anywhere near as thorough as he.

The UPS and FedEx trucks came so often to the Aldersons' house in Dillon, dropping off new boxes of evidence and picking up old ones to pass on to his attorneys and accountants, there were times when Jim felt the business he was running at home was bigger than his job at the hospital. He and Connie learned later that the neighbors had varying theories on the meaning of all this traffic. One had Connie as a compulsive shopper and Jim as the stern husband forcing the return of all her purchases. Another had Jim as some kind of secret agent. There were only seven thousand people in Dillon, and before the Aldersons moved there a FedEx pickup or delivery was considered a major event in the neighborhood.

During those two years, while Jim and his attorneys labored over the river of documentation, Quorum and HCA never varied from their insistence that everything they had done was legitimate. Their argument was that Jim Alderson just didn't understand how cost reports were prepared. They said it was standard industry practice. If there were some minor variations from the way other companies did it, that was because the regulations were gray and subject to interpretation. The government seemed to go along with that argument, treating Jim's lawsuit as a complex Medicare dispute rather than as Jim's attorneys saw it, a case of "good old-fashioned fraud."

In March 1995, Jim got word that his mother, then eighty-four and in a nursing home, had taken a serious downturn. He called his brother in Colorado and told him she was nearing the end. The next day, the doctor confirmed the bleak prognosis. The timing forced Jim into a terrible choice. Elaborate arrangements had been made with his law firm and an attorney from Philadelphia to spend the coming weekend conducting a full review of the Quorum documents he had analyzed over the prior months. Jim and the others were all scheduled to meet in Kansas City that Friday through Sunday. Anguished, he discussed the conflict with his brother and sister. He felt the work with his attorneys that weekend would be critical in convincing the Justice Department to join his lawsuit. If he didn't go, he would not only be letting down the lawyers who had invested in his case, but he was afraid it would be the end of the lawsuit, that all of his efforts and sacrifice of the past two years would go to waste.

Throughout his long ordeal, Jim's mother had been one of his staunchest supporters. He kept her up to date, and she was proud of what he was trying to do. His father had died when Jim was eight. As a widow with three young children, his mother knew what it was like to struggle alone and often against the system. Medicare fraud, she would tell him, was the main reason her insurance premiums kept rising. Often, at the end of their visits when she waved good-bye, she would punch the air half comically with her fist and say, "Go get 'em!"

His siblings talked it over with him, and then told Jim she would have wanted him to go ahead with the meeting. He knew they were right. On Thursday afternoon, he went up to the hospital and said good-bye, sensing it was the last time he would see his mother alive. He left the room in tears and flew that night to Kansas City.

From the thousands of Quorum documents they reviewed, Jim and his attorneys culled a huge stack that they felt clearly showed Medicare fraud and sent copies along with their analysis of the fraud to the Department of Justice. Jim expected the information would be carefully reviewed by all of the Justice Department and other government attorneys involved. When he called to hear how the government attorneys reacted, he was chagrined to learn they were nowhere near as enthusiastic about this evidence as Jim and his lawyers were. Later, the Justice Department attorneys said they had misplaced the packet of documents. When he heard this, Jim barely managed to contain his rage. He told his lawyer, "You tell Marie O'Connell what I was doing that weekend and what I gave up." He saw it as nothing more than a power play, and wondered if he would ever be able to forgive her—or himself, for trading away the chance to be with his dying mother.

Years later, a reporter asked Jim if he had any second thoughts about decisions he had made along his solitary journey. That was one of the few times, he said, when he might have done something different. His son had called him Saturday morning in Kansas City to say that Jim's mother had just passed away. At first Justin called the wrong hotel, and panicked. He was nineteen, calling from school in Los Angeles, and at one of the times in his life when he most needed to talk with his father he was having trouble finding him. The case was swallowing up their lives.

By mid-1995, the case had really started to drag. Jim realized the pressure was mounting for the government to walk away from it, and if that happened, there was no way he could see himself standing up to an army of enemy lawyers with his present legal team. He had three attorneys working for him in Kansas City, and they had never stinted in their commitment. Their credentials were impressive: One had graduated from Stanford and the University of Kansas, one was from Boston College Law

School, and the third was an alumnus of Harvard. He liked and respected all of them. He realized the firm had a lot of money invested in his case, and a lot of energy. But they all knew it was gradually getting away from them. He found himself in a position he once would have considered unimaginable—an accountant from Montana telling the only real allies in his case that the time had come for him to find a replacement.

To his immense relief, they simply said the choice was his. Then one of them asked Jim what he had in mind for his next move.

"Throughout this whole thing, I've always had this 'bird on my shoulder,'" he answered. "It tells me what to do next. As much as I hated making this decision, it's one of the things it told me to do. I realized that if we were to keep on going where we've been headed, this case would just die on the vine."

What he really needed, the bird was telling him, was a law firm that knew its way around in the Justice Department, one that could give his case the kind of boost that would lift it to the top of the wave. And by then, he had a pretty good idea who that firm would be.

Several months earlier, he had gotten an advertisement in the mail for a free trial subscription to the *Wall Street Journal.* Jim felt a little guilty accepting the offer. Jennifer had finished college the previous spring, but they now faced a new siege of tuition payments for Justin's school in Los Angeles, and Jim knew he wouldn't be able to extend the subscription on a paying basis when the trial ended. When the paper started arriving, he read each issue conscientiously. It yielded dividends in the first week. Back in January, he had unfolded it to a front-page story under the headline "Honesty Pays Off." The article described "a growing industry of whistle-blowing," and in particular a lawyer named John Phillips who'd helped draft the False Claims Act. "Of the top eight cases successfully prosecuted by the government," the article said, "Mr. Phillips had a hand in seven."

Several months later, Jim heard from Justin. A similar story had appeared in the *Los Angeles Times,* this one focused on a couple of local false claims cases and the role played by Stephen Meagher, an attorney in the San Francisco office of Phillips's law firm.

Jim read the stories again and again. It wasn't until late October that he finally decided Phillips & Cohen might be his last, best hope.

TWENTY

A DOG OF A CASE

How many times had he already told this story? Jim listened to the ringing on the wire, knowing this could be one of the most important calls he had ever made, and his mind raced ahead to its possible outcome. Phillips & Cohen had just the kind of experience his case had needed from the start. But was the theft too complicated to explain in a single call? And was the case too shopworn to be attractive to yet another firm? Jim's other attorneys had spent several hundred thousand dollars in time and out-of-pocket expenses, but there was still no hint of a commitment from the government. Phillips & Cohen would be the third law firm on a case that had dragged on for two years and still gone nowhere.

To his immense relief, the call went well. After talking with Peter Chatfield, an attorney in the firm's Washington office, Jim explained the case in even greater detail in a conference call with Chatfield and Stephen Meagher, a former federal prosecutor who had opened the Phillips & Cohen San Francisco office the previous year along with another former assistant U.S. attorney, Eric Havian. Neither Chatfield nor Meagher seemed put off by anything Jim told them, including his contract with the other lawyers, the government's reaction to the lawsuit, or even the length of time the case had remained under seal. They were business-like and, for most of the conversation, carefully neutral. They asked the kinds of questions that showed an understanding of the issues, and Jim sensed that the story had piqued their interest. In contrast to the government attorneys, who continued to treat his case like a hot potato, both Meagher and Chatfield actually seemed willing to take hold of it, to turn it over and examine it for its potential. Near the end of the call, Jim sensed that the tone of the conversation had begun to shift, if only slightly, to one of cautious enthusiasm. If Jim came down to San Francisco, Meagher

said, he would ask two of his partners to come in from Washington to
hear his story.

It was the best outcome he could have hoped for, even if it put him
right back in the middle of a familiar dilemma. This was the leading firm
in False Claims Act litigation. If Phillips & Cohen didn't have any interest in his case it wouldn't have invited him out, and it certainly wouldn't
be bringing in people from Washington. Excited, and without a moment's
hesitation, he agreed on a date for the meeting. But once more, he had to
pay his own way. He could barely afford the cost of the plane ticket and a
motel.

The afternoon before the appointment, he packed a heavy briefcase
with the evidence he and his lawyers had culled that long, sad weekend
when his mother died. He carefully folded his best suit and tie into an
overnight bag. He knew that the protocol for travel was a lot more casual
than for a business meeting, so he chose a paisley shirt and brown pants
for the plane ride.

At eight o'clock the next morning in San Francisco, when he came
out of the shower and went to his bag, he realized in a near panic that he
hadn't packed a dress shirt. He rushed from the hotel wearing the same
combination he'd worn on the airplane. There was a clothing store just
down the street, but the next shock was the sign on its door: It didn't open
until nine-thirty. The interview was at ten; it would be tight, but still possible. He waited by the door, and as soon as he got inside he bolted for
the menswear department. The cheapest white shirt in the store was $45;
there probably wasn't a shirt costing that much in the entire state of
Montana, but he had no time left to find a better choice. Back in his room,
he struggled out of his travel clothes, at the same time pulling out the
pins and unfolding his purchase with a combination of resentment and
relief. A few minutes later, on the dot of ten, he arrived at the offices of
Phillips & Cohen. His heart was racing.

The two partners from Washington who joined Meagher and Havian
for the meeting turned out to be the firm's founders, John Phillips and Mary
Louise Cohen. Jim started by telling them frankly that the firm was essentially his last hope. Despite what he considered powerful evidence, the
Justice Department seemed to doubt whether it would be possible to prove
a case of fraud against Quorum or HCA. He then proceeded as methodically as possible to build just such a case, an accountant creating a picture

with numbers, systematic in his presentation and careful with his conclusions. But it wasn't like a business presentation where he had someone else to help with the exhibits or where he could hand off complicated explanations to others. The entire responsibility was his alone—to make the pitch, to back up his claims, to explain and prove the crime.

There was nothing particularly enthusiastic about the response he got from his audience, but neither was it adversarial. The four attorneys were interested and cordial, and they asked every conceivable question relating to what Jim regarded as the case's strengths and weaknesses. Why hadn't anything happened in the past three years? What did he feel about the case now that he had put so much into it? Where did he stand with the prior lawyers? How was his family holding up? How did he view the role of the Justice Department? If it continued to drag on, was he willing to go the distance?

John Phillips told him he was impressed by Jim's tenacity, and by the job he had done in extracting the essence of the case from the cost reports. Jim had told his story with clarity and precision, and in a whistle-blower suit, the ability to explain a complex fraud was a major virtue. Phillips was equally open about his misgivings. The case would require an enormous investment. Alderson's case involved hundreds of hospitals and thousands of cost-report claims; it would take a lot of work to substantiate and prove the false claims. And HCA had recently merged with Columbia Hospital Corp. to form Columbia/HCA Healthcare Corp., the largest for-profit hospital chain in the country. The merged company had very deep pockets and would certainly fight any challenge. In addition, the Justice Department had apparently formed a negative impression of the case and was on the brink of declining to intervene. Changing that opinion would be very difficult, but was essential, because the Justice Department would be a critical factor in the outcome.

Phillips explained why the analysis Alderson and his attorneys had done to date was useful, but was still a long way from meeting the requirements for making a successful case. The false claims involved tens of thousands of dishonest cost reports by hundreds of hospitals over the course of a decade. The pattern of the fraud was diffuse, and one of the biggest challenges would be to clarify how Quorum and HCA had systematically taken advantage of discrete mechanisms in the Medicare structure to steal the money. It added to the complexity of the case that Phillips & Cohen would have to negotiate an arrangement with the lawyers in Kansas City if it was to proceed on his behalf. None of this was news to Jim, but it was still something of a letdown that he would be leaving San Francisco without a clear sense of whether the firm was willing to take him on. All the lawyers said at parting was "We'll get back to you."

Later, Jim tried to evaluate how the meeting had gone. He told Connie he had been impressed, but had no way of telling how the attorneys were going to weigh the pluses and minuses they had discussed in the interview. Then he told her the story of the shirt, and how sick he had felt about spending all that money. Later, when Connie brought in his laundry, she told him the new one didn't iron right and didn't drape properly on the hanger. She said he had far better shirts that had cost less than half as much. They both shook their heads. Each of them wondered whether the trip would turn out to have been worth it.

A few days later, Stephen Meagher called to tell him Phillips & Cohen had decided to take the case. The attorneys had looked through the documents he had left with them, and it was clear that Quorum and HCA knew from the outset exactly what they were doing. Another strong plus, Meagher said, was Jim himself—he was a good, solid relator with strong credentials. Meagher offered to contact the Kansas City law firm to work out a fair arrangement to compensate it if the case succeeded.

Jim was as relieved by this offer as he had been to hear Phillips & Cohen was taking him on as a client. Changing firms had been one of the toughest decisions of his life. Even though the bird on his shoulder had told him it was the right move, he had enormous respect for the other attorneys and wanted to be certain they received a reward in fair proportion to what they had done. Meagher reached an agreement in which the prior attorneys would recover their expenses and retain a share of the relator's reward. All of this was contingent, as was the original agreement, on a successful outcome. Phillips & Cohen formally took over that November.

By that time, Jim had changed his job again. During the summer, after nearly five years in Dillon, he had taken a position with a Catholic hospital on the other side of the state. He and Connie moved to Miles City, a horse and cattle town of ten thousand people some four hundred miles to the east, in Custer County on the banks of the Yellowstone River. By then Jim had begun to feel that his real job was the lawsuit.

In February 1996, Jim flew to Washington for another meeting with the Justice Department. If he approached that event with any hopes that the experience and prestige of his new attorneys might make a difference in how his case was viewed by the government, Marie O'Connell saw to it that they were short-lived. Greeting Jim with her usual coolness, she told him that she and her colleagues were very surprised that Phillips & Cohen had been willing to become involved. She was equally to the point with Meagher, Havian, and Chatfield. It was very unlikely, she told them, that the Justice Department would agree to join in Jim Alderson's action.

The meeting also included auditors from the Health and Human Services' Office of Inspector General, officials of HCFA, and a government-hired expert named Pete Figliozzi. Meagher and Chatfield had experience in measuring the mood of this kind of a gathering, and it was apparent to both of them that with the exception of Figliozzi, the atmosphere was one of extreme skepticism. The other officials seemed as determined as O'Connell to convince them that the case was too difficult to pursue on the grand scale Alderson believed it warranted. One OIG auditor told them, "We've been looking into this case for three years. You have no idea what you're talking about." A Justice attorney added, "The case is too diffuse. You need to find a common type of fraud from hospital to hospital."

On the latter comment, Alderson's attorneys were more or less willing to concede the point. Unless the case could be organized into unifying themes of fraud, it would be extremely difficult to understand, pursue, and prove.

An OIG auditor rolled her eyes when Meagher and Chatfield suggested that the government audit HCA hospitals. "Audits are too expensive and take too long," she objected. "Besides, you can't use the results of an audit at one hospital to prove that another hospital engaged in the same type of fraud."

The OIG auditors even dismissed the document stamps instructing employees to not show them to Medicare auditors. "Only ten percent of the documents were stamped with that," one of them responded.

The one exception in the group was Figliozzi. When a Justice Department attorney argued that it was unclear HCA knew that it was defrauding Medicare, the government's expert muttered under his breath,

"They knew." A moment later the same lawyer said it was unclear to the Justice Department as well whether HCA had indeed committed fraud. Figliozzi said, again sotto voce, "It's fraud."

Figliozzi's sentiments notwithstanding, Alderson's lawyers emerged from the meeting feeling discouraged. The meeting had given them a clear understanding of how hard it would be to get the government behind the case. Still, the meeting did suggest a strategy for persuading the government to join it. Clearly, Justice would be interested in pursuing the case only if Phillips & Cohen could show that each of the HCA and Quorum hospitals had followed the same pattern when they'd cheated Medicare. That kind of pattern had been demonstrated in other Medicare fraud cases. In the medical testing labs case brought by Jack Dowden, for instance, the labs routinely added the same unnecessary tests and billed Medicare the same amount. In the HCA and Quorum cases, however, each hospital made different false claims for reimbursement on its cost reports. In the absence of a revealed pattern, the complexity of the case and the amount of resources that would be required to pursue it made it unlikely that Justice would join the lawsuit.

Meagher and Chatfield weren't the only ones who knew this. The Justice Department attorneys were also talking about the case with their counterparts for the defense. The HCA attorneys were quick to pick up the chorus, insisting the company had done nothing wrong, and signaling that they were prepared to spend whatever resources were necessary to discourage the government from pursuing the case.

Even before the meeting, Alderson's new attorneys had been aware of the government's attitude toward the case, but they were also puzzled by it. They had at least as good a perspective on the evidence as Marie O'Connell did, and it was obvious to them that the potential recovery was vastly higher than what the government apparently thought.

One thing O'Connell did have that they did not was a detailed, $300,000 analysis by government experts of Quorum's and Columbia's cost-report claims. But when Meagher asked O'Connell to provide this analysis to the firm, she refused. She said she had reviewed it, that it was full of gray areas and subtleties, and that it contained nothing of substance that would help Jim prove anything. Later, she would characterize his lawsuit as "a dog of a case."

After the meeting, Meagher shared with Jim his theory on why the suit had stayed so long in limbo and what to expect on the road ahead. Plain and simple, he told him, the Justice Department was reluctant to take a cost-reporting case. The department's client, the Health Care Financing Administration, which administered the Medicare program, was likely to be embarrassed that the program was susceptible to such widespread abuse. In addition, the applicable regulations could be portrayed as too complex and too convoluted and the gray areas too numerous. The Medicare program might also be embarrassed by the ineffectiveness of its audit review process for cost reports. Not only had it failed to uncover these widespread false claims, but it had also failed to realize that these hospitals were essentially keeping two sets of books. Medicare cost reporting was a vast, largely unexplored new territory for law enforcement. The principal players were powerful and well defended, and the Justice Department would be outnumbered and outspent.

The longer the department avoided taking a position, the weaker Jim's case appeared on its merits. O'Connell appeared to be setting the scene for an eventual rejection, or at least a decision to join only part of Jim's case. Whether she knew it or not, her ingrained skepticism about the case was also testing the depth of the new attorneys' commitment.

Phillips & Cohen still wanted to see the reports that Marie O'Connell said formed the basis for the government's doubts, and the attorneys continued to push to get them. After all, they were all on the same side; having the firm's experts review the government reports surely couldn't hurt. A few months later, O'Connell's boss finally agreed to share the experts' analyses. Phillips & Cohen received some, but not all, of the requested reports and documents. As the attorneys expected, the "gray areas and subtleties" cited by O'Connell were few and far between. The analyses clearly showed that a significant portion of the claims were false, and that the companies had known it. Jim Alderson pored over the reports and documents for weeks, analyzing them and looking for ways they could help his case.

When Alderson filed his suit on January 5, 1993, it was his understanding that it would remain under seal for sixty days; he hadn't particularly noticed the phrase "or more, if necessary." The first time the Justice Department had asked for an extension, back when he was representing himself, it was for half again as long as the original period—another three months. But it happened again and again, like tides that kept returning to erode his shoreline and push the horizon ever farther into the distance. There were times when he promised himself, "This is absolutely it," but still the extensions came and went.

Jim talked with his new attorneys about the pressures of not knowing where they were headed, of not being able to share their journey with anyone but one another, and of having to work in secret on what amounted to a second job. All they could tell him in response was what he knew already. If the government declines to join a *qui tam* lawsuit, the relator can prosecute it on his own, but in this case that would mean taking on a company with billions of dollars in the bank and an almost limitless ability to dodge and stall. It would be a mistake to insist on lifting the seal of secrecy in the hope of forcing the government to take a position, because the most likely reaction to that kind of pressure would be its refusal to join the action. However reluctantly, Jim dutifully agreed to the extensions.

He continued at his day job and, as before, put in a second forty-hour week with his lawyers and their hired experts in the tedious task of analyzing the scope and size of the fraud.

But early in 1996, their efforts received an unexpected boost.

TWENTY-ONE

THE FIREMAN

I n February 1995, eight months before Jim Alderson approached Phillips & Cohen, the firm was contacted by a potential whistle-blower from Florida who had read the same *Wall Street Journal* story as Jim about John Phillips and the False Claims Act. The caller, John Schilling, worked for Columbia/HCA Healthcare Corp.

Schilling said Columbia Hospital Corp. had been submitting false cost reports for its facilities and continued to do so after the merger. He too was an accountant, but unlike Jim, he still worked for the company he thought was stealing from the government, and he had not filed a *qui tam* suit.

Schilling had been recruited to Columbia by a headhunter in 1993. From the outside, it had looked like a dream job in a growing for-profit hospital chain that offered a chance for career advancement as well as a higher salary and bonus pay. The company was considered an innovator and a rising star in an industry that was beset by runaway costs and slumping revenues.

Columbia was founded in 1987 by Richard Scott, a brash, thirty-five-year-old lawyer whose initial attempt to purchase HCA had just been rebuffed by Tommy Frist. Scott's partner, Texas billionaire financier Richard Rainwater, had recently ventured out on his own after gaining fame as a financial manager for the Bass brothers of Fort Worth, Texas, where he had increased their fortune from $50 million to $4 billion in sixteen years. Two years after cofounding Columbia, he joined a partnership which included future president George W. Bush to buy the Texas Rangers.

Backed by financing from Wall Street, Columbia purchased two financially strapped El Paso hospitals. Scott and Rainwater figured they could turn them around with better management and by applying standard business practices. The whole industry was hurting, still adjusting to the new Medicare reimbursement system under which they were paid a predetermined amount based on diagnosis, rather than the actual costs of treatment. But Scott was sure he knew what to do to make a profit: strictly control costs; compete fiercely with any rivals, whether nonprofit or for-profit hospitals; give physicians a financial stake in the hospitals so that their professional decisions affected their income; and set up a bonus system to encourage managers to meet ambitious financial goals.

Scott molded the company in his image: lean, driven, and tenacious. In its first few years, the company bought for-profit hospitals as well as ailing nonprofits, primarily in Texas and Florida. In 1992, Scott acquired a small chain, Basic American Medical Inc., or BAMI, which owned four hospitals in the area of Fort Lauderdale, Florida. Two subsequent moves added more than 160 hospitals to the Columbia stable, creating a health care giant: In September 1993, Columbia merged with the for-profit hospital chain Galen Healthcare, formerly known as Humana Corp., a onetime leader in the for-profit hospital industry, and six months after that it merged with HCA. Tommy Frist had been a hard sell, but he knew the deal made good financial sense and that it was sure to increase HCA's stock price.

Scott took the reins of Columbia/HCA Healthcare Corp. as president; Frist took a backseat and became vice chairman. Together Scott and Frist went after the HCA spin-off, HealthTrust, and worked out a merger eight months later, bringing more than a hundred former HCA hospitals back to the company's portfolio. Columbia also acquired other medical businesses, such as home health care and rehabilitation facilities.

Before and after the merger with HCA, Scott and his company were the darlings of Wall Street. Columbia/HCA's stock soared. With its adherence to cost controls, marketing strategies, and profit incentives, it became a model for the rest of the health care industry, essentially forcing the competition to run facilities more efficiently and to control costs. In 1995, just eight years after Scott founded Columbia, Columbia/HCA revenues were almost $18 billion.

But in the nonprofit hospital world, the company's reputation was an entirely different matter. Apace with the company's phenomenal growth, initial misgivings about profit-making hospitals had fast ripened into fear and loathing. Columbia's cocky corporate attitude and no-holds-barred approach to competition rankled more than just the purists. Typical tactics included suing communities that rejected its efforts to acquire hospitals; and, in one case, it kept a money-losing facility open by maintaining only two inpatient beds in order to avoid surrendering a valued operating license. There was a wave of large and sometimes ill-planned mergers intended as a defense against being swallowed up by the giant. "The threat of Columbia was like the Vikings coming on the coast of France, and people made very rash decisions in response," a health care economist told the *New York Times.*

The biggest criticism of Columbia was that it placed profits ahead of patient care. Certainly the company put tremendous pressure on its employees to make decisions that would help Columbia reach its goal of increasing its profits by at least 15 percent annually. To achieve that growth, the company created a bonus structure based on managers meeting aggressive financial targets. Many hospitals didn't offer managers bonuses. Those that did usually tied them to medical standards like mortality rates rather than monetary ones. But if Columbia managers didn't meet their financial goals, not only would they lose their bonuses, but there was also a good chance they would lose their jobs. Some Columbia hospitals that were poor performers financially saw a lot of turnover in administrators as a result.

Despite the criticism, Scott sat on top of the health care world. A hands-on manager, he sent out daily E-mails to employees companywide, containing exhortations and encouragement. In 1996, *Time* magazine named him one of America's twenty-five most influential people. His empire included more than 350 hospitals, 145 outpatient surgery centers, 550 home care agencies, and several other ancillary businesses. The following year, with 285,000 employees, Columbia/HCA was the nation's ninth-largest employer. It was also the largest single biller of Medicare. Medicare reimbursements made up about one-third of the company's revenues.

Columbia hired John Schilling one year before the merger with HCA to be a supervisor of reimbursement services in a division office in Fort Myers, Florida. The division managed five area hospitals, including some that had recently been acquired through the purchase of the BAMI chain. Schilling served the hospitals as an internal consultant, educating and guiding their staffs in Medicare reimbursement and cost reports and assisting Medicare auditors. With his annual bonus, he made $46,000, enabling him and his wife to build their own house.

John's boss, Robert Whiteside, was a friendly, jovial mentor in his first months on the job. A dedicated family man, he seldom kept John working late, making sure the job didn't intrude on his time at home.

Life in Florida was a far cry from life in Menomonee Falls, Wisconsin, where John was born in 1962. His grandfather had come over from Germany in the 1920s and spent most of his working life in the local Allen-Bradley plant, a sprawling complex dominated by the world's largest four-sided clock. John's father and uncle, and eventually one of his sisters, followed in the grandfather's footsteps. During that time the company became a division of Rockwell, and its product line shifted to electronic switches, transistors, and conductors. John's father was there for thirty years as a machinist. His sister still works in the office.

John went through eighth grade at St. Mary's Catholic Grade School, as had his mother, who grew up just one street away from where John did. He graduated from Menomonee Falls North High School, but when many of his old parochial school classmates went on to Marquette, he didn't, because his family didn't have that kind of money. Shortly afterward, his parents ended their twenty-eight-year marriage and his father moved to Fort Myers, Florida.

Despite his earlier hopes for college, John decided a degree wouldn't make all that much difference to his plans for becoming a fireman. He was a volunteer firefighter as soon as he got out of high school, and shortly after that an EMT, positions he held for the next twelve years.

While prepping for the necessary exams in order to get a full-time job in a fire department, he supported himself with a string of odd jobs, bagging at the grocery store and helping a neighbor who was a custodian at the local school to clean or paint classrooms. After about a year he decided to take classes at a technical college in film and communications, and he got into a program called "Telecasting" at a school-run local TV station. He graduated with an associate's degree in directing and producing, but when it came to finding a job he was hardly better off than he had been before. He was finally successful in getting on the Milwaukee Fire Department hiring list, and also started working at a local hospital as an EMT. He then moved up to full-time work with a private ambulance service. He was still living at home.

In 1984 a friend introduced him to a beautiful, sweet, soft-spoken girl named Kirsten. They got married the following year, when John was twenty-three and Kirsten nineteen, and moved into an apartment near his mother's home in Menomonee Falls. Kirsten had a job as a secretary for a car dealership, and the couple decided John should go to university for a four-year degree. He began classes at the University of Wisconsin in the fall of 1986, even though the earlier credits didn't count and it meant starting over.

Near the end of his first year, he learned that his long-standing application had finally been approved for the Milwaukee Fire Department academy. But before he had a chance to act on that opportunity, another event intervened. He was still working part-time as an EMT, and while leaving the scene of a false alarm call in the inner city of Milwaukee he fell down a flight of steps and broke his foot. The academy agreed to move back his admission date to the next class six months later, as long as he passed the medical exam. But by the time that date came around he was a sophomore in college, and he realized the equation had changed. A business career was less dangerous than being a fireman, and it might give him and Kirsten a better life, especially once they had a family. He decided on the degree. By studying summers, he finished the program in three and a half years.

After graduation, he started as a Medicare auditor with Blue Cross/ Blue Shield of Wisconsin. Kirsten was working for an insurance broker by then, but when their first son, Alex, was born a year and a half later, they decided she should stay home. Two years after the baby came, in December 1992, John moved over to St. Mary's Hospital in Milwaukee as a Medicare reimbursement analyst. He was making $35,000.

When John had been on the new job nine months, a recruiter called him about an opening in Florida with a division of Columbia Hospital Corp. John accepted the job, not just because it was appealing in its own right, but also because it was in Fort Myers, the town where his father had retired and remarried.

In the spring of 1994, about six months after starting work for Columbia and shortly after the Columbia and HCA merger, John began to have misgivings about his job and his employer. He was working with several hospitals on a Medicare audit of their cost reports. Typically, there is a lag of a year or two between the filing of a cost report and an audit by a Medicare intermediary, a private company that contracts with the federal government to handle Medicare reimbursements and audits of those who receive Medicare funds. Thuan Tran, an auditor for the intermediary Blue

Cross/Blue Shield of Florida, asked John if he was familiar with the re-opening of cost reports submitted to Medicare by Fawcett Memorial Hospital, a Columbia-owned facility in nearby Port Charlotte. A hospital or Medicare auditor can reopen cost reports to correct certain types of errors, which can result in Medicare's owing the hospital more money or the hospital's owing Medicare more money.

John told Tran he was still relatively new at the job and said he didn't know anything about Fawcett's earlier cost reports. Whiteside was not in the office, so John called the hospital's comptroller, Jim Burns. There had been some previous reopenings, Burns said. He thought they were related to reimbursement claimed for interest paid on certain loans.

When Whiteside returned the next day, John asked him if he knew why the cost reports had been reopened. Whiteside didn't know all of the details but explained that several years earlier an intermediary who was reviewing a Fawcett cost report had made a mistake in the hospital's favor. When the hospital saw the error, it said nothing to the government but secretly reserved about $3.5 million in case the intermediary realized the error and demanded the money back. Columbia was not going to tell the intermediary about the mistake.

John knew that interest payments are treated in one of two ways on a cost report. If they are related to capital expenses, such as the construction of a new hospital wing or the purchase of X-ray equipment, they are reimbursed at a higher rate than if the money was borrowed for everyday operations. The reasoning for this difference is that Medicare already includes interest costs in its formula for reimbursing a hospital's operating expenses, but the formula doesn't include expenses related to capital assets like buildings or machinery. In the case at Fawcett, it appeared that the intermediary had mistakenly accounted all of the interest on the cost report as a capital item, when a large portion of it was not.

John also knew, as did any educated accountant, that Medicare contractors were required by law to notify the government of a significant mistake over a certain dollar amount, regardless of whom it benefited. Even if Medicare regulations hadn't spelled it out, which they had, CPAs are aware of the moral and ethical duty to return undeserved payments; it's like finding a wallet on the street and knowing whose it is. His boss was saying that Columbia would return the wallet only if its owner found out Columbia had it. Whiteside also told him not to get back to the auditor and to let him know if Tran brought the matter up again, and that company policy in this type of situation was to keep quiet and see what happened next. It wasn't the kind of thing John wanted to hear, but he was the new kid. His boss was matter-of-fact and businesslike, an old hand explaining the ropes.

The next day, that tone abruptly changed. Whiteside got a call from Michael Neeb, the chief financial officer at Fawcett. Neeb, who had worked for a big accounting firm before joining Columbia, was in his late thirties, tall, slender, and in good shape—things that Whiteside was not—and he was clearly upset. His comptroller, Jim Burns, had told him about John's question of the day before, and Neeb was worried that the $3.5 million reserve might be at risk. Seconds after the normally low-key Whiteside hung up the phone, he stormed into John's office and slammed the door behind him. "What's going on here?" he yelled. "I told you not to talk about this with anyone." He berated John for putting him on the hot seat. Jobs could be lost, he said, if this got out.

It didn't make any difference that John had contacted Burns in Whiteside's absence and prior to the warning. He told John to get as much information on the cost report as possible from the files, the storage room, wherever he could find it. Neeb summoned Whiteside to his office the following day. Whiteside was going to have to inform Jay Jarrell, CFO of the division office, about the problem. Jarrell, who oversaw the CFOs in each of the hospitals, was farther up the ladder and, at least to Whiteside, even more formidable than Neeb. A trim, intense six-two and an alumnus of Indiana University and Arthur Anderson, he was an intelligent, career-oriented workaholic.

John was worried, but when he got home that night he decided there was no point in upsetting Kirsten. Until he knew if this was really a problem or just his boss's fearful reaction, he decided, it was better to keep it to himself.

The next day, John and Whiteside drove up to Fawcett Memorial Hospital in Port Charlotte. It was a long trip. The older man's rage had abated, perhaps because he had decided John might be more useful as an ally than as a scapegoat. Whiteside was still anxious about what lay ahead, sorting through the files as John drove and asking what he had found in his search. The plan was to meet with Neeb, with Jay Jarrell calling in on a speakerphone from out of town.

Neeb was fairly new at the hospital, so neither he nor Whiteside was familiar with all the details, and neither had been a party to the original transaction. It turned out that the error had occurred when Fawcett was owned by Basic American Medical Inc. Jay Jarrell was an executive with BAMI at the time. When Columbia acquired the company in 1992, he was one of the staff who survived the transition. Thus, Whiteside said, the intermediary's mistake obviously went back to the 1980s. He asked John to repeat exactly what he could remember of what Thuan Tran had said.

The rest of the meeting was given over to planning how to continue the concealment. They started making a "to do" list of ways to divert the auditor's attention. One item on that list was to try moving up the next year's audit. Another was to bombard Tran with questions on new product lines or new services, and to constantly contact her for assistance on other issues in an effort to change the subject. Because they were looking to John as the auditor's primary contact, he sensed with growing unease that he was being recruited into a criminal conspiracy. The clincher came when Jarrell ended the meeting. "Well, if none of this works," he said, "we can always offer her a job with the company."

The trip back began in relative silence. Whiteside was more relaxed now that the meeting was behind them, a chastened, somewhat muted version of his old self. John made a point of apologizing for telling Jim Burns about the auditor's inquiry, but only because it gave him the chance to reiterate that he had done it before Whiteside's warning.

"Don't worry about it," his boss replied, apparently glad for the chance to be magnanimous. "You're still green. A few more years and you'll know what things you can talk about and when to keep quiet."

Over the following weeks, John processed what had happened. He was fourteen hundred miles from home, in a new job with a large company, and if he stood up and said something, there was a good chance he would lose his job and even be blacklisted. But was this an isolated incident or part of a larger pattern? He began measuring some of his other experiences against his new insight from Fawcett, and he realized the misreported interest expense wasn't the only thing that was wrong.

Columbia was doing reserve cost reports throughout the whole company. He began looking more closely at those reserves, and it was obvious that a lot of them were for issues that were basically fraudulent. The company was claiming expenses it knew shouldn't be there, and setting that same amount aside in case it was caught.

His former life, he reflected, had been basically in rescues—the EMT job, the volunteer fire department work—and its purpose had been not to make himself rich but to be useful to others. Now he was working for a health care provider, but he had the sense that he was on the wrong side, that these were the guys who were making the fires instead of putting them out.

But what if Columbia's practices were just the accepted way of doing business in the for-profit health care industry? Was it really wrong, or was he merely overreacting out of inexperience?

A few weeks later, Whiteside moved on to a new job with Columbia in Tennessee. His replacement was fifty-year old Larry Bomar, a twenty-year veteran who came to Columbia from the not-for-profit Tampa General. He was a welcome change, very knowledgeable about the industry and a kind and willing mentor. When Bomar first learned about the reserve cost reports and the Fawcett interest issue, John was delighted that he reacted in the same way he had. Bomar said he had been doing cost reports for twenty years and that this was not the way they were supposed to be prepared.

John was not the only one to recognize that his new boss was a straight shooter. The Columbia comptrollers quickly dubbed him "Bad News Bomar" for his unyielding integrity on what was permissible and what was not. He told John he knew the reserve reports were crooked, but he felt they should try to work within the organization to set things straight.

On his own, before Bomar's arrival, John had written a memo to Columbia's director of reimbursement for Florida, a woman named Trish Lindler. He had outlined his concerns about the interest payments, hoping, he said, to correct what he thought was an honest misperception about what was acceptable practice. His goal was to get the error disclosed to the intermediary and return the reserved money to the government, both without losing his job or being blackballed. He was sure that if had made those same suggestions to Whiteside, Jarrell, or Neeb, he would have been out the door the next day.

Lindler had given John the impression she was working on the issue with corporate headquarters in Tennessee, but the hope of change from

within appeared to fade with her retirement around the time of the acquisition of HCA. Shortly afterward, however, her replacement, Bonnie Reid,
invited John Schilling and Larry Bomar to a reimbursement meeting, and
their hopes rallied when she raised the topic of John's memo. She told them
to bring anything they had on the interest issue, because she had been
instructed to look into it.

At the meeting, she told them she had gotten some indications that
the company's top management was becoming concerned with their misgivings, and she repeated that she had been assigned to deal with the problem. She listened with apparent interest as they told her the background
of the error, and that the company was holding money that belonged to
the government. But as soon as they finished, it became immediately obvious that she intended to settle the matter on the spot. She said she didn't
think the company had any obligation to tell the intermediary that what it
did was wrong. She said there was no reason for Columbia to reopen something that was so far in the past. Maybe going forward, she conceded, the
company would think twice about doing the same thing again.

The two men left the meeting in shock. What Reid had told them, in
effect, was that the company knew the law had been broken and that it was
going to continue looking the other way. The problem she had been com-
missioned to deal with was not the profitable mistake that had been illegally hidden from the government, John thought, but the two potential
troublemakers who kept trying to bring it out of hiding.

John decided to look for other employment. He had collected a number of articles about the sudden growth in *qui tam* suits in health care, and
at around the same time he contacted a recruiter, he decided to call a law
firm. He wanted to find out if what he was looking at was really fraud.

And if it was, did he already know too much to be able to simply walk
away?

The *Wall Street Journal* article prompted Schilling to track down the
Washington law firm. After several conversations with other attorneys in
the firm, he spoke with John Phillips and Mary Louise Cohen. They offered to meet him near his home in Fort Myers to discuss his allegations
and to lay out what would be involved in filing a *qui tam* lawsuit. When
the meeting ended, Schilling told the two attorneys he would need more
time to weigh his options, including the possibility of confronting his misgivings directly with the company or finding another law firm. They parted

with the standard assurances of confidentiality, but with no commitments on either side.

Several months after his initial contact, Schilling called Phillips & Cohen again. He said he was now ready to file a *qui tam* lawsuit, and he wanted the firm to represent him. The lawyers told him it had taken on another relator who had filed a *qui tam* lawsuit against HCA before the merger with Columbia. However, it was possible that the two cases could be different pieces of the same puzzle. The lawyers then called Jim Alderson.

They told Jim they thought the two cases could be mutually supportive in working toward a common goal and that each lawsuit would make the other one stronger. A second *qui tam* suit would increase the scope of his own case to more than twice the size it had been before, making it that much harder, at least in theory, for the Justice Department to continue arguing that it wasn't worth its time.

Jim needed no persuading. If this alliance could finally bring his case out into the light, he could begin reclaiming the parts of his life that had been sacrificed to secrecy. With another relator and a whole new source of supportive evidence, he couldn't imagine that the Justice Department could continue to walk away from its duty.

TWENTY-TWO

ONE-EYED KINGS

J im Alderson and John Schilling liked each other from their first conversation, a conference call arranged by their attorneys. As things progressed, they began telephoning each other on a daily basis and developed a close friendship. Although they were half a generation apart in age and lived at opposite ends of the country, their differences were trifling compared with what they had in common. They were from the same profession, with similar training and like views of their ethical accountability. Their backgrounds were in the same industry, even, arguably, in different parts of what was now the same company. They had both spoken the truth to power, and each had been answered with contempt. Their principal motivation was not the money, but a deeply offended sense of right and wrong.

It quickly became apparent to them both that their attorneys had been right, that their two cases were indeed stronger together than if they had been brought as separate, unrelated actions. The two lawsuits claimed that from 1987 to 1997, Columbia/HCA, its corporate predecessors, and its spin-off companies consistently filed false Medicare claims to boost their revenues.

Stephen Meagher was the lead attorney on the case for Phillips & Cohen. A University of Virginia law school graduate, he had spent three years in private practice before becoming a federal prosecutor. His East Coast counterpart was Peter Chatfield, a Yale Law School graduate who had joined Phillips & Cohen two years before from a major Washington law firm, Williams & Connolly.

On April Fools' Day of 1996, after many phone conversations about the case with the two attorneys, Schilling packed all of his documents into four storage cartons and flew to Washington. It was the first time he had ever met either Meagher or Chatfield face-to-face, and he knew immediately that they were sizing him up. The two attorneys liked what they saw: a quiet, unassuming accountant who thought clearly, spoke carefully, and was committed to stopping the fraud. He would make a good impression on a jury.

A month later, Chatfield attended a seminar on cost reporting to get a better understanding of the applicable Medicare rules and regulations. The program was of particular interest because it was run by KPMG, the accounting firm that had helped Columbia/HCA prepare and file cost reports for a few years at hospitals where Schilling had worked. During a break, Chatfield asked the instructor a hypothetical question that was based on both lawsuits. "If a hospital files a cost report that it later discovers had incorrect claims for reimbursement, is it required to report it?"

The instructor didn't think twice. "Yes," he said firmly. "In fact, I think there's a criminal statute on that point." Chatfield thought it was ironic to learn this at a seminar run by a company involved in cost-report fraud.

On June 26, 1996, Phillips & Cohen filed John Schilling's *qui tam* lawsuit in Tampa. A short time later, the firm filed a motion to move Jim Alderson's case to Florida as well so that the two cases could be worked on more easily together. Eight weeks later, Meagher, Chatfield, and John Schilling met with Marie O'Connell to present Schilling's case to the Justice Department.

John had heard about O'Connell from Jim Alderson, but she was different from what he had envisioned. In her late thirties, she reminded him more of a librarian than a government prosecutor. She was interested and courteous. Although she frequently questioned his statements about the size of the case, most of those challenges were not to him but to his attorneys. There was still no proof, she said repeatedly, that the wrongdoing went any further than the four hospitals with which he had direct experience. John told her of conversations with other reimbursement people, who'd all assured him the pattern was consistent throughout the HCA system. She was unmoved. John knew her history in the Alderson case. He wasn't surprised that she chose to remain just as skeptical in the face of the new evidence.

She called him "Mr. Schilling" throughout the interview, which lasted nearly nine hours. At the end, as though to show him how seriously she was taking his case, she said that she had taken eighteen pages of notes.

John was relieved when it was over. He and his attorneys thought it had gone pretty well.

To give the case some momentum, Meagher tried to interest criminal prosecutors in Schilling's cost-report allegations. He hoped a criminal investigation would keep the Justice Department's Civil Division from simply dropping out of the *qui tam* lawsuits, which he felt it was close to doing. Prosecution of criminal charges would give the cases a different center of gravity and essentially a fresh start with a whole new set of government attorneys. And if the Criminal Division thought there were sufficient grounds for prosecution, it would be hard for the Civil Division to explain why there wasn't an equally strong basis for the recovery of losses. This second front would prove to be a turning point in the case.

From his days as a prosecutor, Meagher knew the FBI's supervising agent for health care fraud, Joe Ford, in connection with a Justice Department task force on health care fraud in northern California which Meagher had chaired. Coincidentally, Ford had recently moved from Washington to Tampa, where the firm had filed Schilling's lawsuit. In late September 1996, Meagher, Chatfield, and Schilling flew down to meet with Ford and a local assistant U.S. attorney, Kathleen Haley, in Fort Myers. Two attorneys from the Civil Division attended as well.

Florida had one of the oldest, sickest populations in the country, making the price of health care a major concern in the state, and the U.S. Attorney's Office there had an outstanding record for investigating and prosecuting large Medicare fraud cases. It was immediately apparent that Ford and Haley were very interested in Schilling's case. They were not afraid to go toe-to-toe with a giant in the industry. In fact, they were already looking into other possible criminal behavior by the same company. Based on what they learned from Schilling—in particular, his story of how Jarrell had suggested offering Thuan Tran a job to steer her away from investigating a false claim—they saw cost-report fraud as the centerpiece of the criminal prosecution. They also recognized that the young accountant would be a good witness. He was knowledgeable about cost reports, and since he had worked for Columbia/HCA right up to a year ago, he could provide them with current insider information.

Schilling's documents, which suggested the company kept two sets of books, gave the government important evidence and probable cause to search many Columbia/HCA offices. In apparent preparation for obtaining search warrants and raiding Columbia/HCA facilities, Ford later drove Schilling around to the different company locations in the area, asking about corporate policies, how cost reports were handled, and the management pecking order. Schilling told him where agents would be able to find specific types of files and other valuable data.

Schilling had left Columbia in August 1995 to join a start-up health care company in Naples, about twenty-five miles away. Columbia was sorry to see him go, and had even made a counteroffer. But in December of the following year, his new employer ran into financial trouble and Schilling found himself out of work. His *qui tam* lawsuit, filed six months earlier, was still under seal, so Columbia was unaware of the case against it or of his cooperation with the Justice Department and the FBI. John had stayed in touch with some of his former coworkers, and when Columbia/HCA began looking for a Medicare reimbursement coordinator in Winter Park, near Orlando, several called to tell him of the opening. Meagher and Ford encouraged him to take it.

He initially went back to work for Columbia on a one-week consulting assignment in January 1997. The company was slow to come to a decision about the full-time job, but offered him other consulting work in February and March. Ford stressed to Schilling that he was there strictly as an observer. He was to advise the FBI on what kinds of files were being processed, where they were located, and who was responsible for what. He was not to copy or remove any documents. At the agent's request, Schilling went into the FBI's office and taped the job interviews he had over the telephone with Columbia employees, who were just two floors away in the same building. In mid-April, Ford provided him with a recorder, which he put in his computer bag to tape a meeting about cost reports with a Columbia/HCA manager during one of his consulting assignments.

John was nervous that he might be caught, and he felt bad about the potential consequences to the lives of the people he recorded. But unlike the Justice Department, the FBI was consistently supportive, and it was obvious it shared his view of the seriousness and scope of the crime he had reported.

Meanwhile, in Washington, Meagher and Chatfield continued in their attempts to convince the Justice Department's Civil Division that Alderson's lawsuit against Quorum was worth pursuing. The law firm was glad to have obtained the government's expert analyses of Quorum's cost reports that previously had been withheld. Despite that token of collegiality, the department's attitude toward the Quorum case was basically unchanged. Marie O'Connell told Meagher and Chatfield that Schilling's case was very attractive, but it was at one of those same meetings that she described Alderson's lawsuit against Quorum as "a dog of a case." Why did she feel that way, Meagher asked, when the cases were based on similar evidence? O'Connell answered that the evidence in the two cases was dramatically different.

That March, the U.S. Attorney's Office convened a federal grand jury in Fort Myers. Schilling was called to testify. The atmosphere was casual; some jurors asked him questions while others appeared to have no interest at all. On the eighteenth, federal agents raided several Columbia/HCA hospitals and other facilities in El Paso and carted off scores of boxes of records and computer files. Although no reason for the raid was made public at the time, its focus was not cost reports but physician kickbacks, which had been alluded to by a different whistle-blower in a separate *qui tam* lawsuit.

Ten days later, the first of many stories on Columbia/HCA by an investigative team headed by reporter Kurt Eichenwald appeared on the front page of the *New York Times*. The government, it said, was questioning the Medicare reimbursement claims of the hospital chain. The *Times*'s own data analysis was included in the story. The story received widespread attention. Other newspapers would later rush to catch up on what was beginning to look like a monumental corporate scandal. (The series was to earn Eichenwald and a colleague, Martin Gottlieb, the Polk Award for business reporting, a major journalism award.)

Even after the first wave of articles, HCA was able to spin its way out of the negative publicity. Two months later, a front-page story on the company appeared in the *Wall Street Journal*. It focused on CEO Richard L. Scott and his big plans for Columbia/HCA's future. The government investigation was mentioned only in passing.

By early summer of 1997, the government had begun to prepare search warrants to seize documents relevant to Schilling's cost-report allegations. About that same time, Marie O'Connell called Schilling and Alderson's attorneys with bad news: She intended to recommend that the Department of Justice not intervene in the case against Quorum. On short notice, O'Connell invited the firm to meet with Justice attorneys for a formal opportunity to discuss the case. Alderson feverishly pored over the eight boxes of Quorum documents and experts' reports recently turned over by the Justice Department, combing them for more ammunition to give his lawyers. They all knew it was their last chance to keep his case against Quorum alive.

At this point, the Phillips & Cohen team was expanded to include Gerald M. Stern. A seasoned litigator, Stern had been the lead counsel for six hundred survivors of a coal mine disaster in West Virginia in the 1970s, and his book on the case, *The Buffalo Creek Disaster,* was widely used in law schools to introduce students to complex litigation. He later served as general counsel and a board member of Occidental Petroleum, and was nominated in 1993 to be an assistant attorney general at the Justice Department, where he served for two years.

O'Connell knew the FBI was interested in the Florida case and that Schilling was cooperating with the agency's criminal investigation. Stern and Meagher argued that a government decision to decline to intervene in Alderson's lawsuit against Quorum might reduce the impact of the government's impending execution of search warrants seeking cost-report documents against Columbia/HCA, since the warrants were directed at the same kind of fraudulent billing practices as those alleged by Alderson. They said that dropping Alderson's case could raise doubts about the government's commitment to eliminating fraudulent health care billing practices and embolden potential targets to oppose rather than cooperate with the FBI's investigation. Meagher presented a summary of Alderson's analysis of the recently delivered documents, showing more false claims. Given the resources the U.S. Attorney's Office was putting into the case against Columbia/HCA, the prospects of a recovery in Alderson's case would be much greater if Justice got involved.

Their arguments prevailed, at least for the moment. The Justice Department agreed to delay its decision on whether to intervene or not.

Just a few days later, a Florida grand jury handed down a sealed indictment of Whiteside, Jarrell, and Neeb. On July 16, the FBI descended on Columbia/HCA offices at thirty-five locations in six states, with the largest number of search warrants ever served simultaneously on a publicly owned corporation. These raids targeted not only cost-report documents but also evidence related to government investigations into company kickbacks to doctors, false Medicare claims involving home health agencies

Columbia/HCA had acquired, and overbilling for lab tests. The latter charges had been made in a separate *qui tam* case Phillips & Cohen brought on behalf of two clients who were emergency room doctors in Utah.

The massive, tightly coordinated raids took the company completely by surprise and made headlines across the country, though little information was made public about the reasons for the raids or the seriousness of their implications. Columbia/HCA shares lost more than 12 percent of their value, falling $4.75 to close at $34.1875. That night, CEO Richard Scott was interviewed on CNN's *Moneyline*. A hands-on manager, he was aware of all of the company's financial practices. But he could only speculate on exactly what the federal investigators were looking for, and he wasn't about to do that on national television. Tough and self-assured, he gave no indication the company's investors had anything to worry about. He said, in effect, that the entire health care industry was under investigation, and that Columbia/HCA just happened to be the most obvious target.

Apparently his directors didn't agree. Tommy Frist, HCA's co-founder and now the company's largest individual shareholder, had reportedly grown increasingly frustrated with Scott's leadership style and his resistance to advice that he tone down his aggressive style. Not only had the government investigations hurt the company's stock price, but the name "Columbia/HCA" was now synonymous with fraud.

A high-profile member of Nashville society, Frist was deeply protective of the public's perception of Columbia/HCA, and the legacy of the company he and his father founded. The search warrants and the negative publicity were the final straw. Just nine days after the raids, Scott and his right-hand man, Columbia/HCA president David Vandewater, quit under pressure from Frist and the board. Their combined severance packages totaled $16 million.

Tommy Frist succeeded Scott as CEO. In personality and management style, Scott and Frist couldn't have been more different, and the latter wasted no time in reshaping the company to fit his image. Scott had seemed to relish his role as the abrasive outsider unconcerned about making enemies while building an empire. Frist, nearly a generation older, had a low-key style and what was described by one old friend as a "good old boy outer shell." He was portrayed as a white knight coming back to reclaim his ravaged company and clean up Scott's terrible mess. "We are going to make significant changes that will show them over the next few weeks and months that we do take [the government's investigation] seriously and we are willing to work with them in any way they deem fit," he told reporters. "Hopefully, I can work with the government to establish some new benchmarks for what is proper behavior in the health care delivery system."

Schilling and Alderson's attorneys were nowhere near as optimistic. By then they knew the long history of the policy of keeping secret reserves for questionable claims in cost reports. It had begun with the original HCA, during Frist's first tenure, long before the company had ever heard of Richard Scott.

After the management change, Columbia/HCA shed its home health business, sold off a third of its nearly 350 hospitals, and eased off its aggressive acquisition efforts. The company had posted a 15 percent growth in annual earnings prior to the news about the federal investigation. Immediately following the management change, quarterly earnings declined.

Frist worked hard to distance himself in demeanor, strategy, and corporate policies from his brash, upstart predecessor. He even dropped "Columbia" from the company name. To represent HCA in the government's Medicare fraud investigation, he hired one of the nation's top defense firms, Latham & Watkins, with its more than fifteen hundred attorneys. Phillips & Cohen knew its new legal adversaries well: Latham & Watkins had represented Teledyne in the *qui tam* case the firm had settled successfully on behalf of Emil Stache just a few years earlier.

Five days after Scott's departure, the identities of the indicted HCA executives became public, and the three were arrested and charged with conspiring to defraud Medicare. A few weeks later, the company's attorneys advised John Schilling they wanted to talk with him. He got in touch with Phillips & Cohen, who arranged for him to be represented in his talks with the company by a law firm in Florida. When his new counsel told the attorneys that Schilling didn't want to be interviewed ("He's just starting his new job—what could he know about the raid?"), his second career at HCA abruptly came to an end. "Tell your client not to take any documents with him when he leaves," the HCA lawyer warned.

Phillips & Cohen attorneys continued to analyze and sort data from Columbia/HCA and Quorum, formulating an approach that would help prove a case if it went to trial. For this mammoth task that would ultimately take years, they worked with government attorneys, government experts, and their own experts. One of their biggest challenges was to clarify the legal standards applicable to determining whether false claims in the cost reports had been filed knowingly, a requirement to proving a case under the Flase Claims Act. Another was determining how much money Medicare had lost as a result.

Meagher and Chatfield also continued to meet periodically with Justice Department attorneys to keep them informed of what evidence the attorneys were uncovering and to try to persuade the department to intervene in the *qui tam* lawsuits.

Phillips & Cohen came across a federal appeals court ruling they hoped would give Alderson's and Schilling's cases more weight. Back in 1996, a federal appeals court had ruled that health care providers were required to clearly note any questionable claims they file with Medicare and to openly challenge the government if they think those claims should be reimbursed. "Nothing less is required if the Medicare reimbursement system is not to be turned into a cat-and-mouse game in which clever providers could, with impunity, practice fraud on the government," the court said. HCA certainly fit the description of a "clever provider."

By early 1998, it had become apparent that the false claims filed by certain Columbia hospitals had been greatly facilitated by the work of outside accountants. From a public policy perspective, Phillips & Cohen felt, and the Justice Department later agreed, it was important to hold outside accountants liable when they played a key role in a health care provider's filing fraudulent claims. In May, the firm filed a *qui tam* lawsuit against accounting giant KPMG on behalf of John Schilling. The complaint charged the firm with helping its client, now called HCA—The Healthcare Company, to prepare and later conceal fraudulent claims worth millions in Medicare cost reports.

That summer, the *New York Times* filed a motion with the Florida court, asking the court to unseal the Columbia/HCA case so that the public would have access to the documents. The Justice Department opposed the motion. The government attorneys tried to argue that they needed the extra time because the case was so difficult and complex. But when the judge saw that the case had been filed in 1993, he waved the objections aside. "This case has already taken longer than World War II," he said. "It can't be that complicated." He gave the government until October 5 to decide whether to intervene.

In August, Alderson's lawyers met in Washington with Joyce Branda, who was in charge of all of the Columbia/HCA litigation at the Justice Department, and other department attorneys to make a last stab at convincing the government to join the case against Quorum. They listened to the government attorneys run through their timeworn litany of doubts, lamenting the complexity of the case, questioning the legal theories, dismissing the evidence as weak, and minimizing the potential recovery. Meagher and Chatfield rebutted their points with additional analyses of cost reports prepared by one of Alderson's accounting experts. But no one seemed to be listening. Branda said the government had insufficient resources to undertake what was likely to be protracted litigation, given that the Quorum case was much smaller than the Columbia/HCA one.

Chatfield said he thought the case was worth tens of millions of dollars.

Justice Department attorney Marie O'Connell scoffed, "It isn't worth even ten million."

Phillips said his firm would put up whatever resources it took to pursue the case. But even after making that commitment, Alderson's lawyers still didn't know whether the government was going to join the case or decline to intervene.

A month later, the Justice Department advised Meagher and Chatfield that the government would be joining Jim Alderson's case, though Branda said the firm, and not the Justice Department, would have to carry the principal burden in prosecuting it.

On October 6, 1998, the seal on Jim Alderson's *qui tam* lawsuit was finally lifted. For the first time, he was allowed to talk to his friends and the press about the case he had filed five years earlier. More than eight years had passed since the fateful breakfast in Juneau when Jim's comfortable life and promising career had suddenly begun their long, dark descent. For both the Aldersons, it was the equivalent of getting out of prolonged solitary confinement.

His first interview was with Kurt Eichenwald, who did a lengthy story in the *New York Times*. Jim thought of its potential impact on his old friends from the long-ago days when they had lived in Whitefish, and on the newer friends from their years in Dillon. If they didn't read the *Times*, they'd see his story on *60 Minutes* two months later, when Mike Wallace allowed Jim to lay out his ordeal to a national TV audience. At long last, he was free to speak the truth.

With understandable reluctance, Quorum was about to step into the light as well. A couple of years had passed since the company had last been contacted by the Department of Justice, and with the more recent focus on HCA, Quorum seemed to have assumed that its problem had simply gone away. The company was right to the extent that it was reading the Justice Department's interest, or lack of it. What it hadn't counted on was the tenacity of the man it had fired eight years earlier and his attorneys. When the company learned that the government was going to intervene on Alderson's behalf, it asked the court to split its part of the case from the action against HCA.

On the last working day of the year, the government joined Schilling's case, and it too was unsealed. Now his former colleagues and old neighbors knew the truth as well: that he was the source behind the criminal case against the Columbia executives awaiting trial.

In early 1999, the court severed Quorum's case from HCA's as Quorum had requested. A new attorney, Arnie Auerhan, took it over for the Justice Department, and Peter Chatfield assumed the lead for Phillips & Cohen. The two groups of attorneys worked in close collaboration. Knowing the defense would argue that the law had not been broken intentionally, the attorneys filed an amended complaint with five binders of exhibits nearly a yard thick. They contained thousands of highlighted examples of how Quorum had knowingly submitted false claims to Medicare. The company responded with a motion to dismiss the case.

In March, while waiting for the court's ruling on that motion, Phillips & Cohen served subpoenas for documents on two hundred hospitals Quorum managed but did not own. Almost immediately, the company sought a protective order to stop these "unduly burdensome" discovery efforts until more motions to dismiss could be filed and heard. The court replied that Quorum lacked standing to complain on behalf of hospitals it did not own. So the company simply encouraged the hospitals to object for themselves and retained counsel to help them do it. That strategy didn't work either. Eventually the hospitals produced documents without further hearings. For almost three weeks, Chatfield was inundated with calls from the hospitals' attorneys, all anxious to be sure they were complying with the order.

While discovery was proceeding against the hospitals it managed, Quorum asked for early mediation in an effort to resolve the matter. Phillips & Cohen and the Justice Department agreed. The judge picked the mediator, but eventually it became clear that Quorum was using the process to drag out the case. Months would go by between mediation sessions.

Meanwhile, in May 1999, Quorum responded to the plaintiffs' joint complaint with a series of five additional motions for dismissal. Justice Department attorneys and virtually every lawyer at Phillips & Cohen pitched in to answer and rebut the factual and legal assertions in those motions. The court never ruled. It appeared that the judge intended to leave the outcome of all substantive motions in doubt while the mediation effort still looked viable.

At nearly the same time, the criminal trial of the Columbia executives charged with defrauding Medicare of nearly $3 million began in Florida. The combined witness list contained more than 150 names. One of them was John Schilling. By then, he and his family had moved back to Wisconsin.

Media interest was high, and the health care industry was following the case closely. Schilling's and Alderson's suits were already having a major impact on compliance with Medicare reimbursement regulations by health care providers. After years of double-digit growth, Medicare spending rose only 1.5 percent in 1998, a record low. In the first six months of 1999, it actually dropped. The head of the Health Care Financing Administration spoke of a "paradigm shift" in Medicare's focus on fraud and abuse, and of a new commitment by providers to educate themselves for better compliance.

The government had three attorneys on the trial team, and at any one point about a dozen agents were working on the investigation. Early in the trial, FBI agent Ford turned to Meagher and said, "We can't lose this. We've got to win."

In the fourth week of trial, the government called John Schilling. It was a day he had been dreading. Kirsten offered to go with him to Tampa, but he said he didn't want her to go all that distance just to see the defense attorneys tear him to pieces. He left for Florida by himself. But Kirsten asked her sister to watch the kids and followed him down two days later. He was glad to have her with him for the little time they could be together.

The lawyers thought he would start on Wednesday, so he sat all that morning in the FBI office, dressed in a suit and tie, twiddling his thumbs, reading the newspaper, and getting more anxious by the minute. Finally, in the afternoon, one of the agents told him, "It looks like you might get on. I've got to get you over there right away." On the way to court, he was aware of the rush of adrenaline, the beating of his heart, and a growing sense of nausea. But once he got there, he was led to the witness room and went right back to waiting. There were no windows. He sat there by himself, unable to hear what was going on in the courtroom, ready to leap up in an instant for a call that never came. At the end of the day, Meagher appeared and told him he would appear the following day, that he was the last witness.

When he walked into the courtroom Thursday morning, everyone else was already there. He could feel the jury, the judge, the attorneys, the defendants, and the observers all watching his every move. When he got up on the witness stand, his mouth was dry, and he poured a glass of water. His hand was trembling a little, but he decided he was going to be okay if this was as bad as it got.

The government attorneys had told him what questions they were going to ask him, and they had given him an idea of what to expect from the defense. The majority of the defense cross-examination, they warned, would be adversarial, and some of it would be outright nasty.

His first questioner was one of the government lawyers who had prepped him, and the exchange was friendly. John focused on the attorney, but occasionally he would look across at the jury members and answer directly to them. He deliberately had little eye contact with the defendants. Their expressions were carefully neutral. The only one who appeared hostile was Bob Whiteside's attorney. On the few times when John glanced over at him during the direct questioning, he met the same hard stare. The defendants would catch his eye from time to time as well, but when that happened he and they both quickly looked away. The government lawyer's questioning lasted almost four hours. When it ended, John sat back in relief. It had gone well.

The cross-examination was nowhere near as easy. The attorneys for Bob Whiteside and Mike Neeb each questioned him for a full day, and Jay Jarrell's lawyer went on for three hours. Just as he had been warned, most of what they asked was intended either to trip him up, to intimidate him, or to paint him as the bad guy. They spoke of all the chances he'd had to set the matter right while he was still working for the company, instead of filing a lawsuit when he left. They accused him of stealing documents, of withholding the truth, of being motivated by greed rather than principle. Schilling's *qui tam* lawsuit against KPMG was unsealed during the trial, so that he could be cross-examined about his financial interest in that case as well. They called him the "lotto man" in reference to the *qui tam* action, a "man of half-truths," and a government agent spying on the company.

Most far-fetched of all, they tried to portray him as the mastermind, if not of the fraud he had reported, then of its aftermath, calling the shots, misleading the others, betraying his trust. They showed him documents he had signed, saying the defendants were relying on him, that he was the expert and he had misled three innocents. They tried to get him to back down from his story about the proposal to hire Thuan Tran as a means of keeping her quiet. Sometimes the attorneys would cut him off in mid-answer. He had been told this would happen, and not to react or argue. Frequently at those times the judge would interrupt as well, telling the defense attorney to let the witness complete his answer. John ended each day's testimony in a state of exhaustion.

When it was finally over, he felt that on balance he had done quite well. The government prosecutors and his own attorneys told him they thought so too.

On July 2, 1999, Joe Ford called Stephen Meagher to tell him the verdict was in. The jury had acquitted Mike Neeb on all counts, but had found Whiteside and Jarrell guilty. The FBI agent was delighted and relieved. The following December, Whiteside was sentenced to two years in prison, plus probation, fined $10,000, and ordered to pay restitution of $600,000. Jarrell was sentenced to thirty-three months in prison, fined $10,000, and ordered to make restitution of $1.3 million. In both cases, the restitution was contingent on the civil suit: If the company paid instead, then they would no longer be personally liable for the money.

While work on the cost-report cases against HCA trudged along, other *qui tam* lawsuits against the chain were resolved. On May 19, 2000, the government announced that HCA had agreed to pay the government $745 million to settle several *qui tam* lawsuits. The settlement covered a small piece of Schilling's case involving fraudulent claims for reimbursement of costs associated with the purchase of home health agencies. But it did not cover any of Alderson's allegations. The lab overbilling case brought by Phillips & Cohen on behalf of two Utah doctors accounted for $92 million of the settlement. Other lawsuits included in the settlement alleged that HCA had engaged in "upcoding," in which false diagnosis codes were used in patient records to get greater Medicare reimbursement, and that it had billed Medicare for home health visits that were not performed or that were made to patients who did not qualify for them.

Paradoxically, the settlement didn't give the expected boost to Alderson's and Schilling's cases. Instead, the company's public comments on the settlement encouraged a misperception that HCA's troubles were over. But that was far from the truth. Two big issues were left unresolved: kickbacks the company was alleged to have paid doctors and the cost-report cases. Those outstanding liabilities, however, seemed to have little effect on Wall Street analysts' comments about the company or on its stock price. As a result, HCA was not under the same shareholder pressure to settle Alderson's and Schilling's lawsuits as it might have been previously.

Several months later, any sort of pressure the government could exert on HCA to settle the cost-report cases shrank even further when the Justice Department settled criminal charges against the company for Medicare fraud. As part of a package deal to finalize the previously agreed-to $745 million settlement of certain civil charges, HCA worked out a deal with the government that an empty corporate subsidiary would plead guilty to Medicare fraud and pay a fine of $95.3 million. That way, the subsidiary rather than HCA would be excluded from the Medicare program, a nonconsequence that would have no effect on HCA. By accepting the criminal plea from a subsidiary, the government relinquished the one major weapon it had to force HCA to the negotiating table to settle the remaining *qui tam* cases.

With the slow pace of the cost-report cases, Alderson was delighted a short while later when the mediator on the Quorum case proposed a "silver bullet" to reach settlement, an approach used when parties are unable to agree on a settlement amount. Each side would offer arguments for a fair settlement value, a somewhat more elaborate version of the method by which Judge Byrne had negotiated the settlement with Teledyne six years earlier. But this time the mediator would choose the number and both sides would have to accept it for there to be a settlement.

The mediator reviewed the arguments, then proposed what he thought was a fair number. Everyone had until the close of business on July 10, 2000 to take it or leave it. Unless there was unanimity, no one would be told if any of the parties had accepted the number. If the silver bullet failed, the mediator would report to the court that eighteen months of effort had resolved nothing.

At nearly 6:30 P.M. on the designated day, the mediator called and said that all three sides had accepted the proposed figure of $77.5 million.

To get the government to release from liability all of the hospitals it managed, Quorum agreed to pay another $5 million, which boosted the settlement amount to $82.5 million. With interest computed from the date of the original settlement announcement, Quorum's final payment to the United States was $85.7 million.

All that remained was to work out the relator's share. Phillips & Cohen was adamant that Alderson deserved the allowable maximum, a full 25 percent of the $82.5 million settlement. The recovery, the firm argued, was due entirely to Jim's persistence over seven years and his attorneys' willingness to assume responsibility for the litigation and refusal to let the case die despite the Justice Department's attitude. Justice countered with 20 percent of the original settlement sum, $77.5 million, still an enormous amount of money, it said, for a case that didn't go to trial.

In May 2001, a hearing on the relator's share was held before U.S. district judge Steven Merryday in Tampa. Meagher and Judy Hoyer, an attorney with the local law firm working with Phillips & Cohen, presented the case. Their most effective witness was Connie Alderson.

"It was like waiting for test results if you have had a medical procedure," Connie said of their long saga. "I felt like we were living in a tunnel and living this traumatized life and not knowing if we were halfway in or halfway out of that tunnel."

Connie acknowledged that her husband would receive millions. "But I also feel that ten years of your life is worth a great deal," she said. She noted that her husband's health had suffered owing to the stress of the case. Since the case had begun, he had had to take medications for high blood pressure and high cholesterol. He was being treated monthly for a psoriasis condition, and he suffered from a sleep disorder.

She also talked about the problems her husband's *qui tam* lawsuit had caused her family and her disappointment with the government's lack of support and appreciation for what they had endured. "The struggles and the turmoil that our family has gone through—I'm not sure you can put a price on that," she said.

"I really have always felt that we had a civic duty to the community . . . and the country . . . to do what [we] could," she continued. "I feel we have been let down by my government. And I feel that . . . I feel we should have been a team."

The government's attorney chose not to cross-examine.

The following afternoon, Marie O'Connell was called as a witness for the Justice Department. If Jim Alderson was awarded the maximum share, the net to the Treasury from the Quorum settlement would be $63.75 million. Meagher asked O'Connell what she thought was an appropriate amount to award Alderson. The difference between the minimum reward of 15 percent and the maximum of 25 percent was, literally, determined by using a scale of 1 to 10. O'Connell replied that the department felt Jim Alderson deserved no more than 17 percent. She was rating his years of sacrifice, suffering and persistence at a meager 2.

"Ms. O'Connell, as you sit here today, having lived through this case for the better part of a decade," Meagher asked, "do you believe that the United States would be in a position to recover sixty-three and three-quarter million dollars absent the efforts of Jim Alderson?"

"I'm sorry," O'Connell replied, "I don't understand the question."

"Do you believe that absent the efforts of Mr. Alderson and his team, the United States today would be in a position to recover sixty-three and three-quarter million dollars from Quorum?"

"You are—again, you are asking a compound question. If Mr. Alderson hadn't brought this matter to our attention in the first place, we might not—we might not have ever taken occasion to investigate it. And then of course we wouldn't be in a position to recover *any* funds for it."

It was a surprising concession in view of her long opposition to the case, but after the past two days of testimony it was hard to imagine any other reply. "So the answer—" Meagher began.

"But you know," O'Connell interrupted, "it is possible that we would have uncovered the practice elsewhere, because since I was assigned to the case I also became aware of other allegations against Quorum over the years, which I am not at liberty to discuss."

Hoyer's summation was brief but powerful.

"This case, Your Honor, is not about dollars," Hoyer said. "But if it were, in the light of that twice-declination decision on the part of the government, shouldn't it be enough for the government to get seventy-five percent, when it would have had nothing absent Jim Alderson?

"And if it is not entirely about dollars, then what is it about? Well, there is some principle here. And to lean on a rather tired cliché, if you look up in the dictionary the word 'resolute,' you may well see a picture of Jim Alderson. And . . . you can picture him, as he went through his testimony yesterday, starting out on this alone—I mean literally alone, because he had to move away from his family—finding out what had happened and trying to put it together alone. And then a little way, as he trudges up this hill carrying this load, he's joined by Nick Bourdeau. And the two of them kind of carry this load up the hill, up the hill. And then they are joined by . . . the first law firm. And now there's a little group of them trudging up the hill, carrying this load.

"And then they are joined by the accountants. . . . And then they get the Phillips & Cohen law firm. And now there's a very large group of people trudging up the hill, trudging up the hill, carrying this load. Until finally, finally, the government says, 'Okay, we're in, we'll go with you.'

"And now they have literally an army trudging up the hill. They meet the enemy and subdue it. And at that point the government says to Mr. Alderson, 'You are worth a two.'

"Does anyone here who listened to his testimony, who saw him, think that Jim Alderson would say, 'Oh, okay,' and walk away? It is not fair. It is not right. And so we are here to ask you for fairness and to ask you for justice."

At the end of the hearing, in an extraordinarily rare gesture, Judge Steven Merryday came down from his bench, crossed the courtroom, and thanked Connie Alderson for her testimony. He was sorry, he told her, that she felt let down by the government. He agreed they should have been a team.

Five months later, he delivered his ruling. The case would never have settled, he said, if it weren't for Jim Alderson's "dogged resolution, eventually supported by competent professionals and an occasionally reluctant government."

The judge noted that "the participation of Alderson's counsel was unusual in several respects." This included dissuading the Justice Department on two occasions from dropping the case and assuming responsibility for the case "essentially equivalent to that of the DOJ attorneys."

"The record establishes that Alderson's counsel contributed significantly in both quality and quantity and at certain moments crucially to this case. That contribution deserves manifest and telling weight in determining the proper relator's award."

The relator's share was set at 24 percent of $85.7 million, for a reward of $20.5 million. The judge had given Jim a 9.

The Aldersons were back in their rented house in Vancouver, Washington, when Jim got the telephone call. More than the money, Judge Merryday had given them the justice Judy Hoyer had asked for.

He and Connie wiped away tears of relief and joy. They got into their 1995 Pontiac and drove to the City Grill, a deli restaurant in a nearby mall. Jim didn't need a menu; it was time to celebrate with his favorite lunch. He ordered the cold meat loaf sandwich.

TWENTY-THREE

FINAL RECKONING

For nearly two years after the federal government joined Alderson's and Schilling's *qui tam* lawsuits, HCA consistently assured the Justice Department and the public that it would prefer settling the cases to fighting them out in court. In conciliatory media sound bites, Frist and other HCA officials repeatedly pledged their cooperation toward that goal. But just as consistently, the company's actions said otherwise.

The growing army of attorneys and consultants for Schilling and Alderson, the government, and HCA, as well as officials from the Health Care Financing Administration and the Department of Health and Human Services, met periodically to discuss evidence of the allegations as a way to work out a settlement. There was only one conference room at the Justice Department's Civil Division headquarters large enough for all twenty-five or thirty of them, so they sometimes chose instead to meet at the more luxurious offices of HCA's defense counsel, Latham & Watkins.

The whistle-blowers' attorneys and their government allies found these sessions increasingly frustrating. At each meeting, they would focus on a few selected claims HCA had made on its cost reports that were representative of the fourteen thousand claims said to be fraudulent, and their experts would present whatever evidence was available up to that point to substantiate the allegations. But HCA's attorneys didn't present evidence of their own to refute them. Instead, they would constantly interrupt with hypothetical justifications for each false claim: It might have been an accident; perhaps there were special circumstances; possibly it was done because the regulations are unclear; an HCA employee might have misunderstood cost-report guidelines. The strategy was short on facts, and HCA's lawyers never presented anything that revealed the true reason the reserves were created. They left it to the relators' counsel and the government to discover and prove what had actually happened. Even after the

company pled guilty in December 2000 to criminal charges related to filing false claims in cost reports, its attorneys rarely conceded any possibility of wrongdoing in the sessions.

One of the company's outside lawyers was John Hellow, a health care
law specialist with the California law firm of Hooper, Lundy & Bookman,
Inc. Over and over again, he would offer possible explanations for each
false claim—what the claimant might have been thinking, what the circumstances might have been—but just as consistently he avoided making
even the simplest statement of the facts in a particular case. He also kept
insisting that the fiscal intermediaries, the contractors who handled the
Medicare reimbursement program, hadn't objected to any of the claims
the whistle-blowers and government said were false. He said this meant
the fiscal intermediaries were fully aware of the claims HCA had made,
essentially approving them.

HCA's in-house counsel, Steve Hinkle, told the government and the
whistle-blowers' attorneys that they would be forced to prove HCA intended to defraud the government on each of the fourteen thousand claims
referred to in the lawsuits. Everybody knew that such an effort would take
years. In effect, HCA was threatening to drag out the case indefinitely by
tying up the opposition with minutiae. This meant that the government's
limited number of salaried attorneys would be unavailable to pursue new
matters piling up on their desks. HCA seemed to be hoping that the Justice Department would decide it wasn't worthwhile to continue fighting
the case and would take whatever it could get to settle.

If the strategy worked, it would be much cheaper for HCA to pay its
attorneys to drag the case out than to simply write a check for the hundreds of millions that the government said it was owed. HCA's attorneys
were paid by the hour, and for them the lawsuits were a gold mine.

In April 2001, the Justice Department decided it had had enough of
the claim-by-claim approach. Government lawyers met with the Phillips
& Cohen attorneys to get their input on what amount they thought the
department should demand from HCA to settle.

John Phillips was acutely aware that imbalances in staffing and fi-
nances had weighed heavily in the department's initial reluctance to join
the civil case and later to move the battle to the courtroom. He now made
clear to the government lawyers that if HCA wouldn't agree to settle for a
reasonable amount, his law firm would secure whatever additional re-

sources were necessary. "We'll give you all the troops you need," he promised. He was determined that his side would not be outresourced on the case.

Later that month, the Justice Department presented HCA with a number that it said it would accept as a settlement.

Meanwhile, as a result of the 2000 presidential election, there was a shift in key players. The incoming Bush administration turned to Thomas Scully, president and chief executive officer of the Federation of American Hospitals, a lobbying group representing the nation's investor-owned hospitals whose biggest member was HCA. Scully had publicly challenged the government's case against HCA and was highly critical of the government's use of the False Claims Act to pursue Medicare fraud by hospitals. In May 2001, he became administrator for the agency that established and implemented Medicare policies and rules.

Scully didn't lose a minute in putting his mark on the agency, renamed the Centers for Medicare and Medicaid Services (CMS). One of his first steps was to move CMS staff who were cooperative with the Justice Department into other jobs. This included CMS officials who were working on the HCA case. He established a strict rule that CMS employees must have an agency lawyer present whenever they met with the Justice Department.

While waiting for the company to respond to the Justice Department's settlement offer, Phillips & Cohen attorneys and their government counterparts continued to build the case against HCA. One seemingly endless task was organizing and analyzing millions of HCA documents, either seized when the government executed the search warrants in 1997 or obtained later as a result of administrative subpoenas. The papers, including internal reports, correspondence, memos, E-mail printouts, handbooks, cost reports, and work papers used to calculate cost-report reserves, were stored in a former bank building in Tampa. Fourteen thousand boxes of HCA documents filled two floors, creating a rat's maze five feet high. The attorneys couldn't help but feel overwhelmed whenever they visited there.

Teams of private and government attorneys and their hired experts sat for days and weeks searching through the mind-numbing documents. Some got to the point where they could recognize the handwriting of executives from scribbled notes on memos. They constructed a painstaking time line of when key individuals learned about certain cost-report claims,

whom they told about them, and who made the decisions on how to char-
acterize the claims. By piecing together thousands of bits and fragments
like the reconstructed wreckage of a giant airliner, they determined the
roles played by each of the participants and traced the process by which
issues were handled at every link in the decision chains within both HCA
and Columbia.

Two months after the Justice Department made its settlement offer,
HCA told Justice that it didn't intend to counter the demand. What this
meant was that the company was essentially walking away from settlement
talks. With the criminal violations no longer a threat and the appointment
of a sympathetic former hospital industry insider as head of CMS, the
company appeared to be openly disavowing its earlier intentions to settle
the rest of its civil liability. The only alternative left to the government
was to go after the company in court, which was likely to be a long-drawn-
out battle.

A short time after HCA's declaration, Mary Louise Cohen and Peter
Chatfield were in Tampa reviewing the stored HCA documents when they
were approached by Marie O'Connell. The Justice Department attorney
asked them if Phillips meant what he had said about filling the gap. Was
the law firm really willing to supply whatever additional resources the
government needed if the case were to go to litigation? Cohen assured her
that the firm would get the Justice Department whatever support it called
for. O'Connell said DOJ needed the equivalent of twenty full-time attorneys to work on the case; the Justice Department could provide only three
full-time equivalents. Since attorneys usually work on many matters at
once, Phillips estimated the case would actually require more than triple
the full-time equivalent, or around sixty lawyers.

With twelve attorneys and many other pending cases, Phillips &
Cohen was too small to staff the entire need internally, so John Phillips
set about lining up other powerful law firms. He was determined to make
clear to HCA—and to reassure the Justice Department—that it was not
going to be able to outlawyer and outresource the government.

One of the first firms to sign on was Heller Ehrman White &
McAuliffe, whose managing partner in Washington was Brent Rushforth,
a founder and codirector with Phillips of the Center for Law in the Public
Interest. With more than six hundred attorneys in twelve offices, Heller

Ehrman usually represented corporate interests, but it also had a vigorous pro bono practice. It was an impressive beginning.

Phillips also enlisted two Los Angeles law firms with strong litigation records that had worked with his firm on other cases: Hennigan, Bennett & Dorman and Irell & Manella. Hennigan represented Orange County, California, in its successful multimillion-dollar lawsuit against its former financial adviser, Merrill Lynch, for advice that led to the county's bankruptcy. The firm was at the cutting edge in its use of technology in complex litigation for document handling and retrieval. Irell & Manella, with more than two hundred attorneys, had a reputation of having the meanest, toughest litigators in L.A.

The fourth member of the legal team was Boies, Schiller & Flexner. Partner David Boies had represented the government in the landmark Microsoft antitrust lawsuit, and his face was known to every American with a television set for his efforts on behalf of Al Gore to win a recount of Florida ballots in the presidential election. In addition, the firm of James, Hoyer, Newcomer & Smiljanich in Tampa was already working with Phillips & Cohen as its local counsel.

To the relief of the Justice Department—and no doubt to the dismay of HCA—the complement of attorneys on the whistle-blowers' legal team quickly grew to more than seventy. The government improved the odds even further, raising the number of its own attorneys assigned to the case to ten. HCA's counsel, Latham & Watkins, was one of the nation's largest law firms, but even it had to scramble to keep up with the combination of government and private legal talent and resources. At one point, one of the opposing lawyers asked Peter Chatfield in exasperation, "How many attorneys do you have on this case?"

The whistle-blowers' legal team was headed by Phillips & Cohen counsel Gerald Stern. For more than an hour every Monday afternoon, thirty or more attorneys would join a weekly conference call to discuss new developments and to coordinate work assignments.

The team decided to shift the focus away from haggling with HCA over whether individual claims were false and instead to look at HCA's Medicare billing practices overall. "This case isn't just about cost reports," Stern reminded the team. "This is a thoroughly corrupt company that cheated the government in every possible way." The attorneys wanted to demonstrate to the court that there was a pattern of Medicare fraud dating back to the time before HCA merged with Columbia, when the original HCA was under the stewardship of Thomas Frist, Jr.

The legal team decided on a two-pronged approach to the case. It would focus initially on a few large, illegal HCA claims that totaled about $100 million and try to get a court ruling on those relatively soon. It would also expand the case through a closer examination of all of HCA's cost-report claims.

By focusing on litigating just a few big-ticket claims to begin with, the legal team wanted to counter a central theme in HCA's defense strategy. HCA's attorneys continually emphasized the enormous breadth of the case, stressing to the Justice Department and to the court that it involved fourteen thousand distinct claims in two thousand cost reports, suggesting the case would take years to try—a daunting prospect for an underfunded Justice Department and an overworked federal judiciary.

By narrowing the initial scope to a few large claims, the whistle-blowers' attorneys hoped to convince a judge to issue a summary judgment—a finding that the facts showed HCA had cheated the government in those instances—and to order HCA to pay tens of millions to the government for the fraud.

At the same time, they continued digging for evidence to link HCA's top management to fraud both before and after the HCA-Columbia merger. It seemed certain that high-level executives had some role in what had happened: The claims were too big to have been the result of decisions by low-level employees.

If the whistle-blowers' attorneys could get a judgment in the range of $100 million against HCA on a few major reimbursement claims and expose top management's role in the fraud, the hospital chain might be inclined to settle all of the allegations sooner rather than later.

Toward that end, the legal team homed in on several schemes it uncovered by digging through documents, analyzing them, and pursuing any leads it was able to glean about other instances of major Medicare fraud. A particularly flagrant example was in the original HCA's corporate reorganization to spin off HealthTrust in 1987.

The goals of the divestiture were to drive up HCA's stock price and make it a less attractive takeover target. When the change went into effect, however, interest rates on loans to former HCA hospitals that were now part of HealthTrust doubled overnight from 8.5 percent to 16 percent. Because the reorganization did nothing to improve patient care, HealthTrust wasn't entitled to reimbursement from Medicare for the difference in interest rates. But the new company claimed reimbursement anyway—and an unquestioning Medicare gave it what it asked for. The government awarded HealthTrust $65 million to pay the higher interest rate on the junk bonds used to finance the corporate reorganization.

In a search of documents in the Tampa warehouse, Phillips & Cohen attorneys found a corporate memo about the reorganization with a hand-written notation clearly indicating the company knew it was not entitled to Medicare reimbursement for the excess interest on the loans. Tom Johnson, HCA's director of reimbursement, cautioned his colleagues that if HCFA were to catch the claim, it would be disallowed.

Other documents recorded that Frist spent 10 percent of his time in one year on the reorganization. With that degree of involvement, it seemed highly unlikely that he managed to remain unaware of the illegal plan to shift reorganization costs to Medicare.

As part of its research, the whistle-blowers' team sought documents that dealt with other instances where HCA had been accused of fraud. In the course of that search, the attorneys came across a deposition of an HCA vice president who referred to another, similar lawsuit against HCA.

But they were stymied in getting further information. HCA refused to give them any documents from the case, saying the matter was irrelevant. And they couldn't get the records from the court, because the case had been sealed as part of a settlement agreement. However, Stern knew the attorney on the other side of the case, who was willing to let them review the unsealed public file after the attorneys subpoenaed the documents. The legal team spent $6,000 just to photocopy the papers. It was worth the cost.

The documents showed that HCA had been sued in 1979 for deliberately manipulating its finanicial statements to lower the amount it had to pay to buy a Florida facility later known as University Hospital. HCA had agreed to pay an additional $1.6 million on top of the selling price if the hospital's profits exceeded a certain amount in any of the first four years of the deal. When the time came to settle accounts, HCA told the seller that the hospital had not fared well financially and so it was not required to make the $1.6 million earn-out payment. The seller sued HCA and its accountant, Ernst & Young, claiming HCA had engaged in numerous sham transactions and accounting practices to present an artificially depressed picture of the hospital's financial condition.

The lawsuit said HCA had donated undeveloped hospital land to the local firefighters association, but the gift was contingent on the group building a very expensive burn center on the property. HCA knew the association, which was essentially a social club, had no funding and no capacity to build a burn center, and that thus the land would eventually revert back to HCA. But the donation, which was made one day before the four-year earn-out period expired, had the effect of lowering HCA's earnings and further depressing the hospital's profits on paper.

In another effort to artificially lower its earnings, the lawsuit said, HCA donated outdated, essentially worthless X-ray equipment from the hospital to the local humane society. It reported the transaction as a straightforward loss, overestimating the equipment's value by $400,000, to further reduce the hospital's bottom line, according to court papers. The humane society apparently never used the equipment, which was engineered for humans rather than animals.

The final amended complaint in that case, which was backed up by internal company correspondence and documents, alleged accounting improprieties directed from the highest levels of HCA, including Frist and another former president and chief executive officer, R. Clayton McWhorter. HCA settled the lawsuit for an undisclosed sum and had the case sealed as part of the settlement agreement.

The revelations in that earlier case bolstered the confidence of the whistle-blowers' attorneys in their present efforts. When companies or people use such trickery to cheat other businesses, they reasoned, it was unlikely they would hesitate to cheat Medicare, where the amounts involved were much larger and the risk of getting caught much smaller.

That logic dovetailed with the second line of attack by the whistle-blowers' legal team, which was to expand the scope of the case by digging into HCA's cost reports and going beyond the false claims that HCA had reserved for on its books. The lawyers also began to develop a system to lay out the basic themes of the fraud in a consistent way. Their goal was to make it clear to a judge that the false claims followed a pattern, and that in identifying the pattern it would become practical to bring the case to trial. This effort was headed by Peter Chatfield.

Phillips & Cohen had known all along that every time HCA had taken a reserve amount on its books, it was a hedge against the possibility the government would discover a false claim and demand repayment. But closer examination of HCA's books revealed that the reserve amounts were only the tip of the iceberg, and that there were several thousand more false claims for which no reserve had been made. Once it was clear the government had failed to catch a false claim on audit, the books showed, the company would often continue to make the same false claim but would no longer bother to set aside a reserve against getting caught. Adding the false claims that were not covered by HCA's reserves boosted the calculations of how much money HCA had defrauded from Medicare by more than $100 million.

The kind of false claims the attorneys found that HCA continued from year to year included Medicare reimbursement for tickets to the Kentucky Derby and other sporting events, country club dues, purposeful double-counting of medical equipment expenses, and claiming as an expense of a home health agency the costs of running a hospital cafeteria that was located thirty miles from the offices of the agency employees who supposedly ate their lunches there.

Buried in one box of documents was an HCA e-mail that the whistleblowers' legal team called "the fifty-million-dollar challenge." A regional division of HCA was essentially told in this e-mail message to go back and manipulate cost reports so that the company could squeeze $50 million more in reimbursement from Medicare.

"The case is getting bigger and stronger," Alderson and Schilling's attorneys repeatedly assured the Justice Department, continually urging their government partners to stay the course. By now there was no question the Justice Department was firmly committed to the battle. Government attorneys were working around the clock. When Chatfield would arrive at 7 A.M. at the office to get a jump on the day's work, he often found e-mails about the case they had sent in the middle of the night.

Alderson, Schilling, and their attorneys settled in for what looked like a long siege of their corporate adversary. But they got good news in late October 2001. KPMG agreed to pay the federal government $9 million to settle Schilling's lawsuit against the accounting firm. It was the first time the federal government had held a Big Six accounting firm liable under the False Claims Act for aiding and facilitating a fraud committed by a client.

Schilling had charged KPMG with knowingly submitting false reports to Medicare and Medicaid on behalf of six HCA hospitals that were first owned by Basic American Medical Inc. and then acquired by Columbia. The accountants had concealed errors from government auditors to enable HCA to illegally keep the Medicare funds.

Two months later, in December 2001, the legal team notified HCA of its intention to depose seventy-nine current and former HCA officers and employees, including Tommy Frist. The judge ordered the two sides to set up a schedule for the depositions. HCA's top officers would go last.

Jerry Stern flew to Nashville, where HCA was headquartered, with Kirk Dillman, a partner in the Hennigan law firm, to start the depositions. The first person on their list was HCA comptroller Milton Johnson. During the deposition, Dillman homed in on whether HCA had followed general accounting practices in its cost reports and financial reporting, as required by the SEC. Under the rules, the company had to take a reserve against its reported income whenever HCA believed that claims it had made for reimbursement from Medicare would probably be denied by Medicare if the federal program audited HCA's cost reports and learned all of the relevant facts. In a way, the rule was a catch-22: By taking a reserve for a cost-report claim, HCA had tacitly admitted that it knew it was probably not entitled to the reimbursement it had received from Medicare. If it were now to try to claim that the reserves were simply the result of overly conservative accountants, then the company would be admitting it had violated SEC financial reporting requirements.

Johnson's deposition lasted two days. The morning after Stern and Dillman finished with him, HCA abruptly canceled the rest of the schedule. Even though such a step required a judge's authorization, the company's decision was unilateral. The depositions raised the risk, HCA's attorney said, that the witnesses might incriminate themselves. Citing the Fifth Amendment, HCA filed a motion for the judge to put the depositions on hold until the U.S. Attorney's Office in Florida closed its criminal investigation of HCA.

The government and the whistle-blowers' attorneys went to court as well, to oppose HCA's motion. But months went by without a ruling from the judge.

Neither side foresaw the advantage this tactic and the subsequent delay would create for the government and for Alderson and Schilling's attorneys. The additional months gave the lawyers and the whistle-blowers more time to dig deeper into HCA's Medicare billing practices, and indeed they found new ammunition for the depositions. For instance, the attorneys uncovered a series of "pros and cons" memos that company officials had written about some of the false claims, providing added proof of the deliberate nature of HCA's fraud. In those documents, which had been scooped up by the government search warrants, officials laid out the potential benefit from a false claim—i.e., how much the company would be reimbursed, versus the risk of legal fees and other consequences of possibly being caught.

Meanwhile, HCA and Scully—without the participation of the Justice Department—put together a deal that allowed HCA to avoid audits of more than two thousand cost reports, excluding those covered by the *qui tam* lawsuits. HCA announced on March 28, 2002 that it would pay $250 million to resolve all HCA cost reports from 1993 to 2001 that were not covered by Alderson's and Schilling's complaints. After the FBI raids in 1997, CMS had stopped processing all of HCA's cost reports, including those that were in the pipeline going back to 1993. HCA said the settlement "would resolve the net difference between what HCA would likely owe CMS and what CMS would likely owe HCA."

It was an astonishing agreement; many of those reports had never been audited by the government. Without an audit, the government would never know how much HCA had overcharged the Medicare program.

The approval of the Department of Justice was needed to finalize the settlement. It was not forthcoming. Senator Grassley, who had maintained his strong interest in whistle-blower cases, questioned the basis for the settlement and said his office would investigate. "This information is especially troubling," he said, "in light of the fact that the deal CMS has negotiated is with a company that has already entered several guilty pleas relating to Medicare cost-report fraud."

The relators' team was equally alarmed by the agreement. At a time when it was trying to put pressure on HCA, the company essentially was being given a pass on more than two thousand cost reports.

By August, the criminal investigation in Tampa had shut down, and depositions resumed. The relators' legal team and government attorneys took the testimony of more HCA corporate executives, as well as of employees at individual hospitals who'd prepared the cost reports. In the detailed questioning, the legal team was gradually proving that the pattern and practice of false cost reports extended not just back to the heady days of Richard Scott but all the way back to the pre-merger regime of HCA partriarch Thomas Frist, Sr. HCA's defenses were crumbling.

The company had hoped it could rely on the depositions of employees of fiscal intermediaries, acting as the government's auditors, to say that Medicare reimbursement regulations were unclear, thus excusing HCA's fraudulent claims. That didn't happen. The fiscal intermediary witnesses provided no excuses at all. Instead they testified that they had known nothing about the claims and that they wouldn't have allowed them if they had been informed.

Depositions of HCA's accounting firm and financial auditor hurt the company's position even further. They said that they relied on HCA to tell them what claims the company wanted to file for Medicare reimbursement and which ones it wanted to reserve for because those claims were likely to be rejected if discovered. Low-level HCA employees swore they had been directed on what to include when filing claims. The finger of blame was pointing ever upward.

The date to depose Frist and other top HCA executives grew closer. The relators' and government attorneys were ready to put ex-CEO Tommy Frist and other executives under oath to ask them a range of questions regarding their knowledge of and participation in the fraud or any other questionable practices that showed a pattern over time. Hardly anyone likes being deposed, and it is an especially unpopular process when it involves the possibility of criminal prosecution, or at the very least a damaged reputation.

About six weeks before Frist was scheduled to be deposed, HCA threw in its hand. The company announced an agreement to pay $631 million to the federal government to settle its remaining false claim cases, including the cost-report lawsuits. As part of the deal, the Justice Department approved the earlier settlement of $250 million that HCA had worked out with CMS. The settlement would bring the total amount HCA would pay the government since the 1997 search warrants to $1.7 billion—by far the most ever paid to the government by a company to settle false claims.

While Jim Alderson was thrilled to hear that HCA had settled, he knew from his Quorum experience that he might face yet another battle, this time with Justice Department lawyers over his relator share.

His attorneys didn't know what portion of the settlement the Justice Department would attribute to Schilling and Alderson, which would affect the whistle-blowers' reward. Despite its repeated requests to the department for information, Phillips & Cohen remained in the dark for weeks.

Two months after the HCA settlement was announced, the department's director of commercial litigation called John Phillips. Undoubtedly mindful of Judge Merryday's ruling in the Quorum case, the government offered to pay Alderson and Schilling a combined total of $100 million.

It, too, was a record.

T W E N T Y - F O U R

W H A T   H A P P E N E D   N E X T

J im Alderson happened to be visiting friends in Whitefish when the government made its offer, ending his saga where it had begun more than a decade earlier. Both he and Schilling accepted the $100 million, relieved and delighted their battles were over. Out of that amount, 35 percent went straight back to the Treasury for federal taxes, and in addition they had to pay their attorneys' contingency fees.

Never before had a *qui tam* case been fought so long and so hard for such a large recovery.

The relators' attorneys received more than their contingency fee. In addition, the company paid Phillips & Cohen and its cocounsel $28.4 million in legal fees and expenses, which covered more than eighty-five thousand hours and $7 million out of pocket that the relators' attorneys had spent on the case over ten years. HCA paid more than $347 million for legal and other costs related to the federal investigation and *qui tam* lawsuits.

Emil Stache, whose story begins this book, bought some small apartment buildings after receiving his part of the relator's share and went into the real estate development business in southern California. He invested his money carefully, and it grew. He moved his company into a suite in a low, modern office building which he owned, under the shadow of high, blue-black mountains that rise dramatically from the farmland and desert about forty miles east of Los Angeles. In the spring of 2000, six years after his case ended, he was asked how he felt about the way it had all turned out.

He took a long pull on his cigarette and thought about the question. His hair had thinned and grayed, but he was still as skinny and taut as he had been in his army days. For the interview, he had dug out the picture his friend had taken outside the field hospital in Vietnam, and he glanced down at it on his desk. He was smoking then as well. There was a hint of bemusement on the face in the old photo, the look of someone who had just discovered he was both fragile and unstoppable. "You see?" it seemed to say. "I have a hole through my body but I'm still here. I've lived to tell the story."

He knew that a lot of Teledyne employees blamed him and Al Muehlhausen for ruining their careers and their lives. "Teledyne is the one they should blame," he said. "They were cheating, and in the end they admitted to it. But for some of the dummies, I'm still the guy that spoiled the party. That kind of anger doesn't go away."

Emil expressed pride in both what he had done and the effectiveness of the False Claims Act. "It changed the entire defense industry. It gave some consequence to the things these companies were doing. Prior to this, nothing would happen to them. Even if they were caught, all they would give back was exactly the amount that was caught."

People were wrong, he said, to think that whistle-blowers file *qui tam* lawsuits to become instant millionaires. "The money is nice, but it doesn't really change all that much, and it doesn't buy you anything that counts. You still work hard to keep it and to make good decisions. I'm fifty-two; I still have another thirteen years to work."

He put out the cigarette and looked again at the picture before returning it to a dog-eared file folder. "I like to think I did some good."

As things turned out, he had far less time than the years he had assumed. The pressures of his life, answered in part by years of heavy smoking, collected an early toll. He died of a heart condition at the age of fifty-four in the summer of 2002.

Emil Stache was the only client attorney Ann Carlson ever stayed in touch with when a case had ended. Several years after she had left the law firm and was teaching at the University of California-Los Angeles law school, Emil made a $75,000 contribution to the law school in her honor, to fund tuition and living expenses for a student pursuing a career in public interest law. "He wanted to encourage young lawyers," she said, "to provide the kind of representation he felt he had received . . . who were up against big corporate interests and trying to do the right thing."

*   *   *

Al Muehlhausen stayed in California for a while after the settlement. His father had Alzheimer's and his mother was confined to a wheelchair, so he brought them out from Chicago and set them up in a rest home. He wasn't as successful as Emil in his investments, but he was older than Stache and ready to retire. After his parents died, he moved to Florida.

Jack Dowden was the first person to blow the whistle on the independent clinical diagnostic testing labs for fraud against Medicare and other government health insurance programs. As a result of his initial lawsuit against NHL and the subsequent settlement, the federal government formed an interagency task force for a large-scale investigation of billing practices by independent labs. It was known as "Operation LabScam."

From 1992 to 1997, independent labs paid more than $800 million to settle false claims charges brought by whistle-blowers and the federal government. The real payoff was that Dowden's lawsuit and the resulting government investigation into the industry saved the Medicare program billions by stopping the fraud and deterring similar practices by other labs.

Jack is still living well in his house above San Diego Harbor.

For his work on the GE case, lead investigator Stephen Kosky was given the "Director's Award for Excellence in Investigation" by the FBI in 1994. When GE complained to the director of the FBI that Kosky's citation was unnecessarily harsh on the company and its lawyers, the Bureau responded by changing the wording.

Chet Walsh's tribulations did not end with the payment of his relator's share. In September 1997, he dropped in on John Phillips and Mary Louise Cohen at their law firm's offices in Washington. It seemed the visit was mostly a trip down memory lane. He recalled with gratitude the work Mary Louise had done, and how the firm had secured a release on his behalf, saving him from the everlasting vengeance of his former employer. But the meeting had a subtext: He had lost most of his money through bad investments. Now in his late sixties, he found himself looking for something to do.

The two lawyers took him to lunch. They crossed the street behind the office to a small restaurant with the Italian-sounding name of BeDuCi, actually a humorous near-acronym for its location Below Dupont Circle.

Almost as an afterthought, Chet brought up the subject of Taxpayers Against Fraud, the public interest organization that had received the legal contingency portion of his recovery. John said the organization was doing well. It was at the forefront defending the law in both Congress and the courts and was a great resource for all whistle-blowers and their attorneys. Chet made a few seemingly pointless comments about TAF's relationship to the case; they sounded like reminiscences. The conversation moved to other subjects—their families, how well they all looked, how Chet and his wife were doing in Florida. John and Mary Louise felt sorry for him, listening to the story of his financial losses. When they parted after lunch they all wished each other well.

Three months later, on Christmas Eve, John was sitting at the desk in his office, idly sorting through the mail before turning out the lamp and heading home. He came upon a Federal Express envelope from a law firm, and after almost putting it aside he decided it might be something important.

It contained a notice from a new attorney who had been engaged by Chet Walsh. John and Mary Louise's old client had finally decided on something to do. He was suing Phillips & Cohen for a conflict of interest with TAF in the way the firm had represented him in the GE case. He was demanding that the firm give to him all of the money it had made on his case.

As John read the letter, he kept thinking about the countless hours Mary Louise had spent with Walsh, poring over documents, spending weeks in Cincinnati away from her young children, fighting on his behalf and working hard to get him as big a reward as possible so that he would be financially set for the rest of his life. She had worked hard to keep the Justice Department from indicting him and to obtain the release that would stop GE from pursuing him to his grave. He had walked away a free man with $6 million in his pocket. Now he was turning on his defenders.

John felt sickened and saddened. He debated whether to ruin Mary Louise's Christmas and show her the letter now. Leaning back in his chair, he recalled the meeting and the long, leisurely luncheon at BeDuCi.

He wondered if Chet had come to that meeting, as he had to similar conversations with his old friends at GE years ago, wearing a wire.

John walked over to Mary Louise in the adjoining office to show her the letter. He handed it to her without explanation. After she skimmed through it, she looked up at him with an expression of disbelief. "What a Christmas present. . . . "

Walsh and his attorney had badly miscalculated. John and Mary Louise were determined to fight the lawsuit and not reward either of them for what they saw as a shakedown and betrayal. A brief was filed in response to the suit. It quoted the record of Walsh's earlier statements under oath about the treatment he had received from his old law firm. His attorneys, he had told the court, were some of the "finest people" he had ever met. "Your Honor, I am a lucky man. I had the best legal talent in the business." He had referred to the two partners as "outstanding lawyers," and to John Phillips in particular as a "knight in shining armor." In direct contradiction of his subsequent suit, he had said that he benefited from TAF's involvement in the case.

Chet Walsh's case against Phillips & Cohen went to court and was dismissed. Walsh appealed, and it was dismissed again. He appealed one final time to the California Supreme Court and was turned down. The process took two years and cost Phillips & Cohen $350,000 in fees to other attorneys to defend themselves.

The key Israeli figure in the GE case, former air force general Rami Dotan, had been reduced in rank to private at the time of his sentencing to thirteen years in prison. In 2001 he came up before a military parole board, which voted to release him four years early for reasons of poor health. Following protests by his former comrades in arms, the board's decision was overturned by the Supreme Court. On October 26 of the following year, he finally was set free, at the age of fifty-six. He was taken to a hospital in central Israel to be treated for a heart condition.

One year after attorney Theodore Olson successfully defended the constitutionality of the False Claims Act before the Supreme Court, he would make another kind of history in the same venue. This time he was representing George W. Bush in the case that decided the 2000 presidential election. In the new administration, he became the U.S. solicitor general.

On March 22, 2002, a federal appeals court in Florida overturned the criminal convictions of John Schilling's old boss, Bob Whiteside, and Jay Jarrell, ruling that "competing interpretations of the applicable law are far too reasonable to justify these convictions."

They never paid the fine or made restitution.

Neither of them ever went to prison.

In early 2003, Phillips & Cohen received an e-mail from an American woman working at a hospital in the Middle East. Driven by misgivings about another expatriate who had recently become the hospital's CEO, she had done a Web search and found information on him at the law firm's Internet site. She learned that he had been a key figure in the lawsuit that exposed the biggest Medicare fraud in history. She thanked the lawyers for their service to the public in making the facts available. Her new boss's name was Clyde Eder—Jim Alderson's old nemesis in Whitefish.

The 2002 *Forbes* list of the four hundred richest Americans, published in September, ranked Thomas Frist, sixty-four, of Nashville, at number 113. Frist's personal fortune, based on his ownership interest in HCA, stood at $1.7 billion—the same amount, coincidentally, that HCA paid to the U.S. Treasury to settle all of the fraud charges and related *qui tam* cases.

Two weeks after the announced settlement, on the day before Christmas Eve, Frist's brother Bill, also a physician but with no history of involvement in the company that earned his family's fortune, was elected majority leader of the United States Senate.

Phillips & Cohen continues to represent whistle-blowers in the enforcement of the law John Phillips helped bring back to life. Cases brought by the firm's clients account for about a third of the total amount returned to the United States Treasury as a result of *qui tam* lawsuits since the act was revised.

TURNING UP THE LIGHT

BY

Senator Chuck Grassley

AND

Congressman Howard Berman

S tanding up for the truth is a democracy's greatest liberty, and the
ultimate test of citizenship. Like every other freedom, its price can
be high. For whistle-blowers, speaking out can cost them their reputations, friendships, marriages, even their whole livelihood.

This book comes at an appropriate time, at the intersection of
massive betrayals of the public trust by some of our most powerful
corporations, and the successful completion, under the amended False
Claims Act, of the largest fraud recovery in American history. It offers a
timely forum for restating the vision of Congress in passing the 1986
amendments to the law.

Simply put, we expected that whistle-blowers, often with specialized
insider knowledge or industry expertise, would actively provide assistance
to the government. We expected, too, that the Justice Department would
take full advantage of the insight, knowledge, and legal and financial
resources of the relator's counsel. And we expected that where appropriate,
whistle-blowers would be compensated for their efforts in successful cases.

The revised False Claims Act provides a means and an incentive for
reporting fraud against the public treasury. For thousands of individual
whistle-blowers, it offers the only alternative to fearful silence or the near
certainty of terrible consequence. It protects and rewards those with the
courage to cast their light in dark places. It levels the playing field in the
contest between corporate greed and personal conscience.

It has been eighteen years since we took the lead in the Senate and the House, respectively, in bringing the False Claims Act back to life. Protecting the Treasury from fraud represents a priority for Republicans and Democrats alike. Our bipartisan 1986 amendments strengthened whistle-blowers' incentives and improved their partnership with the government in ferreting out and prosecuting fraud and abuse. Of the more than $12 billion recovered by the act through 2003, some $8 billion was a direct result of the enhanced whistle-blower features of the law. If it were not for the courage and commitment of citizens like those described in this book, the United States taxpayer would today be $8 billion poorer.

And that $8 billion is just the tip of a much larger iceberg. For far longer than there has been a False Claims Act, there has been a basic ambivalence in human nature about the age-old contest between integrity and greed. We all agree that one is to be encouraged and the other punished, but too often, greed has reaped the rewards, while integrity paid the price. Under the revised act, that pattern is being reversed. Studies estimate the fraud deterred thus far by the *qui tam* provisions runs into the many hundreds of billions of dollars. Instead of encouraging or rewarding a culture of deceit, corporations now spend substantial sums on sophisticated and meaningful compliance programs. That change in the corporate culture—and in the values-based decisions that ordinary Americans make daily in the workplace—may be the law's most durable legacy.

The False Claims Act was originally called "Mr. Lincoln's Law" because its strongest early advocate was Honest Abe. It is fitting that a new generation of heroes—not just courageous whistle-blowers like Emil Stache, Jack Dowden, and Jim Alderson, but their equally committed allies in compliance and enforcement—is now arising from the law that once bore one of this country's most honored names.

I. THE LAW

FEDERAL FALSE CLAIMS ACT
31 USC 3729-3733

§ 3729. False claims

(a) Liability for Certain Acts.—Any person who—

(1) knowingly presents, or causes to be presented, to an officer or employee of the United States Government or a member of the Armed Forces of the United States a false or fraudulent claim for payment or approval;

(2) knowingly makes, uses, or causes to be made or used, a false record or statement to get a false or fraudulent claim paid or approved by the Government;

(3) conspires to defraud the Government by getting a false or fraudulent claim allowed or paid;

(4) has possession, custody, or control of property or money used, or to be used, by the Government and, intending to defraud the Government or willfully to conceal the property, delivers, or causes to be delivered, less property than the amount for which the person receives a certificate or receipt;

(5) authorized to make or deliver a document certifying receipt of property used, or to be used, by the Government and, intending to defraud the Government, makes or delivers the receipt without completely knowing that the information on the receipt is true;

(6) knowingly buys, or receives as a pledge of an obligation or debt, public property from an officer or employee of the Government, or a

member of the Armed Forces, who lawfully may not sell or pledge the property; or

(7) knowingly makes, uses, or causes to be made or used, a false record or statement to conceal, avoid, or decrease an obligation to pay or transmit money or property to the Government, is liable to the United States Government for a civil penalty of not less than $5,000 and not more than $10,000, plus 3 times the amount of damages which the Government sustains because of the act of that person, except that if the court finds that—

(A) the person committing the violation of this subsection furnished officials of the United States responsible for investigating false claims violations with all information known to such person about the violation within 30 days after the date on which the defendant first obtained the information;
(B) such person fully cooperated with any Government investigation of such violation; and
(C) at the time such person furnished the United States with the information about the violation, no criminal prosecution, civil action, or administrative action had commenced under this title with respect to such violation, and the person did not have actual knowledge of the existence of an investigation into such violation; the court may assess not less than 2 times the amount of damages which the Government sustains because of the act of the person. A person violating this subsection shall also be liable to the United States Government for the costs of a civil action brought to recover any such penalty or damages.

(b) Knowing and Knowingly Defined.—For purposes of this section, the terms "knowing" and "knowingly" mean that a person, with respect to information—

(1) has actual knowledge of the information;

(2) acts in deliberate ignorance of the truth or falsity of the information; or

(3) acts in reckless disregard of the truth or falsity of the information, and no proof of specific intent to defraud is required.

(c) Claim Defined.—For purposes of this section, "claim" includes any request or demand, whether under a contract or otherwise, for money or property which is made to a contractor, grantee, or other recipient if the United States Government provides any portion of the money or property which is requested or demanded, or if the Government will reimburse such contractor, grantee, or other recipient for any portion of the money or property which is requested or demanded.

(d) Exemption From Disclosure.—Any information furnished pursuant to subparagraphs (A) through (C) of subsection (a) shall be exempt from disclosure under section 552 of title 5.

(e) Exclusion. - This section does not apply to claims, records, or statements made under the Internal Revenue Code of 1986.

§ 3730. Civil actions for false claims

(a) Responsibilities of the Attorney General.—The Attorney General diligently shall investigate a violation under section 3729. If the Attorney General finds that a person has violated or is violating section 3729, the Attorney General may bring a civil action under this section against the person.

(b) Actions by Private Persons.—(1) A person may bring a civil action for a violation of section 3729 for the person and for the United States Government. The action shall be brought in the name of the Government. The action may be dismissed only if the court and the Attorney General give written consent to the dismissal and their reasons for consenting. (2) A copy of the complaint and written disclosure of substantially all material evidence and information the person possesses shall be served on the Government pursuant to Rule 4(d)(4) of the Federal Rules of Civil Procedure. The complaint shall be filed in camera, shall remain under seal for at least 60 days, and shall not be served on the defendant until the court so orders. The Government may elect to intervene and proceed with the action within 60 days after it receives both the complaint and the material evidence and information. (3) The Government may, for good cause shown, move the court for extensions of the time during which the complaint remains under seal under paragraph (2). Any such motions may be supported by affidavits or other submissions in camera. The defendant shall not be required to respond to any complaint filed under this section until 20 days after the complaint is unsealed and served upon the defendant pursuant to Rule 4 of the Federal Rules of Civil Procedure. (4) Before the expiration of the 60-day period or any extensions obtained under paragraph (3), the Government shall—

(A) proceed with the action, in which case the action shall be conducted by the Government; or

(B) notify the court that it declines to take over the action, in which case the person bringing the action shall have the right to conduct the action. (5) When a person brings an action under this subsection, no person other than the Government may intervene or bring a related action based on the facts underlying the pending action.

(c) Rights of the Parties to Qui Tam Actions.—(1) If the Government proceeds with the action, it shall have the primary responsibility for prosecuting the action, and shall not be bound by an act of the person bringing the action. Such person shall have the right to continue as a party to the action, subject to the limitations set forth in paragraph (2). (2)(A) The Government may dismiss the action notwithstanding the objections of the person initiating the action if the person has been notified by the Government of the filing of the motion and the court has provided the person with an opportunity for a hearing on the motion. (B) The Government may settle the action with the defendant notwithstanding the objections of the person initiating the action if the court determines, after a hearing, that the proposed settlement is fair, adequate, and reasonable under all the circumstances. Upon a showing of good cause, such hearing may be held in camera. (C) Upon a showing by the Government that unrestricted participation during the course of the litigation by the person initiating the action would interfere with or unduly delay the Government's prosecution of the case, or would be repetitious, irrelevant, or for purposes of harassment, the court may, in its discretion, impose limitations on the person's participation, such as—

(i) limiting the number of witnesses the person may call;

(ii) limiting the length of the testimony of such witnesses;

(iii) limiting the person's cross-examination of witnesses; or

(iv) otherwise limiting the participation by the person in the litigation. (D) Upon a showing by the defendant that unrestricted participation during the course of the litigation by the person initiating the action would be for purposes of harassment or would cause the defendant undue burden or unnecessary expense, the court may limit the participation by the person in the litigation. (3) If the Government elects not to proceed with the action, the person who initiated the action shall have the right to conduct the action. If the Government so requests, it shall be served with copies of all pleadings filed in the action and shall be supplied with copies of all deposition transcripts (at the Government's expense). When a person proceeds with the action, the court, without limiting the status and rights of the person initiating the action, may nevertheless permit the Government to intervene at a later date upon a showing of good cause. (4) Whether or not the Government proceeds with the action, upon a showing by the Government that certain actions of discovery by the person initiating the action would interfere with the Government's investigation or prosecution of a criminal or civil matter arising out of the same facts, the court may stay such discovery for a period of not more than 60 days. Such a showing shall be conducted in camera. The court may extend the 60-day period upon a further showing in camera that the Government has pursued the criminal or civil investigation or proceedings with reasonable diligence and any proposed discovery in the civil action will interfere with the ongoing criminal or civil investigation or proceedings.

(5) Notwithstanding subsection (b), the Government may elect to pursue its claim through any alternate remedy available to the Government, including any administrative proceeding to determine a civil money penalty. If any such alternate remedy is pursued in another proceeding, the person initiating the action shall have the same rights in such proceeding as such person would have had if the action had continued under this section. Any finding of fact or conclusion of law made in such other proceeding that has become final shall be conclusive on all parties to an action under this section. For purposes of the preceding sentence, a finding or conclusion is final if it has been finally determined on appeal to

the appropriate court of the United States, if all time for filing such an appeal with respect to the finding or conclusion has expired, or if the finding or conclusion is not subject to judicial review.

(d) Award to Qui Tam Plaintiff.—(1) If the Government proceeds with an action brought by a person under subsection (b), such person shall, subject to the second sentence of this paragraph, receive at least 15 percent but not more than 25 percent of the proceeds of the action or settlement of the claim, depending upon the extent to which the person substantially contributed to the prosecution of the action. Where the action is one which the court finds to be based primarily on disclosures of specific information (other than information provided by the person bringing the action) relating to allegations or transactions in a criminal, civil, or administrative hearing, in a congressional, administrative, or Government (FOOTNOTE 1) Accounting Office report, hearing, audit, or investigation, or from the news media, the court may award such sums as it considers appropriate, but in no case more than 10 percent of the proceeds, taking into account the significance of the information and the role of the person bringing the action in advancing the case to litigation. Any payment to a person under the first or second sentence of this paragraph shall be made from the proceeds. Any such person shall also receive an amount for reasonable expenses which the court finds to have been necessarily incurred, plus reasonable attorneys' fees and costs. All such expenses, fees, and costs shall be awarded against the defendant. (FOOTNOTE 1) So in original. Probably should be "General". (2) If the Government does not proceed with an action under this section, the person bringing the action or settling the claim shall receive an amount which the court decides is reasonable for collecting the civil penalty and damages. The amount shall be not less than 25 percent and not more than 30 percent of the proceeds of the action or settlement and shall be paid out of such proceeds. Such person shall also receive an amount for reasonable expenses which the court finds to have been necessarily incurred, plus reasonable attorneys' fees and costs. All such expenses, fees, and costs shall be awarded against the defendant. (3) Whether or not the Government proceeds with the action, if the court finds that the action was brought by a person who planned and initiated the violation of section 3729 upon which the action was brought, then the court may, to the extent the court considers appropriate, reduce the share of the proceeds of the action which the person would otherwise receive under paragraph (1) or (2) of this subsection, taking into account the role of that person in advancing the case to litigation and any relevant circumstances pertaining to the violation. If the person bringing the action is convicted of criminal conduct arising from his or her role in the violation of section 3729, that person shall be dismissed from the civil action and shall not receive any share of the proceeds of the action. Such dismissal shall not prejudice the right of the United States to continue the action, represented by the Department of Justice. (4) If the Government does not proceed with the action and the person bringing the action conducts the action, the court may award to the defendant its reasonable attorneys' fees and expenses if the defendant prevails in the action and the court finds that the claim of the person bringing the action was clearly frivolous, clearly vexatious, or brought primarily for purposes of harassment.

(e) Certain Actions Barred.—(1) No court shall have jurisdiction over an action brought by a former or present member of the armed forces under subsection (b) of this section against a member of the armed forces arising out of such person's service in the armed forces. (2)(A) No court shall have jurisdiction over an action brought under subsection (b) against a Member of Congress, a member of the judiciary, or a senior executive branch official if the action is based on evidence or information known to the Government when the action was brought. (B) For purposes of this paragraph, "senior executive branch official" means any officer or employee listed in paragraphs (1) through (8) of section 101(f) of the Ethics in Government Act of 1978 (5 U.S.C. App.). (3) In no event may a person bring an action under subsection (b) which is based upon allegations or transactions which are the subject of a civil suit or an administrative civil money penalty proceeding in which the Government is already a party. (4)(A) No court shall have jurisdiction over an action under this section based upon the public disclosure of allegations or transactions in a criminal, civil, or administrative hearing, in a congressional, administrative, or Government (FOOT-

NOTE 2) Accounting Office report, hearing, audit, or investigation, or from the news media, unless the action is brought by the Attorney General or the person bringing the action is an original source of the information. (FOOTNOTE 2) So in original. Probably should be "General". (B) For purposes of this paragraph, "original source" means an individual who has direct and independent knowledge of the information on which the allegations are based and has voluntarily provided the information to the Government before filing an action under this section which is based on the information.

(f) Government Not Liable for Certain Expenses.—The Government is not liable for expenses which a person incurs in bringing an action under this section.

(g) Fees and Expenses to Prevailing Defendant.—In civil actions brought under this section by the United States, the provisions of section 2412(d) of title 28 shall apply.

(h) Any employee who is discharged, demoted, suspended, threatened, harassed, or in any other manner discriminated against in the terms and conditions of employment by his or her employer because of lawful acts done by the employee on behalf of the employee or others in furtherance of an action under this section, including investigation for, initiation of, testimony for, or assistance in an action filed or to be filed under this section, shall be entitled to all relief necessary to make the employee whole. Such relief shall include reinstatement with the same seniority status such employee would have had but for the discrimination, 2 times the amount of back pay, interest on the back pay, and compensation for any special damages sustained as a result of the discrimination, including litigation costs and reasonable attorneys' fees. An employee may bring an action in the appropriate district court of the United States for the relief provided in this subsection.

§ 3731. False claims procedure

(a) A subpena requiring the attendance of a witness at a trial or hearing conducted under section 3730 of this title may be served at any place in the United States.

(b) A civil action under section 3730 may not be brought—

(1) more than 6 years after the date on which the violation of section 3729 is committed, or

(2) more than 3 years after the date when facts material to the right of action are known or reasonably should have been known by the official of the United States charged with responsibility to act in the circumstances, but in no event more than 10 years after the date on which the violation is committed, whichever occurs last.

(c) In any action brought under section 3730, the United States shall be required to prove all essential elements of the cause of action, including damages, by a preponderance of the evidence.

(d) Notwithstanding any other provision of law, the Federal Rules of Criminal Procedure, or the Federal Rules of Evidence, a final judgment rendered in favor of the United States in any criminal proceeding charging fraud or false statements, whether upon a verdict after trial or upon a plea of guilty or nolo contendere, shall estop the defendant from denying the essential elements of the offense in any action which involves the same transaction as in the criminal proceeding and which is brought under subsection (a) or (b) of section 3730.

§ 3732. False claims jurisdiction

(a) Actions Under Section 3730.—Any action under section 3730 may be brought in any judicial district in which the defendant or, in the case of multiple defendants, any one defendant can be found, resides, transacts business, or in which any act proscribed by section 3729 occurred. A summons as required by the Federal Rules of Civil Procedure shall be issued by the appropriate district court and served at any place within or outside the United States.

(b) Claims Under State Law.—The district courts shall have jurisdiction over any action brought under the laws of any State for the recovery of funds paid by a State or local government if the action arises from the same transaction or occurrence as an action brought under section 3730.

§ 3733. Civil investigative demands

(a) In General.—

(1) Issuance and service.—Whenever the Attorney General has reason to believe that any person may be in possession, custody, or control of any documentary material or information relevant to a false claims law investigation, the Attorney General may, before commencing a civil proceeding under section 3730 or other false claims law, issue in writing and cause to be served upon such person, a civil investigative demand requiring such person—

(A) to produce such documentary material for inspection and copying,

(B) to answer in writing written interrogatories with respect to such documentary material or information,

(C) to give oral testimony concerning such documentary material or information, or

(D) to furnish any combination of such material, answers, or testimony. The Attorney General may not delegate the authority to issue civil investigative demands under this subsection. Whenever a civil investigative demand is an express demand for any product of discovery, the Attorney General, the Deputy Attorney General, or an Assistant Attorney General shall cause to be served, in any manner authorized by this section, a copy of such demand upon the person from whom the discovery was obtained and shall notify the person to whom such demand is issued of the date on which such copy was served.

(2) Contents and deadlines.—

(A) Each civil investigative demand issued under paragraph (1) shall state the nature of the conduct constituting the alleged violation of a false claims law which is under investigation, and the applicable provision of law alleged to be violated.

(B) If such demand is for the production of documentary material, the demand shall—

(i) describe each class of documentary material to be produced with such definiteness and certainty as to permit such material to be fairly identified;

(ii) prescribe a return date for each such class which will provide a reasonable period of time within which the material so demanded may be assembled and made available for inspection and copying; and

(iii) identify the false claims law investigator to whom such material shall be made available.

(C) If such demand is for answers to written interrogatories, the demand shall—

(i) set forth with specificity the written interrogatories to be answered;

(ii) prescribe dates at which time answers to written interrogatories shall be submitted; and

(iii) identify the false claims law investigator to whom such answers shall be submitted.

(D) If such demand is for the giving of oral testimony, the demand shall—

(i) prescribe a date, time, and place at which oral testimony shall be commenced;

(ii) identify a false claims law investigator who shall conduct the examination and the custodian to whom the transcript of such examination shall be submitted;

(iii) specify that such attendance and testimony are necessary to the conduct of the investigation;

(iv) notify the person receiving the demand of the right to be accompanied by an attorney and any other representative; and

(v) describe the general purpose for which the demand is being issued and the general nature of the testimony, including the primary areas of inquiry, which will be taken pursuant to the demand.

(E) Any civil investigative demand issued under this section which is an express demand for any product of discovery shall not be returned or returnable until 20 days after a copy of such demand has been served upon the person from whom the discovery was obtained.

(F) The date prescribed for the commencement of oral testimony pursuant to a civil investigative demand issued under this section shall be a date which is not less than seven days after the date on which demand is received, unless the Attorney General or an Assistant Attorney General designated by the Attorney General determines that exceptional circumstances are present which warrant the commencement of such testimony within a lesser period of time.

(G) The Attorney General shall not authorize the issuance under this section of more than one civil investigative demand for oral testimony by the same person unless the person requests otherwise or unless the Attorney General, after investigation, notifies that person in writing that an additional demand for oral testimony is necessary. The Attorney General may not, notwithstanding section 510 of title 28, authorize the performance, by any other officer, employee, or agency, of any function vested in the Attorney General under this subparagraph.

(b) Protected Material or Information.—

(1) In general.—A civil investigative demand issued under subsection (a) may not require the production of any documentary material, the submission of any answers to written interrogatories, or the giving of any oral testimony if such material, answers, or testimony would be protected from disclosure under—

(A) the standards applicable to subpoenas or subpoenas duces tecum issued by a court of the United States to aid in a grand jury investigation; or

(B) the standards applicable to discovery requests under the Federal Rules of Civil Procedure, to the extent that the application of such standards to any such demand is appropriate and consistent with the provisions and purposes of this section.

(2) Effect on other orders, rules, and laws.—Any such demand which is an express demand for any product of discovery supersedes any inconsistent order, rule, or provision of law (other than this section) preventing or restraining disclosure of such product of discovery to any person. Disclosure of any product of discovery pursuant to any such express demand does not constitute a waiver of any right or privilege which the person making such disclosure may be entitled to invoke to resist discovery of trial preparation materials.

(c) Service; Jurisdiction.—

(1) By whom served.—Any civil investigative demand issued under subsection (a) may be served by a false claims law investigator, or by a United States marshal or a deputy marshal, at any place within the territorial jurisdiction of any court of the United States.

(2) Service in foreign countries.—Any such demand or any petition filed under subsection (j) may be served upon any person who is not found within the territorial jurisdiction of any court of the United States in such manner as the Federal Rules of Civil Procedure prescribe for service in a foreign country. To the extent that the courts of the United States can assert jurisdiction over any such person consistent with due process, the United States District Court for the District of Columbia shall have the same jurisdiction to take any action respecting compliance with this section by any such person that such court would have if such person were personally within the jurisdiction of such court.

(d) Service Upon Legal Entities and Natural Persons.—

(1) Legal entities.—Service of any civil investigative demand issued under subsection (a) or of any petition filed under subsection (j) may be made upon a partnership, corporation, association, or other legal entity by—

(A) delivering an executed copy of such demand or petition to any partner, executive officer, managing agent, or general agent of the partnership, corporation, association, or entity, or to any agent authorized by appointment or by law to receive service of process on behalf of such partnership, corporation, association, or entity;

(B) delivering an executed copy of such demand or petition to the principal office or place of business of the partnership, corporation, association, or entity; or

(C) depositing an executed copy of such demand or petition in the United States mails by registered or certified mail, with a return receipt requested, addressed to such partnership, corporation, association, or entity at its principal office or place of business.

(2) Natural persons.—Service of any such demand or petition may be made upon any natural person by—

(A) delivering an executed copy of such demand or petition to the person; or

(B) depositing an executed copy of such demand or petition in the United States mails by registered or certified mail, with a return receipt requested, addressed to the person at the person's residence or principal office or place of business.

(e) Proof of Service.—A verified return by the individual serving any civil investigative demand issued under subsection (a) or any petition filed under subsection (j) setting forth the manner of such service shall be proof of such service. In the case of service by registered or certified mail, such return shall be accompanied by the return post office receipt of delivery of such demand.

(f) Documentary Material.—

(1) Sworn certificates.—The production of documentary material in response to a civil investigative demand served under this section shall be made under a sworn certificate, in such form as the demand designates, by—

(A) in the case of a natural person, the person to whom the demand is directed, or

(B) in the case of a person other than a natural person, a person having knowledge of the facts and circumstances relating to such production and authorized to act on behalf of such person. The certificate shall state that all of the documentary material required by the demand and in the possession, custody, or control of the person to whom the demand is directed has been produced and made available to the false claims law investigator identified in the demand.

(2) Production of materials.—Any person upon whom any civil investigative demand for the production of documentary material has been served under this section shall make such material available for inspection and copying to the false claims law investigator identified in such demand at the principal place of business of such person, or at such other place as the false claims law investigator and the person thereafter may agree and prescribe in writing, or as the court may direct under subsection (j)(1). Such material shall be made so available on the return date specified in such demand, or on such later date as the false claims law investigator may prescribe in writing. Such person may, upon written agreement between the person and the false claims law investigator, substitute copies for originals of all or any part of such material.

(g) Interrogatories.—Each interrogatory in a civil investigative demand served under this section shall be answered separately and fully in writing under oath and shall be submitted under a sworn certificate, in such form as the demand designates, by—

(1) in the case of a natural person, the person to whom the demand is directed, or

(2) in the case of a person other than a natural person, the person or persons responsible for answering each interrogatory. If any interrogatory is objected to, the reasons for the objection shall be stated in the certificate instead of an answer. The certificate shall state that all information required by the demand and in the possession, custody, control, or knowledge of the person to whom the demand is directed has been submitted. To the extent that any information is not furnished, the information shall be identified and reasons set forth with particularity regarding the reasons why the information was not furnished.

(h) Oral Examinations.—

(1) Procedures.—The examination of any person pursuant to a civil investigative demand for oral testimony served under this section shall be taken before an officer authorized to administer oaths and affirmations by the laws of the United States or of the place where the ex-

amination is held. The officer before whom the testimony is to be taken shall put the witness on oath or affirmation and shall, personally or by someone acting under the direction of the officer and in the officer's presence, record the testimony of the witness. The testimony shall be taken stenographically and shall be transcribed. When the testimony is fully transcribed, the officer before whom the testimony is taken shall promptly transmit a copy of the transcript of the testimony to the custodian. This subsection shall not preclude the taking of testimony by any means authorized by, and in a manner consistent with, the Federal Rules of Civil Procedure.

(2) Persons present.—The false claims law investigator conducting the examination shall exclude from the place where the examination is held all persons except the person giving the testimony, the attorney for and any other representative of the person giving the testimony, the attorney for the Government, any person who may be agreed upon by the attorney for the Government and the person giving the testimony, the officer before whom the testimony is to be taken, and any stenographer taking such testimony.

(3) Where testimony taken.—The oral testimony of any person taken pursuant to a civil investigative demand served under this section shall be taken in the judicial district of the United States within which such person resides, is found, or transacts business, or in such other place as may be agreed upon by the false claims law investigator conducting the examination and such person.

(4) Transcript of testimony.—When the testimony is fully transcribed, the false claims law investigator or the officer before whom the testimony is taken shall afford the witness, who may be accompanied by counsel, a reasonable opportunity to examine and read the transcript, unless such examination and reading are waived by the witness. Any changes in form or substance which the witness desires to make shall be entered and identified upon the transcript by the officer or the false claims law investigator, with a statement of the reasons given by the witness for making such changes. The transcript shall then be signed by the witness, unless the witness in writing waives the signing, is ill, cannot be found, or refuses to sign. If the transcript is not signed by the witness within 30 days after

being afforded a reasonable opportunity to examine it, the officer or the false claims law investigator shall sign it and state on the record the fact of the waiver, illness, absence of the witness, or the refusal to sign, together with the reasons, if any, given therefor.

(5) Certification and delivery to custodian.—The officer before whom the testimony is taken shall certify on the transcript that the witness was sworn by the officer and that the transcript is a true record of the testimony given by the witness, and the officer or false claims law investigator shall promptly deliver the transcript, or send the transcript by registered or certified mail, to the custodian.

(6) Furnishing or inspection of transcript by witness.—Upon payment of reasonable charges therefor, the false claims law investigator shall furnish a copy of the transcript to the witness only, except that the Attorney General, the Deputy Attorney General, or an Assistant Attorney General may, for good cause, limit such witness to inspection of the official transcript of the witness' testimony.

(7) Conduct of oral testimony.—(A) Any person compelled to appear for oral testimony under a civil investigative demand issued under subsection (a) may be accompanied, represented, and advised by counsel. Counsel may advise such person, in confidence, with respect to any question asked of such person. Such person or counsel may object on the record to any question, in whole or in part, and shall briefly state for the record the reason for the objection. An objection may be made, received, and entered upon the record when it is claimed that such person is entitled to refuse to answer the question on the grounds of any constitutional or other legal right or privilege, including the privilege against self-incrimination. Such person may not otherwise object to or refuse to answer any question, and may not directly or through counsel otherwise interrupt the oral examination. If such person refuses to answer any question, a petition may be filed in the district court of the United States under subsection (j)(1) for an order compelling such person to answer such question. (B) If such person refuses to answer any question on the grounds of the privilege against self-incrimination, the testimony of such person may be compelled in accordance with the provisions of part V of title 18.

(8) Witness fees and allowances.—Any person appearing for oral testimony under a civil investigative demand issued under subsection (a) shall be entitled to the same fees and allowances which are paid to witnesses in the district courts of the United States.

(i) Custodians of Documents, Answers, and Transcripts.—

(1) Designation.—The Attorney General shall designate a false claims law investigator to serve as custodian of documentary material, answers to interrogatories, and transcripts of oral testimony received under this section, and shall designate such additional false claims law investigators as the Attorney General determines from time to time to be necessary to serve as deputies to the custodian.

(2) Responsibility for materials; disclosure.—(A) A false claims law investigator who receives any documentary material, answers to interrogatories, or transcripts of oral testimony under this section shall transmit them to the custodian. The custodian shall take physical possession of such material, answers, or transcripts and shall be responsible for the use made of them and for the return of documentary material under paragraph (4). (B) The custodian may cause the preparation of such copies of such documentary material, answers to interrogatories, or transcripts of oral testimony as may be required for official use by any false claims law investigator, or other officer or employee of the Department of Justice, who is authorized for such use under regulations which the Attorney General shall issue. Such material, answers, and transcripts may be used by any such authorized false claims law investigator or other officer or employee in connection with the taking of oral testimony under this section. (C) Except as otherwise provided in this subsection, no documentary material, answers to interrogatories, or transcripts of oral testimony, or copies thereof, while in the possession of the custodian, shall be available for examination by any individual other than a false claims law investigator or other officer or employee of the Department of Justice authorized under subparagraph (B). The prohibition in the preceding sentence on the availability of material, answers, or transcripts shall not apply if consent is given by the person who produced such material, answers, or transcripts, or, in the case of any product of discovery produced pursuant to an express demand for such material, consent is

given by the person from whom the discovery was obtained. Nothing in this subparagraph is intended to prevent disclosure to the Congress, including any committee or subcommittee of the Congress, or to any other agency of the United States for use by such agency in furtherance of its statutory responsibilities. Disclosure of information to any such other agency shall be allowed only upon application, made by the Attorney General to a United States district court, showing substantial need for the use of the information by such agency in furtherance of its statutory responsibilities. (D) While in the possession of the custodian and under such reasonable terms and conditions as the Attorney General shall prescribe—

(i) documentary material and answers to interrogatories shall be available for examination by the person who produced such material or answers, or by a representative of that person authorized by that person to examine such material and answers; and

(ii) transcripts of oral testimony shall be available for examination by the person who produced such testimony, or by a representative of that person authorized by that person to examine such transcripts.

(3) Use of material, answers, or transcripts in other proceedings.— Whenever any attorney of the Department of Justice has been designated to appear before any court, grand jury, or Federal agency in any case or proceeding, the custodian of any documentary material, answers to interrogatories, or transcripts of oral testimony received under this section may deliver to such attorney such material, answers, or transcripts for official use in connection with any such case or proceeding as such attorney determines to be required. Upon the completion of any such case or proceeding, such attorney shall return to the custodian any such material, answers, or transcripts so delivered which have not passed into the control of such court, grand jury, or agency through introduction into the record of such case or proceeding.

(4) Conditions for return of material.—If any documentary material has been produced by any person in the course of any false claims law investigation pursuant to a civil investigative demand under this section, and—

(A) any case or proceeding before the court or grand jury arising out of such investigation, or any proceeding before any Federal agency involving such material, has been completed, or

(B) no case or proceeding in which such material may be used has been commenced within a reasonable time after completion of the examination and analysis of all documentary material and other information assembled in the course of such investigation, the custodian shall, upon written request of the person who produced such material, return to such person any such material (other than copies furnished to the false claims law investigator under subsection (f)(2) or made for the Department of Justice under paragraph (2)(B)) which has not passed into the control of any court, grand jury, or agency through introduction into the record of such case or proceeding.

(5) Appointment of successor custodians.—In the event of the death, disability, or separation from service in the Department of Justice of the custodian of any documentary material, answers to interrogatories, or transcripts of oral testimony produced pursuant to a civil investigative demand under this section, or in the event of the official relief of such custodian from responsibility for the custody and control of such material, answers, or transcripts, the Attorney General shall promptly—

(A) designate another false claims law investigator to serve as custodian of such material, answers, or transcripts, and

(B) transmit in writing to the person who produced such material, answers, or testimony notice of the identity and address of the successor so designated. Any person who is designated to be a successor under this paragraph shall have, with regard to such material, answers, or transcripts, the same duties and responsibilities as were imposed by this section upon that person's predecessor in office, except that the successor shall not be held responsible for any default or dereliction which occurred before that designation.

(j) Judicial Proceedings.—

(1) Petition for enforcement.—Whenever any person fails to comply with any civil investigative demand issued under subsection (a), or

whenever satisfactory copying or reproduction of any material requested in such demand cannot be done and such person refuses to surrender such material, the Attorney General may file, in the district court of the United States for any judicial district in which such person resides, is found, or transacts business, and serve upon such person a petition for an order of such court for the enforcement of the civil investigative demand.

(2) Petition to modify or set aside demand.—(A) Any person who has received a civil investigative demand issued under subsection (a) may file, in the district court of the United States for the judicial district within which such person resides, is found, or transacts business, and serve upon the false claims law investigator identified in such demand a petition for an order of the court to modify or set aside such demand. In the case of a petition addressed to an express demand for any product of discovery, a petition to modify or set aside such demand may be brought only in the district court of the United States for the judicial district in which the proceeding in which such discovery was obtained is or was last pending. Any petition under this subparagraph must be filed—

(i) within 20 days after the date of service of the civil investigative demand, or at any time before the return date specified in the demand, whichever date is earlier, or

(ii) within such longer period as may be prescribed in writing by any false claims law investigator identified in the demand. (B) The petition shall specify each ground upon which the petitioner relies in seeking relief under subparagraph (A), and may be based upon any failure of the demand to comply with the provisions of this section or upon any constitutional or other legal right or privilege of such person. During the pendency of the petition in the court, the court may stay, as it deems proper, the running of the time allowed for compliance with the demand, in whole or in part, except that the person filing the petition shall comply with any portions of the demand not sought to be modified or set aside.

(3) Petition to modify or set aside demand for product of discovery.—
(A) In the case of any civil investigative demand issued under subsec-

tion (a) which is an express demand for any product of discovery, the person from whom such discovery was obtained may file, in the district court of the United States for the judicial district in which the proceeding in which such discovery was obtained is or was last pending, and serve upon any false claims law investigator identified in the demand and upon the recipient of the demand, a petition for an order of such court to modify or set aside those portions of the demand requiring production of any such product of discovery. Any petition under this subparagraph must be filed—

(i) within 20 days after the date of service of the civil investigative demand, or at any time before the return date specified in the demand, whichever date is earlier, or

(ii) within such longer period as may be prescribed in writing by any false claims law investigator identified in the demand. (B) The petition shall specify each ground upon which the petitioner relies in seeking relief under subparagraph (A), and may be based upon any failure of the portions of the demand from which relief is sought to comply with the provisions of this section, or upon any constitutional or other legal right or privilege of the petitioner. During the pendency of the petition, the court may stay, as it deems proper, compliance with the demand and the running of the time allowed for compliance with the demand.

(4) Petition to require performance by custodian of duties. - At any time during which any custodian is in custody or control of any documentary material or answers to interrogatories produced, or transcripts of oral testimony given, by any person in compliance with any civil investigative demand issued under subsection (a), such person, and in the case of an express demand for any product of discovery, the person from whom such discovery was obtained, may file, in the district court of the United States for the judicial district within which the office of such custodian is situated, and serve upon such custodian, a petition for an order of such court to require the performance by the custodian of any duty imposed upon the custodian by this section.

(5) Jurisdiction.—Whenever any petition is filed in any district court of the United States under this subsection, such court shall have

jurisdiction to hear and determine the matter so presented, and to enter such order or orders as may be required to carry out the provisions of this section. Any final order so entered shall be subject to appeal under section 1291 of title 28. Any disobedience of any final order entered under this section by any court shall be punished as a contempt of the court.

(6) Applicability of federal rules of civil procedure.—The Federal Rules of Civil Procedure shall apply to any petition under this subsection, to the extent that such rules are not inconsistent with the provisions of this section.

(k) Disclosure Exemption.—Any documentary material, answers to written interrogatories, or oral testimony provided under any civil investigative demand issued under subsection (a) shall be exempt from disclosure under section 552 of title 5.

(l) Definitions.—For purposes of this section—(1) the term "false claims law" means—

(A) this section and sections 3729 through 3732; and

(B) any Act of Congress enacted after the date of the enactment of this section which prohibits, or makes available to the United States in any court of the United States any civil remedy with respect to, any false claim against, bribery of, or corruption of any officer or employee of the United States;

(2) the term "false claims law investigation" means any inquiry conducted by any false claims law investigator for the purpose of ascertaining whether any person is or has been engaged in any violation of a false claims law;

(3) the term "false claims law investigator" means any attorney or investigator employed by the Department of Justice who is charged with the duty of enforcing or carrying into effect any false claims law, or any officer or employee of the United States acting under the direction and supervision of such attorney or investigator in connection with a false claims law investigation;

(4) the term "person" means any natural person, partnership, corporation, association, or other legal entity, including any State or political subdivision of a State;

(5) the term "documentary material" includes the original or any copy of any book, record, report, memorandum, paper, communication, tabulation, chart, or other document, or data compilations stored in or accessible through computer or other information retrieval systems, together with instructions and all other materials necessary to use or interpret such data compilations, and any product of discovery;

(6) the term "custodian" means the custodian, or any deputy custodian, designated by the Attorney General under subsection (i)(1); and

(7) the term "product of discovery" includes—(A) the original or duplicate of any deposition, interrogatory, document, thing, result of the inspection of land or other property, examination, or admission, which is obtained by any method of discovery in any judicial or administrative proceeding of an adversarial nature;

(B) any digest, analysis, selection, compilation, or derivation of any item listed in subparagraph (A); and

(C) any index or other manner of access to any item listed in subparagraph (A).

II. QUI TAM STATISTICS

(*Source: Department of Justice, through 9/30/02*)

Total amount recovered where there is an associated *qui tam* **case:** $7.9 billion

Total amount recovered in cases that the Department of Justice (DOJ) entered or otherwise pursued: $7.5 billion

Total amount recovered by relators in cases declined by DOJ: $362 million

Total number of *qui tam* **cases filed:** 4,281

Qui tam **cases filed (by fiscal year):**

1987:	33
1988:	60
1989:	95
1990:	82
1991:	90
1992:	119
1993:	132
1994:	222
1995:	277
1996:	363
1997:	533
1998:	470
1999:	482
2000:	367
2001:	310
2002:	326

Recoveries in *qui tam* cases pursued by DOJ (by fiscal year):

1988: $355,000
1989: $15 million
1990: $40 million
1991: $70 million
1992: $134 million
1993: $171 million
1994: $379.6 million
1995: $245 million
1996: $125 million
1997: $622.7 million
1998: $432.7 million
1999: $454 million
2000: $1.2 billion
2001: $1.16 billion
2002: $1.4 billion

Recoveries in cases declined by DOJ (by fiscal year):

1988: $35,431
1989:   0
1990: $75,000
1991: $69,500
1992: $994,456
1993: $5.9 million
1994: $1.8 million
1995: $1.8 million
1996: $14 million
1997: $7 million
1998: $29.2 million
1999: $62.5 million
2000: $1.8 million
2001: $125.8 million
2002: $25 million
2003: $85 million

Relators' awards when DOJ intervened in or otherwise pursued the case, in cases where shares have been determined (total): $1.2 billion

Relators' awards when government declined to intervene (total): $89 million

DOJ's decision on qui tam cases:
Intervened or otherwise pursued: 750 cases

Active:	79
Settled or judgment:	639
Inactive:	3
Unclear:	2
Dismissed, no recovery:	27

Declined: 2,653

Active:	268
Settled or judgment:	153
Inactive:	10
Unclear:	38
Dismissed, no recovery:	2,184

Under investigation: 891

Recoveries in *qui tam* cases involving health care fraud and defense fraud:

Health care:

Cases filed:	2,200
Government recovery:	$5.2 billion
Relator share:	$851.6 million

Defense:

Cases filed:	1,277
Government recovery:	$1.59 billion
Relator share:	$291 million